EUROPEANIZATION OF BRITISH DEFENCE POLICY

Dedicated to the memory of Anne and Ron Dover

Europeanization of British Defence Policy

ROBERT DOVER
King's College London, UK

ASHGATE

© Robert Dover 2007

All rights reserved. No part of this publication may be reproduced, stored in a retrieval system or transmitted in any form or by any means, electronic, mechanical, photocopying, recording or otherwise without the prior permission of the publisher.

Robert Dover has asserted his moral right under the Copyright, Designs and Patents Act, 1988, to be identified as the author of this work.

Published by
Ashgate Publishing Limited
Gower House
Croft Road
Aldershot
Hampshire GU11 3HR
England

Ashgate Publishing Company
Suite 420
101 Cherry Street
Burlington, VT 05401-4405
USA

Ashgate website: http://www.ashgate.com

British Library Cataloguing in Publication Data
Dover, Robert
  Europeanization of British defence policy
  1. Great Britain - Military policy 2. Great Britain - Foreign relations - 1997- 3. Great Britain - Foreign relations - European Union countries 4. European Union countries - Foreign relations - Great Britain
  I. Title
  355'.033541

Library of Congress Cataloging-in-Publication Data
Dover, Robert, 1977-
  Europeanization of British defence policy / by Robert Dover.
    p. cm.
  Includes bibliographical references and index.
  ISBN 978-0-7546-4899-4
  1. Great Britain--Military policy. 2. National security--Europe. 3. Europe--Military policy. I. Title.

  UA23.D683 2007
  355'.033041--dc22

2007003826

ISBN 978-0-7546-4899-4

Printed and bound in Great Britain by MPG Books Ltd, Bodmin, Cornwall.

Contents

Preface   *vi*
Acknowledgments   *vii*
List of Abbreviations   *viii*

Introduction   1

1   The Framework, Sources and Approach   11

2   Domestic Policy Formulation: Pörtschach and Saint Malo   21

3   Intergovernmental Bargains: Concepts and Preparations   39

4   Saint Malo and Nice: The Machinery of Negotiating   53

5   Why Governments Transfer Sovereignty: Formal Europeanization   75

6   The Iraq War – The Problem of National Interests for Europeanization   95

7   The Europeanization of the Arms Trade   117

Conclusion   143

Bibliography   *155*
Index   *187*

Preface

I wrote this book to shed light on an under-explored part of Europeanization. To some, the idea of domestic defence policy becoming Europeanized is both abhorrent and an anathema. The challenge of this book has been to capture the diverse range of institutions, actors, and processes involved in the Europeanization of defence and similarly, to show how the pace of Europeanization changes from issue to issue.

One of the surprising elements of this research has been the extent to which different processes and actors feature in formal Treaty amending integration and informal day-to-day Europeanization of defence. Both this formal and informal Europeanization is having a transformatory effect on national governments and the way they conduct their defence policies.

Formal integration is causing national governments to reform their bureaucracies, armed forces and security policy. Informal integration – particularly through the transformation of the arms trade – is removing agency from national governments and placing it in the hands of committees attached to the European Commission, including the European Defence Agency. Thus far, these committees have produced policies that are broadly in line with British government preferences. The potential remains, however, for these agencies to create an internationalized arms trade, removed from the control or influence of national governments.

One of the fascinating elements for me, writing this book, has been to interview current and former officials and politicians and to try to unravel the wiring of domestic policy formulation, and understand something of bureaucratic culture in the UK and EU more widely. It is my hope that I have conveyed some of this thinking and analysis in a way that attracts further research from others on this and related topics.

Robert Dover, November 2006

Acknowledgments

I would like to thank the Economic and Social Research Council for the Post-Graduate Research Award, R42200034110 (2000-2003) that funded the research that went into this book.

Importantly, I would like to acknowledge and thank all the analysts, politicians and officials who have been willing to take the time to be interviewed and who are cited in the text and in the bibliography.

Professionally, I would like to thank Professor Anthony Forster who proved to be a fine supervisor during my doctoral research. I would also like to thank Professors Richard Aldrich, Michael Clarke, Erik Jones and Dr Mark Wickham-Jones for their advice and mentoring.

On a personal note, I would like to thank my parents, Janet and Richard Dover for their unfailing support during all my studies and for sparking my interest in these issues many years ago. In a similar vein, I would like to thank Richard Paterson for being one of those inspirational teachers one never forgets.

I would like to thank Anna Stavrianakis for her love, support and intellectual stimulation. Finally, I would like to thank Sarah Childs and Andrew Monaghan for very kindly critiquing work I have sent them. Of course all errors and omissions remain mine.

List of Abbreviations

AFV	Armoured Fighting Vehicles
ASD	Aerospace and Defence Industries Association of Europe
ASEAN	Association of South East Asian Nations
BAE	British Aerospace Systems
C3	Command, Control and Communications
C4ISTAR	Command, Control, Communication, Computing, Intelligence, Surveillance, Target Acquisition and Reconnaissance
CAP	Common Agricultural Policy
CER	Centre for European Reform
CFSP	Common Foreign and Security Policy
CIA	Central Intelligence Agency (US)
COREPER	Permanent representation to the European Union (Comité des Représentants Permanents)
CT	Counter-terrorism
DA	Defence Attaché
DESO	Defence Export Services Organisation
DESP	Directorate of Export Services Policy
DFID	Department for International Development
DIS	Defence Intelligence Staff (UK)
DSACEUR	Deputy Supreme Allied Command Europe
DTI	Department for Trade and Industry
ECJ	European Court of Justice
EDA	European Defence Agency
(E)DOP	Cabinet Sub-Committee on European Issues
EP	European Parliament
EPC	European Political Co-operation
EPOL	European Policing Missions
ESDP	European Security and Defence Policy
ESRAP	European Security Research Advisory Board
EU	European Union
EU3	Britain, France and Germany.
EUJUST LEX	European Union 'Rule of Law' Mission to Iraq
EUMC	EU Military Committee
EUMS	EU Military Staff
EURO	European Single Currency
FCO	Foreign and Commonwealth Office
FOI	UK Freedom of Information Act
FPC	Foreign Policy Centre
FP7	Seventh Round of EU Framework Funding Programme

List of Abbreviations

G8	Group of Eight 'wealthy nations'
GBP	United Kingdom currency, Pounds Sterling
GDP	Gross Domestic Product
GWOT	Global War on Terror
HUMINT	Human intelligence
IGC	Intergovernmental Conference
LI	Liberal Intergovernmentalism
MEP	Member of the European Parliament
MP	Member of Parliament
MOD	Ministry of Defence
NATO	North Atlantic Treaty Organisation
NGO	Non-Governmental Organisation
PLP	Parliamentary Labour Party
PM	Prime Minister (UK)
PSC	EU Political and Security Committee
PSO	Peace Support Operations
QMV	Qualified Majority Voting
REACH	An EU agreement on chemical processing
RIIA	Royal Institute of International Affairs
RUSI	Royal United Services Institute
SDR	Strategic Defence Review
SFO	Serious Fraud Office
SIGINT	Signals intelligence
UAV	Unmanned Aerial Vehicles
UKREP	The UK's Ambassador to the European Union
UN	United Nations
WEU	Western European Union
WMD	Weapons of Mass Destruction

Introduction

The Europeanization of defence is an undernourished element of the relatively new field of Europeanization studies. The majority of the extant Europeanization literature covers the extent to which membership of the European Union affects the policies produced by member states, and similarly the way that states configure their bureaucracies in responding to EU policy initiatives. As a result the underlying assumption of Europeanization is that this phenomenon is top-down. Pressure is exerted from EU institutions, European law or by expectations on national governments to engage in EU issues means that member states are compelled to alter their policies to reflect and deliver a 'Europeanized' agenda.

This book shows these assumptions to be incorrect. The Europeanization of British defence policy (1997-2005) demonstrates that these presumptions can be reversed with member governments uploading their preferences into the EU and effectively locking the other Members into their 'uploaded' preferences. Uploading domestic preferences provides full weight to Alan Milward's thesis of the 'The European Rescue of the Nation-State' in which he argued that in placing national policy competencies at the European level national governments saw a multiplication of their influence as a result (Milward 1999). Furthermore this book highlights the inconsistencies between what this study describes as 'formal' and 'informal' Europeanization. Formal Europeanization occurs at Intergovernmental Conferences (IGC), through the creation or amendment of treaties or through Presidency Conclusions. Informal Europeanization is that which occurs outside of IGCs, but that has a transformatory affect on the political or bureaucratic behaviour of national governments or supranational institutions. So, for example, whilst the ESDP was negotiated as a discreet item of formal Europeanization separate from other Nice IGC business, the deepening integration of defence has been intimately linked to disagreements over the war in Iraq and the reform of the Common Agricultural Policy (see Chapter 6).

Most accounts of Europeanization emphasize the link between the national and supranational levels, on a governmental basis. Chapter 7, which deals with the Europeanization of the arms trade demonstrates that the influence of big business can steer both national and European policy away from stated strategic objectives and opens up new sites of Europeanization for further research, as well as demonstrating the ways in which entrepreneurial policy actors can go outside of conventional Europeanization routes. This book therefore provides a multi-dimensional analysis of the Europeanization phenomena and a detailed explanation of the developments in Britain's European defence policy.

There is very little published analysis of the UK government's role in the development of the ESDP (Dover 2005). The analysis that does exist has concentrated on the implications for transatlantic relations, the prospects for a so-called 'Euro-Army' and the possible economic impact from a common defence policy. The missing element within the literature is a study of the diplomacy and statecraft involved in developing the policy domestically within the MoD, FCO and Cabinet Office, bilaterally (between the UK and French governments) and at the Nice Intergovernmental Conference (December 2000). This empirically driven research looks further at the bilateral and often personal interactions between entrepreneurial officials and the extensive 'back channel' communications between the foreign and defence ministries of the respective member states. It then builds an analysis of how these interactions culminate in a Europeanized defence policy and the extent to which there is cohesion, at the European level, for these policies.

This book centres on activities in the defence sphere between 1998 and 2005. The crucial moments in the development of a Europeanized British defence policy occurred between 1998 and 2000 and the early stages of this book are given over to a detailed exploration of the internal UK government and external negotiations between January 1998, and the Nice Intergovernmental Conference in December 2000. It pays close attention to the circumstances surrounding the development of the Saint Malo policy particularly as the announcement in December 1998 was contrary to published Labour Party policy prior to and directly after the 1997 General Election. Moreover, the Saint Malo initiative was also counter to the provisions of the Amsterdam Treaty signed by Tony Blair. The policy initiative (emanating from the UK civil service) can therefore be seen in terms of it being a shift in UK government policy. This research provides an account of how such a shift emerged; and with it provides an important explanation of the politics of the core executive. More particularly it highlights the 'Napoleonic' style of Tony Blair's premiership. This book demonstrates how Blair, in this policy sphere, added overwhelming political motivation and mobilization to the policy shift (performing a role of seeking win-sets and support from key stake-holding groups within Whitehall) for a policy initiated by an entrepreneurial group of policy officials in the UK MoD.

The later sections of the book explore the challenges posed to the Europeanization of defence by the 2003 Iraq war, and particularly how this manifested itself during the 2005 Presidency of the EU which was held by the British government. This chapter shows the problem of incohesion in an intergovernmental political system and the linkages between diverse issues areas are brought out starkly within this case study.

The final section examines the Europeanization of the arms trade and in doing so argues that this element of defence policy represents the fast and slow track of Europeanization. The British government is wedded to an isolationist model of the trade that focuses on the success of national industries and the export of materials while the manufacturers themselves pursue internationalization and the Commission aggressively pursues the Europeanization of the trade. This example also highlights the potential for producer groups to gain overwhelming influence over policy formulation at the national and supranational levels.

A Liberal Intergovernmentalist Approach

This research approaches Europeanization from a Liberal Intergovernmentalist (LI) perspective. It utilizes the work of Andrew Moravcsik to provide the framework around which explanations for why the British government sought to Europeanize their defence policy – something that most commentators would have judged unthinkable given the transatlanticist preferences of the British government since 1945. Moravcsik claims, through LI, to offer an explanation of European integration from the formulation of domestic policies, the creation of national negotiating positions, the government's conduct during negotiations and the motivations for transferring sovereignty to the EU (Moravcsik 1993, 1995, 1997, 1998; Moravcsik and Nicolaidis 1998). This research calls on this body of work to show the way in which Europeanization has occurred in the defence sphere.

LI's explanation of domestic politics rests on a dual concept of policies and preferences. In accounting for the British government's development of a Europeanized defence policy these concepts, particularly the impact that preferences have on government policy will be closely examined, and it will be argued here that the British government's preference for transatlantic defence solutions have not been breached by the policies of the previous seven years. Indeed, in adopting innovative 'Europeanized' policies the British government has been able to secure a preservation of the pre-eminence of the nation state in European security and defence issues and the continued dominance of the NATO Alliance in Europe. Within 'preferences' are stable government policy paradigms that inform policies made in that issue area and a description of how government policies are formulated (Moravcsik and Nicolaidis 1998, 63). According to this conception government policies are created by pressure from issue-specific domestic producer groups who exert their preferences on the government. Having received this domestic producer group pressure, the government aggregates the various policy preferences into a government policy. LI also argues that positive and negative externalities impact on the formulation of government policy. A policy has 'external effects' when it has substantial positive or negative impacts, on people outside the territorial boundaries of the political system of the actor or actors pursuing the policy. LI argues that these effects are taken into account by policy makers during the policy formulation process (Moravcsik 1998). These assumptions receive critical attention in Chapter 2 and Chapter 7, particularly where policy formulation lineage is traced.

An intergovernmentalist approach also places governments as the principle units of analysis in Europeanization and particularly those in which developments are codified through negotiations. Further, that governments' have issue-specific competencies and strengths to dominate particular international bargains. Issue specific capabilities, finance, historical experience and institutional affiliations all contribute to a government becoming an influential actor in any particular set of negotiations. Following on from this rationale, the negotiated outcomes between governments are the result of a convergence of governmental interests and occur when an internationalized policy has more benefits for a government than a unilateral solution. It is from these assumptions that the evidence of the Anglo-French summit at Saint Malo (4-5 December 1998), the pre-Nice IGC negotiations and the negotiations at the Nice European Council as well as the impacts of the Iraq war and the arms trade will be used to explain the Europeanization of British defence policy.

Intergovernmentalist explanations focus on causal explanations for governmental behaviour in this area through a series of rational expectations. These expectations include the government's wish to secure credible international action thus solving problems associated with intergovernmental policy co-ordination and the desire to transfer and pool sovereignty in the EU. Furthermore, when a government faces small costs in co-ordinating policies in an international forum there is a greater likelihood of further EU integration occurring. This book tests these explanations of why governments seek to transfer sovereignty through the prism of UK defence policy and UK government's desire to co-ordinate elements of this policy within an EU framework.

Key Contests

This book focuses on some key empirical and theoretical contests. It argues that the liberal intergovernmentalist framework is helpful in explaining the Europeanization of British defence policy between 1997 and 2005; particularly the UK government negotiating team's approach to defence negotiations at the Nice European Council. Chapter 2 reformulates domestic policy making as a result of the evidence from 1997-2000 and the negotiations over the ESDP, arguing that the core executive and policy entrepreneurs have a great deal of control over domestic Europeanization to the exclusion of domestic producer groups. The contrary is true in the case of the Europeanization of the arms trade.[1] It is also argued that Europeanization has paradoxically removed and strengthened competencies and autonomy in security and defence from European member states. The internationalization of the arms trade and aggressive Europeanization by the European Commission has removed state control whilst the negotiation of the ESDP solidified and enhanced member state sovereignty in this area; particularly for the British government who managed to successfully upload their defence and security preferences into the EU, locking in their partner governments.

Part of the liberal intergovernmentalist explanation for domestic policy formulation is that pressure from domestic interest groups are aggregated by the government into policy. In the case of the arms trade the pressure exerted by producer groups is imported directly into government policy whilst in the example of ESDP the government created the changes in UK defence policy and then sought explicit or tacit support from domestic interest groups. This corrective adds an important level of understanding to the relationship between the UK government and domestic interest groups in defence policy. Moreover, it also helps to open the black box of the state to explore the internal dynamics of government involved in the policy making

---

1   Moravcsik uses the term domestic producer groups to describe groups outside of the government with influence on government policy. Only the case study involving the arms trade has traditional 'producer groups'; the Saint Malo process and the Iraq conflict did not involve domestic producer groups but instead involved interest groups like the armed forces, research institutes and think-tanks.

process, illuminating the role of large personalities within the government and the role of international business interests in Europeanization.

In exploring why the British government has pursued decisions that lead to a Europeanization of its defence and security policy this book argues that the motivation for change in UK defence policy was mostly driven by the influence of positive externalities. A key concern was to ensure that the EU had credible capabilities with which to intervene in humanitarian crises, like those in the Balkans, and similarly to encourage European governments to re-shape their armed forces as the UK armed forces had done following the Strategic Defence Review (SDR) of 1998 and to support US-led coalitions of the willing in expeditionary warfare. The changes to the EU defence industrial base have come from the Commission's desire to be engaged in the defence sector to promote high technology industries and from the manufacturers to improve the health of their order books.

The second major area of contestation concerns international bargaining. Intergovernmentalist approaches argue that international negotiations are dominated by major governments (in the European context Britain, France and Germany) and that the outcomes of intergovernmental negotiations are lowest common denominator agreements (Moravcsik 1998, 482). Revisions to this analysis focus on redefining what constitutes a 'major' government; LI suggests that a major government can exert considerable influence on an international negotiation through intrinsic factors, such as financial strength, population, and geographical location. However, this study adds issue specific factors, such as preference intensity, membership of relevant international organizations and the effect their unilateral action has on the international system (Moravcsik 1998, 476-478). Furthermore this research suggests that the intensity of preferences and influence of unilateral action are key aspects within the issue-specific factors and that these factors result in dominance of the UK, France and Germany in the Europeanization of defence policy and also explain, conversely, that when the 'Big Three' disagree on policies, like Iraq, the negative effect this has on Europeanization is very marked.

The liberal intergovernmentalist explanation of domestic policy formulation centres on a concept of preferences, which are historically stable government policy paradigms that inform policies, the everyday decisions, made in that issue area (Moravcsik and Nicolaidis 1998, 59). The development of UK defence policy to include the pro-European dimension of the Saint Malo Initiative is said to threaten the sanctity of the NATO Alliance by some analysts and political opponents of the Labour Government. However, Chapter 2 argues that the British government pursued this policy shift within, and to strengthen, the preference for transatlantic solutions. It did so in order to strengthen the Alliance by creating European based capabilities that could be used with or in the absence of US / NATO capabilities, and/or when the US did not wish to be involved. The concept of preferences is therefore theoretically and empirically useful in explaining the development of UK defence policy and the continuity of the NATO paradigm, but arguably requires tightening. It can be used to argue that the Saint Malo process was either a fundamental shift in preferences or a tactical shift in policy that remained within the transatlantic paradigm. The concept of preferences in this case study remains contestable, but the overwhelming weight of evidence points towards the Saint Malo process being an innovative policy solution within the transatlantic framework.

LI explanations are effective in explaining the codification of defence Europeanization at the 2000 Nice IGC. The IGC and its outcomes demonstrate that governments are the principal units in the formal Europeanization of defence policy. The supranational component in the negotiations was largely absent as a consequence of the closed intergovernmental nature of this bargaining with governments excluding participation by the European Parliament's observers.

Moreover, through a self-denying ordinance the European Commission declined involvement in a subject it viewed as being the preserve of member governments, something it reversed after the Nice Treaty was signed. Chapter 3 argues that the conceptualization of negotiations as the lowest common denominator of respective individual government positions is a simplistic view of international negotiating. A more accurate view is to challenge a 'one-model fits all' approach and to compare those governments with intensive preferences who do reach lowest common denominator agreements, with those governments with less-intensive policy preferences and who do not need to reach lowest common denominator positions. The key factors in shaping the intensity of preferences are the need to ensure domestic support for negotiated positions, the level of capabilities the government holds in the particular issue and the ability of the government to create coalitions in support of a particular policy area. However, the Iraq case study shows that large disagreements between governments can scupper integration, even when there is preference convergence on that specific policy. The Europeanization of the arms trade demonstrates the potential for Europeanization outside of the control of member governments highlighting the complexity of Europeanization.

The fourth core argument is that LI's explanation of why governments seek to transfer domestic sovereignty to international institutions, one element of Europeanization, is validated by the example of British defence policy. Intergovernmentalist explanations argue that the motivations for transferring domestic sovereignty are based on the ambition to secure credible international action on particular policy areas (Moravcsik 1998, 473). Within this general aim of securing credibility, the more specific objectives are to solve the problems associated with the international co-ordination of policy and governments. The result of this objective is to make the costs of co-ordination small and the benefits from joint working large. On a meta-level LI argues that the EU is an opportunity structure to achieve national government policies (Moravcsik 1998, 473; Correspondence with Moravcsik 2003).[2] Following on from this, the British government viewed the Saint Malo initiative and the Europeanized policy (ESDP) as a means to achieve three defence related objectives: to co-ordinate national defence and security policies within the EU, across a limited range of peacekeeping and peace-building issues; to improve EU member states' autonomous defence and security capabilities; and to strengthen the EU's role within NATO. Moreover, the UK Ministry of Defence

---

2 Moravcsik notes that the principal motivation is domestic commercial interests. He goes further to suggest, in correspondence that commercial interests are a primary motivator in defence integration with geopolitical issues also having an importance.

was hopeful that a move towards a common EU policy on defence and security would result in military reforms across the EU to reflect the changes made by the British military after the Strategic Defence Review (SDR), something which is now being done. The UK government's desire to transfer sovereignty on the issue of the ESDP is best conceptualized as being based on a rational aggregation of UK national interests – the benefits of sovereignty transfer outweigh the potential costs to the UK because of the desire to create a framework for domestic policy co-ordination at the international level.

The arms trade introduces tension into the transfer of sovereignty. This is an area in which Chapter 7 argues that the Commission and manufacturers have effectively consumed some state sovereignty. They now shape the state's strategic direction through a research and development focus on homeland security and network centric capabilities. The Commission has successfully linked the arms trade to a cross-pillar agenda of improving and extending trade and industrial co-operation in the European area. Projects like the Eurofighter Typhoon and Airbus 400 that incorporate pan-European design and manufacturing aspects are good examples of where the trade dimension of the EU can assist in spreading design and manufacture costs, output and risk and fit broadly within the Lisbon agenda. Similarly, the development of a European Defence Agency (EDA) aims to improve cooperation between European member governments and their defence procurement efforts. The design and operation of the EDA has been dominated by the influence of a 'state-private' network of manufacturer interests and national and supranational officials but has resulted in a pro-trade organization that dovetails with the export interests of member states like the UK.

The arms trade provides an interesting take on Europeanization. In many ways the arms trade is a prime example of where national governments pursue increasingly isolationist policies and treat their fellow European member states as competitors; employing, in the case of the British government, covert measures against competitors in securing business for British companies. There are strategic and economic reasons for the isolationist policies pursued by EU governments in the arms trade; strategically an independent defence industrial base is seen as essential to giving a country independent strategic defence capabilities (and thus a sensible off-set against the financial savings that can be delivered through buying so-called 'off the shelf' solutions from the United States, for example). Economically, governments and manufacturer lobbyists argue that the defence industries provide an essential economic element to national and supranational wealth – the unit price of defence equipment being so large that the benefits to UK based defence companies are irreplaceable. Moreover, that electorally the number of defence jobs in key UK Parliamentary constituencies are such that a reduction in the defence industrial base could have the affect of marginalising a key number of voters and thus the party political make-up of the House of Commons, a clear echo of American style 'pork-barrel' politics. The net benefit to the UK economy of the defence manufacturers and those employed in the defence industries is subject to a large amount of debate which will be explored in Chapter 7. The extraordinary influence of the European Commission and the manufacturers will similarly be examined to highlight the alternative methods through which the Europeanization of British defence policy occurs.

The diplomatic and military build-up to the US-UK led invasion of Iraq is a case-study in failure of the Europeanization of defence and security policy. In contrast, the aftermath of the Iraq war – the so-called Phase Three operations (post-conflict reconstruction and peace-keeping) – has shown greater levels of cohesion amongst EU member governments. The effects of the build-up to war brought into stark relief the effect and balance of the transatlantic alliance on the EU and the very real divisions between, as Secretary of Defense Donald Rumsfeld put it, 'new' and 'old' Europe. The effect of the intra-EU diplomatic schism has been seen in both defence and security terms – with the French government refusing further co-operation with the UK government on deepening defence and security policy integration and more widely with an obstinate approach to budget and Common Agricultural Policy negotiations – seen as being directly related to a cooling of diplomatic relations around the Iraq war. This case study will show in Chapter 6 the positive and negative possibilities surrounding diplomatic Europeanization – particularly with the strong influence of a non-EU actor. Positively, the Europeanization of diplomacy serves as a multiplier of European influence on the world stage. Negatively it can produce 'blow-back' that affects the progress of diplomacy within the EU on important issues such as negotiating the Union's budget and the future of the CAP.

Book Structure

This book is split into three case-study driven sections. The first chapter introduces the methodological and theoretical debates this book feeds into. It describes how the research for this book was collected along with the questions and challenges this has produced. Moreover, it outlines the theoretical premise and assumptions that underpin this book's explanation of 'Europeanization'.

The structure of the first case-study – the development of the ESDP – is spread over chapters 2, 3, and 4 and echoes the structure of the formal Europeanization of British defence policy. Chapter 2 explores the formulation of the British approach to the ESDP, including the instigation of the Saint Malo process in 1998 and how this impacts on the concept of 'national preferences' (Moravcsik and Nicolaidis 1998, 63). Established accounts of the formulation of government policies are achieved through a process of aggregating the policy positions and preferences of individual interest groups. This account of the domestic policy formulation process has been criticized as being weak by many notable commentators (Wallace 1999; Wincott 1995). Chapter 2 uses elite interviews, contemporary open source material, academic literature and quality news media reports, through a framework derived from liberal intergovernmentalist accounts, to argue that UK defence policy formulation is not created in accordance with these explanations and was, in this example, established by a small cadre of officials and politicians within the core executive of Number 10 Downing Street, the Cabinet Office, and the Ministry of Defence and Foreign and

Commonwealth Office and then officials tested the support for this policy amongst domestic interest groups and political supporters (Rhodes and Dunleavy 1995, 2).[3]

Chapter 3 explores the process of intergovernmental negotiating, more particularly the negotiations between 1998 and 2000, culminating in the Nice IGC. Within the framework used by this book, the British government should be able to achieve more of its key aims within the negotiations as a consequence of its relative strength in voting rights, economic strength and perceived elevated status in foreign and military affairs. This chapter argues that the relative bargaining strengths of the British, French and German governments represented the strongest preferences within the negotiations. Close contextual analysis of the negotiations showed that the three strongest governments dominated the proceedings through alliance building and link-issue trade-offs to achieve the majority of their negotiating aims. Moreover, Chapter 4 advances the argument that during the negotiations the European Commission opted not to exercise its influence over the direction of ESDP, demonstrating the pre-eminent position of governments in the formal Europeanization of defence.

Chapter 4 explores the outcome of the Nice IGC negotiations and the decision of governments to transfer and pool national sovereignty on defence and security policy. The empirical and analytical elements of this chapter are the most straightforward of those tackled in this book. The reason for this is equally straightforward – analysis of treaty outcomes is a key test of how closely outcomes match initial policy preferences. In the context of this book, governmental preferences are discussed in the light of open sources, newspaper reports, government documents, and elite interviews. Chapter 4 argues that the outcomes of the Nice IGC matched UK government's preferences very closely. It also shows that ESDP negotiations were not linked in any tangible way to other policy areas and therefore the UK government was not asked to absorb bargaining 'losses' in other policy areas in exchange for bargaining 'successes' in the defence sphere.

Furthermore, Chapter 5 focuses on institutional decisions to distribute sovereignty. This deals retrospectively with the decision of national governments to pool or delegate their sovereignty into supranational organizations. The rationality within this analysis lends itself to a decision to pool sovereignty based on the maximization of economic or issue-specific benefits (Forster 1998, 386). On the basis of the information and data available this research suggests that the decision to pool and delegate minor amounts of sovereignty and decision making apparatus to the ESDP was taken on the basis of global strategic ambitions, inter-European political ambitions and as a part of a recalibration of domestic economic and political necessity.

Chapter 6 focuses on the Europeanization of diplomacy with particular reference to the diplomatic build-up and fall-out from the US-UK led invasion of Iraq in March 2003 to the present day. It explores the levels of EU-wide cohesion on this policy and the diplomatic efforts being made by the US-UK to secure European support for their actions. The chapter situates these diplomatic efforts within the UK's

---

3 The core executive is 'all those organization and procedures which coordinate central government policies and act as final arbiters of conflict between different parts of the government machine'.

Presidency of the EU in 2005 to demonstrate the effects of diplomatic schisms on the Europeanization of issues even where there is pre-existing policy convergence. This chapter argues that the disparate EU policy areas are closely linked leading to a conclusion that the law of unintended consequences as regards the war in Iraq has had a negative impact on EU cohesion across the full spectrum of policy competencies.

Chapter 7 examines the Europeanization of the arms trade; through the political and economic drivers for this trade and also through an analysis of the politics of arms transfers. It explores the effect of the EU as a trading bloc in providing a pro-trade discourse and incentives for manufacturers to continue producing and exporting military and dual-use equipment; particularly through the Lisbon agenda and the European Defence Agency. It also explores the protectionist steps taken by governments to insulate and promote their indigenous defence manufacturers to the detriment of other EU based firms and the acceleration of Europeanization through the policy entrepreneurship of the Commission and the manufacturers.

The concluding chapter deals with the three core concerns of this book; first, a critical evaluation of Europeanization and an explanation for how the phenomenon works in relation to defence and security policies. Second, an analysis of domestic British defence policy making as it relates directly and indirectly to the European Union; and third, an analysis of the Europeanizing machineries of government both within the UK and within the EU.

Chapter 1

The Framework, Sources and Approach

This chapter seeks to set out how this research was conducted and its findings were established. The method employed by this book is straightforward and robust. The research within the book is based on over fifty elite interviews – conducted with officials and politicians directly involved with the domestic, bilateral and intergovernmental negotiations addressing the development of the European Security and Defence Policy, the transfer of arms to third countries and the development of the coalition efforts concerning Iraq – and a large number of government documents, contemporaneous reports and secondary sources used to triangulate these empirical findings.

Without dwelling on esoteric methodological debates, this research has applied an 'as-if' positivist framework to the three broad case studies which are used to explain the Europeanization of British defence policy (Mann 1996, 222; Bartley 1964, 5; Popper 1963, 33-39). The basis of this approach is that there are at core, discoverable truths but that these are difficult to expose because of the presence of researcher and interviewee bias (Bettis and Gregson 2001, 8). As a consequence 'as if' positivism retains an aspiration to 'scientificity' in social science research, a search for objective truths without the wholesale rejection or problems with finding verifiable facts (Bettis and Gregson 2001, 12). Another significant approach that could have been adopted is post-positivism (Smith 1996, 11-47). This approach includes a critical analysis of theory building as a practice in itself (Moravcsik 1998, 77-85; King, Keohane and Verba 1994, 35-38). James Scheurich describes the difference between positivism and post-positivism in the following way:

> I take positivism (which I also call the 'traditional' or 'conventional' approach) to assume that the individual interview context (including, for instance, the personality or gender of the interviewer) is not a critical consideration and that a category-based reduction of the verbal text of the interview can be taken as a valid representation of the interview itself and of the perceptions of the interviewee. In contrast to positivism, I take post-positivism, following Mischler (186), to assume that interviews are highly contextualised events and, thus, the representations of such events must be contextualised. But both positivism and post-positivism make the modernist assumption that the appropriate research method will yield the real or best meaning of an interview. Postmodernism, in contrast, suggests that there is a radical indeterminacy at the heart of the interview interaction which cannot be overcome by any methodology (Scheurich 1997, 75).

Post-positivism is more sophisticated in its construction than positivism. It acknowledges that individual views are informed by experiences and biases and so 'knowable truths' are difficult to observe and validate (Crotty 1998, 40). Through a process of triangulation, more secure evidence is sought to evaluate positions.

Furthermore, post-positivism draws our attention to a closer analysis of the motivations and biases of individuals or institutions and therefore provides a more nuanced and complete analysis. More particularly, a post-positivist approach leads to the conclusion that trying to theorize European integration is fraught with intellectual problems. Indeed post-positivism suggests that facts are relative leading to situation specific comprehension, 'This argument [...] depends on the positivist assumption that a non-power-related truth game is possible. It is doubtful, however, at least in the social sciences, that such a power-free truth game has ever existed.' (Scheurich 1997, 35). Whilst positivism has been declared obsolete by Karl Popper and Denis Phillips there remains many useful aspects of this approach to theory testing; namely the aspiration of objectivity and a search for untainted and explicit evidence (Popper 1974; Philips 1983, 4-12). The approach applied here – 'as if' positivism – adds critical nuances to positivism without accepting all the constructivist aspects of post-positivism.

In applying 'as if' positivism the high empirical standards demanded by Andrew Moravcsik, in his book 'The Choice for Europe' are met throughout this book (Moravcsik 1998, 10; Moravcsik and Nicolaidis, 1998, 58).[1] The three key indicators established by Moravcsik for research that seeks to advance a theoretical understanding of European integration,

> In each case, a consistent set of competing hypotheses is derived from general theories; the decision is aggregated to generate sufficient observations to test those hypotheses; and, wherever possible, potentially controversial attributions of motive or strategy are backed up by 'hard' primary sources (direct evidence of decision making) rather than 'soft' or secondary sources (public statements and journalistic or academic commentary in which authors have less incentive to report motivations accurately) (Moravcsik 1998, 10).

The research presented in this book follows these three prescriptions to produce a study that is acceptable, on these grounds, as a credible means to examine and explain Europeanization.

Sources

This book tackles some sensitive and contemporary issues; which are documented through a small amount of extant documentation which is limited because of the various 30 and 50 year rules in operation for some British government documents. As a result this research has called upon a significant number of elite interviews with key actors to provide the primary research on which to build its analysis. In using the 'as-if' positivism as the methodological basis of this study it must be accepted that 'facts' are constructed through the biases and experiences of individuals and therefore to make judgements on evidence, then this evidence should be triangulated to minimize errors (Smith 1996, 35).

---

[1] Indeed in 'The Choice for Europe' and associated articles Moravcsik calls for critiques of LI but only from those who are prepared to reach the high empirical standards he sets.

The challenge of reaching sensitive information from people placed at heart of decision making frameworks is significant. The proximity between the events being explained and this research poses problems for several key stakeholder groups. Civil service officials from the Ministry of Defence, Foreign and Commonwealth Office and Cabinet Office are still engaged in the formulation and implementation of the ESDP, arms trade policy and the Iraq conflict and the UK's approach to it. As a result, they might be unwilling to reveal the true nature of the policy negotiations or their role within them. The politicians involved might similarly be conscious that the issues being discussed in this book are 'live' political issues and as such a research publication exploring this policy in-depth might become subject to interest from the media and, by extension, electoral interest. The book overcomes this challenge through anonymising officials – with their consent – who held sensitive positions and also by triangulating their evidence through other interview and secondary evidence.

The secondary accounts available about the UK's approach to ESDP and the policy itself have been weak because of the lack of in-depth research on these areas. Published investigations into the arms trade, for example, have been generated largely by NGOs and campaign groups, with there being only two major studies into the subject; one by Davina Miller on the Scott Report and the other by Mark Phythian who explored the politics behind the British arms sales. The build up and prosecution of a war against Saddam Hussein's regime in Iraq has attracted a huge amount of news-media analysis and academic analysis – this book examines the specific policy formulation aspects of the campaign and the effect the build-up to war has had on the Europeanization of defence and other policy competencies. In placing a large reliance on interview evidence this book aims to provide robust levels of corroborative evidence and also to conform to the professional standards on how researchers should approach collecting interview evidence established by both the Institute for Contemporary British History and the British Sociological Association.[2]

---

2 The Institute for Contemporary British History have produced a set of guidelines for Officials participating in scholarly interviews and witness seminars. The Principles this document sets out for participation in interviews and seminars are first, compliance with the law – both Official Secrets Act and related obligations; and privacy and defamation considerations; second, compliance with the duty of confidentiality, including any employment contract terms; third, respect for the loyalty owed by officials in close working relationships with Ministers; fourth, primacy of the truth. The general guidelines set down are that first, there is a balance to be struck between discretion and the need for accuracy and balance; second, that contemporary history carries some remaining potential for political controversy. This should not be regarded as an automatic bar on taking part but it requires careful judgement as regards the auspices of the interview, the track record of the institution and the standing of the interview; third, closeness in time to the particular event. Events which still concern the government of the day will for the most part make it difficult for former officials to participate; fourth, where the subject matter has attracted a high security classification, or is of lasting live political controversy, it may still be possible for officials to participate to some extent, although exercising discretion. 'Guidelines for Former Officials at Scholarly Interviews and Witness Seminars', Institute for Contemporary British History, 9 December 2002. Similarly

As previously stated, the common problem of access and 'party line' bias encountered when attempting to gain contemporary views of government positions from ministers or senior officials is partly overcome by the use of anonymous quotable sources.[3] Establishing the UK government's negotiating positions on ESDP, and operational positions on the Iraq and arms trade case studies, is based on extensive triangulation of primary and secondary evidence. Primary evidence has been obtained from the relevant desk and high-ranking officials in the Foreign and Commonwealth Office, Ministry of Defence, Cabinet Office, Number 10, the intelligence agencies, interest groups and industry.[4] Evidence was also sought from government officials from EU member governments notably France and Sweden. In addition to these sources, interviews with officials from NATO, the CFSP secretariat (part of the Council's Secretariat), and the European Commission are used to cross-reference the UK government's positions.

---

the British Sociological Association have produced a 'Statement of Ethical Practice for the British Sociological Association' which deals with how social researchers should use interview evidence. The relevant sections for this study are: Section 16 – As far as possible participation in sociological research should be based on the freely given informed consent of those studied. This implies a responsibility on the interviewer to explain in appropriate detail, and in terms meaningful to participants, what the research is about, who is undertaking and financing it, why it is being taken, and how it is to be disseminated and used. Section 17- Research participants should be made aware of their right to refuse participation whenever and for whatever reason they wish. Section 18 – Research participants should understand how far they will be afforded anonymity and confidentiality and should be able to reject the use of data-gathering devices such as tape recorders and video cameras. Section 19 – Sociologists should be careful, on the one hand, not to give unrealistic guarantees of confidentiality and, on the other, not to permit communication of research films and records to audiences other than those to which the participants have agreed. Section 22 – Interviewers should clarify whether, and if so, the extent to which research participants are allowed to see transcripts of interviews and field notes and to alter the content, withdraw statements, to provide additional information and to add glosses on interpretations. 'Statement of Ethical Practice for the British Sociological Association', The British Sociological Association, (London) March 2002.

3 This thesis quotes the sources in full. The published version will render these quotes anonymous in line with 'Chatham House Rule'. According to the Royal Institute of International Affairs '…the new amendment means that participants are free to use the information received and can now also state that it was received at a Chatham House meeting. This provides clarity for participants and will allow summaries of meetings to be prepared. The Chatham House Rule reads as follows: 'When a meeting, or part thereof, is held under the Chatham House Rule, participants are free to use the information received, but neither the identity nor the affiliation of the speaker(s), nor that of any other participant, may be revealed'. http://www.riia.org/index.php?id=14

4 The term 'desks' is often based on two or more officials and is used to describe a narrow but deep understanding of a particular issue area within the Departments. For example, within the MoD there are desks for every country in the world and each of these desks can provide detailed intelligence, information and analysis on their country of expertise. In this thesis the crucial 'desks' were the Security Policy desks in the MoD and FCO as well as the European policy desks in both institutions. Notionally a Grade 5 civil servant is in charge of that particular brief and is responsible to the policy director of the department and ultimately the Permanent Under Secretary.

Informed by the different level of officials involved in each phase and the various political and bureaucratic affiliations of the officials participating in these phases determined where the interview evidence for this book should arise. Interviewees were also selected from various levels of seniority within their institutional frameworks. The selection provided a breadth of experience from different institutional perspectives and insights into how each department viewed the issues under debate and external perspectives from different levels of seniority within the relevant departments.

At the very centre of the UK decision-making framework on the issue of 'Europeanizing' UK defence were key civil service and political appointments. Within the Downing Street Policy Unit, Roger Liddle the Prime Minister's personal political advisor on European affairs, Cabinet Office officials with responsibilities for European policy issues, and Sir Stephen Wall, the Prime Minister's advisor on European issues, whose roles are substantially analysed (Downing Street Briefing 2000; White, 2001). Cabinet Office officials are civil service appointments and thus had a duty of confidentiality to the government and the Prime Minister. Liddle was a political appointment and whilst paid by the civil service a Labour party spokesperson in close day-to-day proximity to the Prime Minister. His interview evidence was inevitably informed by a desire to position his employer and party in a positive light (Mann 2001; Evans-Pritchard 2001). Liddle's position within the Downing Street Policy Unit overlaps in terms of scope and responsibilities with the role of Wall.[5] In answers given to the Lobby Briefing in June 2001 the Prime Minister's official spokesman accepted that the two roles appeared close, but also stated that Wall and Liddle had slightly different roles in advising the Prime Minister about European issues and that Wall retained seniority over Liddle (Downing Street Lobby Briefing 2001). The selection of Liddle and officials in the Cabinet Office as interviewees was based on a need to analyse evidence from those who most closely advised the Prime Minister and who were directly involved in inter-departmental debates between the Cabinet Office and the MoD and FCO. Cabinet Office interviewees, who played key roles in co-ordinating a set of UK government positions to be negotiated around at Saint Malo, centred around the European Secretariat of the Cabinet Office, with responsibilities for EU public diplomacy and EU institutions and Stephen Wall the Head of the European Secretariat and the Prime Minister's advisor on Europe (Cabinet Office 2002).[6]

---

5 From 2002 called the Strategy and Innovation Unit.

6 The main functions of the European Secretariat, which is headed by the Prime Minister's policy advisor on EU matters, are to drive forward the Prime Minister's European agenda, and to ensure that the Government's policy on EU issues is co-ordinated across Departments. In doing this, the Secretariat provides the Prime Minister, his officials and other Ministers with advice on the substance and presentation of EU issues, and supports the Foreign Secretary in his role as Chairman of the Ministerial Committee dealing with EU matters. A feature of the Secretariat's co-ordination work is a weekly meeting held with the UK's Permanent Representative to the EU and senior officials in Whitehall Departments, to discuss the tactics and handling of key issues coming forward for discussion in the Council of Ministers and elsewhere in the week ahead and beyond.

The interview strategy for this book was based on involvement and proximity of sources to the key debates surrounding the development of a Europeanized British defence policy 1997-2005. Particularly important, in the chapters that cover the development of the ESDP, was the interviewee's involvement in negotiating the policy objectives with other European governments both bilaterally and in the multilateral negotiations at the Nice IGC. Such interviewees included Grade 6 to Grade 3 officials within the MoD, FCO and Cabinet Office. Interviews also included officials who were part of the MoD team who initially proposed the Saint Malo initiative, those officials in attendance at Saint Malo and those present at subsequent negotiations, including at Nice. In some key aspects of the development of UK policy, this research has also used interview data from officials present at important meetings providing a rich empirical base to critically evaluate the development and negotiation of UK defence policy preferences.

The process of triangulation and cross-referencing ensures that interview evidence is verified against information that can be gained from quality sources within the news media such as *'Agence France Presse'*, *'Bulletin Quiotidien'*, *'The International Herald Tribune'*, *'The Guardian'*, *'The Daily Telegraph'*, and *'The Financial Times'* as well as UK government reports and press releases. Thus, a varied and extensive collection of primary sources are provided to triangulate and cross-reference the main contentions within this book (Schwandt 1997; Neuman 2000).[7] Nonetheless, the standard caveat for this sort of work should be adopted here too, namely that this research provides a provisional account of the Europeanization of British defence pending the opening of the archives under the 30-year rule in 2028 and beyond.

A reliance on elite interviews raises some notable methodological problems, which are more acute when dealing with sensitive areas of government policy, although only marginally more difficult than securing elite interviews within the mainstream of Whitehall (Dorril, 2000; Dover, 2005a). A considerable amount of government documentation, as with interview evidence, should however be viewed with some scepticism by the researcher; some government papers kept at the National Archives have been subject to 'sanitization' to remove evidence of individuals involvement in the cases they discuss (Aldrich 2001, 6; Davies 2001, 73-4). Supplementary documentary evidence that might be shown to the researcher, such as Cabinet Committee or Departmental minutes, do not often reveal individual positions or areas of tension between politicians and officials and therefore miss some of the rich tapestry of bureaucratic politics. It is therefore necessary, as other scholars have done, to use elite interview data as a means to supplement sparse and

---

7 Triangulation is a research method used to establish the trustworthiness of both qualitative and quantitative data. The aim of triangulation is to 'examine a single social phenomenon from more than one vantage point'. The triangulation approach argues that collecting data from different perspectives adds weight to the credibility of the analysis based on an foundation principle that no single source which is influenced by bias, priorities, and experiences can provide an accurate account of a situations but that by triangulating multiple sources contentions can be verified to a closer degree of accuracy.

deliberately obtuse official documentary evidence (Scott and Jackson 2004, 153; Smith 1996; Hennessy 2002).

Constructing a usable set of interview sources is also problematic – the availability of research subjects is highly restricted and developing new avenues of enquiry often dependent on a 'snowballing' strategy – that is, each respondent recommends one or two additional points of contact (Davies 2001, 76; Scott and Jackson 2004, 140). All the interviewees in this research have been given a random serial number and the comments attributed to them are referenced accordingly (following Davies 2001, 77). Interviewees were contacted more than once to ensure the accuracy of the comments attributed to them. In limited circumstances alternative primary sources were not available, but wherever possible interview evidence has been triangulated with additional primary and documentary evidence to provide corroborated accounts.

How to Explain Europeanization

This research has adopted an intergovernmentalist framework because this provides the most convincing available explanation of Europeanization. Anthony Forster argues that theorists have struggled with the complexity of Europeanization and that theorising has rather unhelpfully been split into considerations of institutions or policymaking (Forster 1999, 14). Anne Branch and Jorgen Øhrgaard take this criticism a step further by arguing that the focus of established European research should be on processes of governance rather than actors within government (Branch and Ohrgaard 1999, 129). Against established research and integration theories however, liberal intergovernmentalist theories fair very well.

In the so-called 'Classical Debate' within European studies of neofunctionalism versus intergovernmentalism the focus is on the process of European integration. The main difference between intergovernmentalists and neofunctionalists is the focus on different actors within the process. Neofunctionalists believe that supranational entrepreneurs are key to integration, whilst intergovernmentalists believe that supranational entrepreneurs hinder, rather than facilitate European integration. Thus governments are the principal actors in European integration. The second key difference is that intergovernmentalists believe that Europeanization is a carefully controlled phenomenon with governments controlling the pace and direction of integration, while neofunctionalists believe that Europeanization has an internal momentum with functional effectiveness being the main drivers. The final difference concerns the perceived global aim of the integration process. Neofunctionalists believe that the aim of European integration is to create a federal state, whereas intergovernmentalists see Europeanization as a framework through which national governments can be strengthened. Neofunctionalism had been, according to Roy Pryce, confined 'to the dustbin of history' in the 1980s (Pryce 1989, 2). Many academics have concluded that neofunctionalism offers no predictive capability because of the process of central institutions gaining more powers and competencies as a consequence of their existing competencies though it has had fleeting resilience in the last decade.

Just as liberal intergovernmentalist theories have been subject to revised theoretical ambitions during the 1990s, neofunctionalism and its hybrids have been similarly revised so that it can now be said that there is a collection of hybrid theories that share common features. Scholars like Wayne Sandholtz and Paul Pierson argue that neofunctionalism convincingly explains the Single European Act (SEA) and the creation of the single currency whilst acknowledging that the theoretical aspects of neofunctionalism are subject to criticism (Sandholtz 1993; Pierson 1996, 158). Ultimately though, neofunctionalists see Europeanization as a means by which to replace national governments rather than as a framework to strengthen them, as LI argues. Importantly neofunctionalism is unable to explain the formal Europeanization of defence and foreign policy integration as these are areas that are subject to high political considerations and thus have remained in the preserve of member governments rather than, as neofunctionalism suggests, increasingly under the control of the EU's supranational institutions. The obvious corrective to this is the case of the EU's defence industrial base which has been Europeanized through the efforts of the manufacturers and the European Commission (see Chapter 7).

Some analysts have proposed a diversification of theories and processes to explain Europeanization. For example, Anand Menon proposes that a sensible resolution to the intergovernmental / supranational dichotomy is that LI explains the processes and outcomes of IGCs, while neofunctionalism explains the processes and outcomes of everyday policy making (Kassim, Menon and Peters 2001; Menon and Weatherill 2002). However, if IGCs really do codify everyday policy making, it is counter intuitive to suggest that neofunctionalism can be completely separated from LI. If IGCs codify everyday policy making, as LI argues, there is logically no need to analyse this dynamic. LI's explanation assumes that all the important elements of routine policy making are included in the outcome of the IGC, this necessarily obviates the need for neofunctionalist studies of everyday policy making.

A more recent theoretical contender to LI, and a development of neofunctionalism, is what might be termed the supranationalist explanation. The supranationalist debate focuses on non-governmental supranational actors, but notably highlights the European Commission, and places these at the heart of the integration project. The rationale for this is that the European Commission is the broker between national governments and central institutions (Sandholtz 1992; Majone 1993). Similarly, as a result of policymaking concerning highly specialized and technical issues, the European Commission is also perceived to hold dominance over the supply of information, a point that it arguable validated by the cross-pillar approach to the arms trade (Kohler-Koch 1996).

Further recent theoretical contributions that attempt to supplant LI's dominance in this field, have sought to change the focus of EU research from explanations routed in governmental actors to explanations based around a political process. Consequently, they switch focus to research questions concerning why and how integration occurs rather than who formulates and implements the policies (Branch and Ohrgaard 1999). By changing the research focus, the governance-led debate seeks to explain why there are varying speeds of integration across different policy areas. The conclusion to this book picks up these threads and provides a basis for further research.

Of the main theoretical approaches to Europeanization a liberal intergovernmentalist framework remains the strongest in an increasingly congested field. The advantage of this framework for the study of the Europeanization of British defence policy is the clear, as are its explicit foundations. These foundations identify important institutions and actors in the Europeanization process and similarly provide clear lines of causation. An intergovernmentalist framework pushes the researcher to examine Europeanization in three stages: domestic policy formulation, intergovernmental bargaining and pooling of sovereignty into supranational institutions. The next three chapters do this whilst examining the formulation, negotiation and codification of the ESDP. The final two case studies adopt a liberal intergovernmentalist framework to analyse government and supranational behaviour in the Europeanization of British defence policy more widely.

Chapter 2

Domestic Policy Formulation: Pörtschach and Saint Malo[1]

This chapter explores the British government's intra-departmental debates and preparation of the so-called Saint Malo process. In doing so it will evaluate the argument that the Labour Party sought to project its pro-EU preferences with a proposed defence policy initiative as a direct trade-off to not being able to pursue the single currency project. It will argue that the Europeanized UK defence policy originated in the UK MoD, the product of an entrepreneurial policy official in the ministry, in response to a Cabinet Office memo seeking pro-European policies across Whitehall. Moreover, it argues that the Prime Minister drove this policy forward, providing key political motivation, whilst leaving trusted officials to negotiate the detail of the policy both within Whitehall and then without with the French and other EU governments (ultimately at the Nice IGC 2000). This chapter shows how Europeanization can strengthen and entrench the interests of national governments – thus enhancing, rather than degrading the interests of sovereign governments as per Alan Milward's 'European rescue of the nation state' thesis (Milward 1999).

The chapter also argues that the actors within the UK core executive, including the Prime Minister Tony Blair, took the decisions to 'Europeanize' British defence policy because they believed it provided the best option for strengthening NATO (their key defence preference). They thought that by providing key European support and thereby removing the mainstay of the burden for European security from the Americans that it would effectively lock-in continued American support for NATO. Moreover, ESDP would improve the EU's independent military capabilities (a much needed and strong reaction to a failed policy in the Balkans) and as a reaction to the perception that if Britain did not lead on this project then it was likely that the French and German governments would shape it to suit their preference. This fear was based on pressure from French and German officials during the 1990s on UK government policy makers to act positively on formulating deeply integrated EU external relations policies. These three factors provided significant motivation for the UK government's core executive to engage pro-actively on these issues (Dover 2005a).

This chapter particularly focuses on whether the UK government's preference for collaborative defence to be conducted through the transatlantic status-quo remained

---

1 A version of this chapter has appeared in Robert Dover (2005), 'The Prime Minister and the Core Executive: A Liberal Intergovernmentalist Reading of UK Defence Policy Formulation 1997-2000', *The British Journal of Politics and International Relations*, 7(4), 508–525. Many thanks to Blackwell Publishing for the permission to use this material.

stable between 1997 and 2000 (Howarth 2002, 1). This includes an analysis of whether the Saint Malo process represents a radical change in governmental preferences or merely a tactical shift of policy to achieve other European policy goals.[2] Interview evidence is used to describe how the British government developed the Saint Malo initiative that led to the ESDP. This evidence convincingly shows that the UK government stayed within established preferences and sought to find an innovative policy solution to meet its ideological, strategic and geopolitical ambitions.

The liberal intergovernmentalist approach argues that governments aggregate domestic pressures into governmental policy and preferences (Moravcsik 1998, 3). It draws a subtle difference between the concepts of governmental 'preferences' and governmental 'policy' (Moravcsik 1998, 3-9). Preferences are the stable positions held by governments, traceable over a large number of years, regardless of the political hue of the government, as discussed in the introduction (Moravcsik 1998, 5-6; Wallace in Hogwood and Gunn 1984, 19; Hogg and Hill 1995, 98). To discover that core UK government preferences changed during the Saint Malo process would be significant within LI's framework, as it would suggest that the Saint Malo process was a radical departure from the fifty-year history of the transatlantic paradigm.

Examining the sixty year post-war history of British defence policy leads to the following suggestions for what core British government defence preferences are: first, Europe's positive and engaged role in global affairs (McElvoy 1997, 27; McInnes 1998, 828; Blair 1995; Robertson 2004; Bailes 1996, 55-64); Second, Britain's preparedness to engage in the fluctuating balances of power and to intervene militarily as part of international coalitions. This is a demand led analysis of European security and a desire for collectivism within defence which, for the last 50years, has been through NATO (Bailes 1996, 56). This latter preference, a security guarantee underwritten by the transatlantic Alliance is, according to mainly Conservative party politicians, strained by the Saint Malo Process as it has the potential to adversely affect the relationship between the EU and the US (Redwood 2002; Rifkind 2004; Hunter 2002, 73; White 1999; Hatfield 2000; Lindley-French 2002, 67; George 2003, Key 2003). As will be later shown by later chapters of this book the strain on the transatlantic alliance, did not manifest itself through the ESDP, indeed just after the attack on New York in 2001, there was an unparalleled degree of EU-US unity. These good relations were subsequently eroded by the war on Iraq (Chapter Six) because of the levels of disagreement and opprobrium heaped on both sides by each other.

In contrast to preferences, policies refer to the issue specific positions of governments that, in Europeanization terms, are rationally pursued at Intergovernmental Conferences (IGCs) (Moravcsik 1998, 3). Liberal conceptions of Europeanization also argue that governments are rational actors who bargain to maximize their national interest (Moravcsik 1993, 480). Moreover, that governments

---

2 The 'Saint Malo Process' describes the bilateral negotiations between the British and French governments between July and December 1998 that resulted in a joint 'Letter of Intent' declaring that both governments would work towards improving European military capabilities. The 'Saint Malo process' also includes negotiations between governments up to and including the Nice Intergovernmental Conference (IGC).

aggregate the policy preferences of domestic interest groups into their national policy (Moravcsik 1993, 481). Government policies are thus shaped by the value of the benefits to be gained from co-operation with other governments, the certainty of these costs and benefits and the relative influence of the interest groups on areas of policy formulation (Moravcsik 1993, 481). Thus, co-operation at the EU level only occurs when governmental interests converge and furthermore argues that negotiations concerning EU policy areas are disconnected (Moravcsik 1998, 74; Olsen 2000, 191-198; Richardson 1996, 3-23; Key 2003; Redwood 2002).

This chapter calls on the work of Charles Lindblom to illuminate the processes behind British defence policy formulation and argues that the Europeanization of this policy sector conforms closely to Lindblom's 'successive limited comparisons' framework (Lindblom 1959, 76-8). His thesis was a reaction to the growth of studies offering rational explanations of policy-making. Lindblom highlights the flaws with rational accounts: that policy makers are very rarely faced with neat problems described by rational theories, they do not have all the necessary information to make a rational choice, they do not necessarily have the time or resources to consider all the possible policy options, nor might they be sufficiently objective to make a rational decision (Lindblom 1959, 76-8). Moreover, once a policy has been made, rational choice theories do not allow for the possibility that the policy might fail or might need amendment. Thus, Lindblom argues that an alternative approach might consider policy making as a process of successive limited comparisons – that is the development of policy through successive trial and error (Lindblom 1959, 79).

This chapter advances five central contentions. First, that the Saint Malo initiative reflected a tactical shift of UK defence policy within fixed government preferences concerning the transatlantic security guarantee. Second, that the PM centralized the defence policy decision making process within a core executive that comprized the PM and his senior political advisors, the European Secretariat of the Cabinet Office, the Secretaries of State for Defence and Foreign and Commonwealth Affairs, and their respective Policy and Political Directors, Richard Hatfield and Emyr Jones-Parry. Third, that the Prime Minister was central to the development of the pro-European British defence policy, motivated as he was by the geopolitical and exogenous factors of the external security situation in Kosovo and by the desire to place Britain 'at the heart of Europe' but did not tightly control the detail of the policy. Importantly, the PM gave his support to the direction of the policy and left officials, on trust, to negotiate the detail of the policy within the parameters he was prepared to support. Fourthly, that the presentation of the pro-European defence policy to the domestic electorate, other European governments, the US President, Defense Department and the US State Department was conducted by advocating the elements of the policy that appealed to the lowest common denominators between all the parties. Fifth and finally, that liberal intergovernmentalist explanations of Europeanization fail to encapsulate the exact nature of domestic policy formulation. The Europeanization of British defence policy and the parallel development of common European security and defence policy can be seen as a process of 'successive limited comparisons'. Short term politically expedient goals were met with pragmatism and efforts to find alternative policy areas to the single currency were pursued and in which the government could positively engage with Europe followed by the development of a pro-European defence policy to meet this overall aim.

The Saint Malo Initiative as a Tactical Policy Shift

The contention that the Saint Malo initiative was a tactical shift of policies, is important to Labour party politicians engaged in the policy formulation process – because it underplays the risks they took with a policy area that touches on core national sovereignty as well as being a necessary element of continued transatlantic diplomacy. The 'special relationship' between the UK and US, for politicians and officials on both sides of the Atlantic, has to remain 'special' in the public discourse in order to serve as a useful political tool, justifying some of the decisions taken in relation to some homeland security measures associated with the 'Global War on Terror', and wars on Afghanistan and Iraq following the terrorist attacks on New York. UK-US co-operation on homeland security measures have continued to publicly emphasize the closeness of the 'special relationship', the Europeanization of British defence policy continues to put some strain on the relationship between some sections of the US and UK defence and foreign policy bureaucracies. Indeed, a former high-ranking official, said in conversation about EU initiatives to acquire intelligence related satellite imagery, that 'any support from your government on this or other EU measures will ensure that the special relationship becomes very un-special' (Interview S). His critique of the UK's Europeanization was that the government had lost sight of the importance of the transatlantic alliance and that American security hegemony provides the UK and the EU with the best form of collective defence available. For the Labour Government and Prime Minister Blair, in particular, who has made particularly strong efforts to be the bridge between the EU and America the perception of undermining the Alliance are damaging, particularly in the context of the US-UK actions on Iraq (see Chapter Six) where British diplomacy served to alienate a large number of European governments and reinstated the UK to the position of 'awkward partner' in Europe.

This section examines the argument that the Saint Malo initiative was a tactical shift in policies rather than a shift in core government preferences. The factors that appear in support of the argument that this was a policy shift were the speed of the decision, absence of economic considerations, and that the initiative ran contrary to explicit Labour Party policy. These are attractive factors but not strong enough to amount to a preference shift. Further, positive evidence that this initiative was a tactical shift of policy can be found in the need to find alternatives to the single currency that the UK government could support. The geopolitical and security rationale behind the policy in addition to the careful negotiations conducted by UK officials makes the case for these being a tactical shift of policy a strong one.

The Saint Malo initiative was announced with a perception of undue haste, especially in the context of defence policy being seen to be a traditionally slowly evolving policy area, subject to long policy reviews and internal consultations. The vast majority of policy initiatives are rigorously analysed for their strategic and economic implications before being brought before Parliament and implemented

(Hopkinson 2003; Rifkind 2004). The Prime Minister, by contrast, gave a speech that provided the motivation for greater Anglo-French defence cooperation and therefore effectively announced the Saint Malo initiative, at the Pörtschach press conference on 25 October 1998 at a time when the debate between the MoD and FCO concerning the policy remained unresolved, but did allow the FCO an 'elegant withdrawal from the debate' (Interview A 2002; Robertson 2004).

The initiative was formally announced at Saint Malo (6 December 1998) with a similar perception of haste. This was partly because it ran contrary to published Labour party policy both before and immediately after the 1997 general election (Labour Party 1996, 11-15). These two factors suggest that the initiative was not under active consideration until the spring of 1998 (Clark 1997; Interview B 2002; Interview C 2003). Furthermore, major changes in defence policy, from 1946, had their origins in the government's desire to reduce or maintain the defence budget. (Dorman 2001, 192). Indeed many, including former Chief of Defence Staff Charles Guthrie argue that the primary motivation for defence reviews are the desire to reduce defence budget spending within a framework of changing strategic considerations (Garden 2003; Guthrie 2003). In the context of the historically identifiable imperative of budgetary considerations – particularly equipment and manpower budgets – it would be reasonable to assume that these factors would play a role in the Europeanization of British defence policy in 1998, as they have done in arms trade policy more widely (Chapter 7).

The Labour party's approach to defence policy leading up to the 1997 election had been to place a great emphasis on the economic benefits that could be derived from a revised defence policy, to be realized through an improvement to the defence and high technology industrial bases they argued had been neglected by the Conservative government (Labour Party Manifesto 1997, 11-15). To commentators, notably Stefano Silvestri and Matthew Uttley, the continued success of the defence industrial base is the key to the 'Europeanization' of the defence sphere (Silvestri 1999, 20; Uttley in Croft, Dorman, Rees and Uttley 2001, 126-7). They argue that the UK, French and Italian governments have guarded their defence industries and as a result failed to produce a pan-European defence industrial base to rival the dominance of the American military industrial complex (Silvestri 1999, 19; Uttley 2001, 126-7). Such a failure results in the collective EU defence capability being significantly lower Euro for Euro than that of the United States; of course this belies a political reality that there is no united states of Europe as there is a United States of America, and therefore the comparison is arguably false. Consolidation across Europe would however produce an estimated cost saving of some 10-12% (Hartley in House of Lords Report 2000, 38). Indeed the likely result of failing to address diminishing defence budgets (produced through year on year stability of the budget coupled with a rising equipment cost base) is to see UK military capabilities eroded 'beyond which the maintenance of a military capability for anything other the most local defence requirements will become impossible.' (Alexander and Garden 2001, 513-515: Ministry of Defence Performance Review 2000, 43; Garden 1989, 38-39; Sandler and Hartley 1995, 185-7; Taylor 1998, 41). Projections show that if British GDP grows at 3% for the next 15 to 20 years and defence spending is maintained at current levels, the defence budget as a share of GDP will have decreased from

2.4% in 2000 to 1.3% by 2015 against the historic NATO aspiration of defence spending to be 5% of GDP but an established actual commitment of 2% of GDP (Alexander and Garden 2001, 520). This analysis is supported by interviewees such as Lord Brittan and Pol de Witte from NATO, who take it to its logical conclusion that greater defence co-operation should lead to a more cost-effective provision of defence across the EU (Brittan 2003; Interview C 2003; de Witte 2004).

Economic analyses of European defence fail to take into account the very strong influence of historical contingency, strategic reality, national pride and military independence when considering the current configuration of European defence forces and procurement practises. The separation of the EU into component nation states presents a large barrier to the Europeanization of defence policy across the Union. Eurosceptics cite the numerous wars between EU states in the last three hundred years of European history, the proximity of the second world war to the present day in relative terms and that the European project is post-conflict reconstruction project and thus subject to potential failure. Moreover, it is an article of faith within the armed forces that it is necessary for sovereign governments to ensure the security of defence equipment supply through developing and retaining an active defence industrial base. It is possible to buy 'off-the-shelf' equipment from American manufacturers, for example, but the security of maintenance contracts and spare parts are dependent on the goodwill of the American government – which adds complications to a government's foreign policy preferences, although not insurmountable ones (Page 2006, Conclusion). Thus many European governments seek to maintain and independent defence industrial base not only to retain their foreign policy independence and security of equipment supply, but also as part of their wider economic and trade policy to sell equipment and thereby garner a positive defence equipment trading balance. Consolidating defence industries does not provide a long-term fix to the gap between European and American capabilities, which are primarily financially focussed, the 'Europeanization' of British defence policy might delay the erosion of domestic defence capabilities and would produce a greater level of capabilities for comparable funding.

Achieving budgetary savings from the defence budget would have been electorally rational, as it would have also allowed Labour to focus spending on electorally significant issues notably the National Health Service, education and pensions (Denver 2003, 100). With voter concern on defence only coming seventeenth out of nineteen priority areas, securing financial savings from the defence budget would have been rational and expedient (Cowley and Quayle 2002, 58). However, there is very little evidence that budgetary considerations played a significant or even minor role in the formulation of UK defence policy between 1997 and 2000, including in the Strategic Defence Review (SDR), feeding into a conclusion that the Saint Malo initiative was a shift of policy rather than of preferences (Interview A 2002; Interview B 2002; Interview I 2002; Interview M 2002).

The most significant policy issue facing the EU in 1997 was the development of the single currency. The UK government's defence initiatives can be seen as a pragmatic response to the politically untenable single currency project; the tenability of which is a highly contested point and one that appears to have been decided internally within the Cabinet level of the government. Standing on a pro-EU election platform

Labour had been keen to show principled support for the project but had added important economic caveats regarding membership, borne of Treasury concerns over convergence criteria and public dissatisfaction with the EU (Young 1999; Milner 2002). This meant that in the big EU policy area of 1997 the Labour government felt that is was unable to demonstrate its pro-European credentials. This perception led to the consideration of alternative policy areas in which the UK government could demonstrate European policy entrepreneurship (Duncan-Smith 2001, 3-4; Interview A 2002; Interview D 2003; Interview M 2002; Redwood 2003). The pro-European defence initiative should, therefore, be seen as part of the government's broad European policy rather than a solely defence based initiative, although one in which the government believed that real benefits to collective European defence and security capabilities could be accrued.

Strategic considerations formed a large part of the UK government's, and particularly the PM's willingness to support the Saint Malo initiative. Not only did the policy demonstrate the government's willingness to engage positively with the EU and its member governments but also to build up real capabilities that could be used to intervene in humanitarian crises such as those in the Balkans. The escalation of Serbian hostility towards the ethnic Albanian population in Kosovo population in 1997 caused the British government to contemplate possible actions against the Yugoslavian government in Belgrade in December 1997 and then again in September and October 1998 (Interview C 2002; Interview I 2002; Garden 2003; Wallace 2003). A realization within the FCO of President Clinton's unwillingness to engage with this issue, without onerous conditions being placed on military operations[3] and further, with the President's attention being drawn towards the fallout from the 'Lewinsky affair' at home, led British policy makers to consider alternatives (Interview E 2003).

In confronting the frustrations over Kosovo, and the realization that the EU governments were unable to act to prevent and extinguish conflict on their geographical backdoor, the Prime Minister announced at the informal EU meeting at Pörtschach a revolutionary message that he claimed would strengthen European defence and the transatlantic Alliance (Silvestri 1999, 14; Lichfield 1998; Cole 1998, 5; Rutten 2001, 1-3). Thus, in the context of the situation in the Balkans, the Saint Malo initiative was a reaction to strategic stimuli and not a radical departure from the stable governmental preferences founded in the transatlantic alliance.

The Centralization of Roles to Number 10 and the Cabinet Office

A key feature of the Europeanization of British defence policy in the post-1997 era was the way the Prime Minister centralized UK European defence policy formulation within the core executive; a select group of politicians and officials drawn from Number 10, the Cabinet Office, FCO and MoD. This centralization is

---

3 The American conditions on military action were broadly that the campaign should be conducted predominantly from the air and that the use of infantry should be highly restricted; indeed it is not clear that the American President, Department of Defense and State Department, acting as one, would have not vetoed this as a policy option.

particularly notable as it places the Europeanization of this policy area firmly away from 'standard policy formulation' thinking which highlights routine aspects of the defence policy making process and into a debate which views it as representing a 'centralized' or 'Presidential' form of policy making.

That a change to the strategic direction of defence policy was allowed to be nurtured at all is somewhat surprising given the context of the Labour Party's recent historical electoral legacy of 'unilaterism' in the early 1980s.[4] The policy entrepreneurship of officials like Richard Hatfield must, therefore, have emanated from alternative sources than a supportive party political environment as part of the Labour party's success in the 1997 election was to remove defence as a major area of debate during the campaign, whilst retaining a commitment to a defence review (Interview I 2002; Interview M 2002). This may have been surprising as the Armed Services were severely overstretched – but relatively under-utilized in comparison to 2003-6 – unable to retain personnel and were similarly unable to re-equip due to major equipment programmes being both late and over-budget (McInnes 1998, 829). Once in power the government signalled a strong desire to be positive on defence. This included the announcement of the Strategic Defence Review and statements that major savings would not be immediately sought from the defence budget (Clarke 1998; Freedman in Seldon 2001, 289-305; Ministry of Defence Expenditure Plans 2003)[5] During the 1997 Labour Party conference, the PM in his headline speech argued that Britain should fulfil its historic legacy '…to lead at the heart of Europe' (Anne McElvoy 1997). This statement of intent presented an opportunity for astute civil servants, like Richard Hatfield, to bring the MoD and the defence agenda to the forefront of the government's policy making agenda, with a Europeanizing core, and also to please their new political masters early in the new term of government.

The 'Presidential' style of government, as described by Anthony Seldon and Peter Hennessy, has produced a heavily laden top-down approach to policy making (Seldon 2001, vii-viii; Hennessy 2000, 477; Liddle and Mandelson 1995, Chapter 9; Hennessy 2003; White 2003). The use of small cabinet sub-committees and informal meetings between cabinet ministers, senior civil servants (Grade 3 and above) and special advisors routinely take favoured subjects out of the sphere of normal civil service decision-making processes and into small centralized policy making for a, which emphasizes the role of the Prime Minister or the Minister in charge (Interview M 2002; Blunkett 2006). This centralized style of government is particularly pertinent to defence policy formulation. Government and opposition politicians and officials close to the process highlighted the centrality of the PM's role in this policy development (Interview I 2002; George 2003; Palmer 2002).

Following Blair's 'Heart of Europe' speech at the 1997 Labour Party conference there was a meeting of key Cabinet Ministers and senior civil servants engaged

---

4 Unilateralism being the discursive shorthand for the range of anti-nuclear armaments policies the Labour Party included in its manifesto for the 1983 General Election and is referred to as being one of the key reasons Margaret Thatcher's Conservative Party won a large majority in that particular election.

5 The MoD's resource budgets in Financial Years 99-03 are: 1999-00; £31,967, 459,000; 2000-01; £32,949, 615,000; 2001-02; £34,299, 438,000; 2002-03; £34,257, 993,000.

in co-ordinating EU policy within the Cabinet and Foreign Office (Interview A 2002; Interview B 2002). This meeting was in response to a memorandum sent round Whitehall by Number 10 asking for areas in which the UK could positively engage with EU policy initiatives. At this meeting Tony Blair asked the assembled Permanent Under-Secretaries to implement a change in operating rationale (Interview B 2002; Interview I 2002; Robertson 2004). Blair's instructions centred on finding policy areas in which Britain could be more co-operative or, indeed, lead in the EU (Interview B 2002; White 2003).[6] One Foreign and Commonwealth Office interviewee said this process aimed to put 'water into the policy wine', that is to say, to take a bold statement of pro-European intent from the PM and to use this to seek possible ideas from senior civil servants that would lead to European initiatives without compromising core British interests (Interview B 2002).

This process was managed through a version of the (E)DOP Committee whose remit was to review the approach of each government department to the EU.[7] This committee agreed with the view of Secretary of State for Defence, George Robertson, primed by Richard Hatfield, who had identified defence as being an area in which Britain could usefully lead. This was partly to reduce the pressure on the government from European colleagues about their reticence both on the issue of the single currency and to act positively on defence integration issues (Interview B 2002; Interview M 2002). The Treasury and Cabinet Committees reviewing British EU policy had quickly concluded that the government could not join the single currency project for electoral and economic reasons (Black 2003; White 2003; Interview M 2002). The civil service officials interviewed for this research argued that there was no link between the decision to adopt a conservative approach to the single currency and the decision to act positively on defence policy (Interview B 2002; Interview D 2003; Interview G 2002; Interview M 2002). These officials are, in the main, still engaged in defence policy making or diplomatic careers and therefore may have felt constrained in the responses they could give. Roger Liddle, the Prime Minister's then personal advisor on EU issues, was decidedly more strident in arguing that there was no link between the Europeanization of defence and a reticence towards the single currency project – this interview evidence is heavily tainted by political bias and the desire, in a very small way, to assist in securing a particular view of the Prime Minister's historical legacy. Other interviewees did not adopt such absolute positions. Robertson, for example, argued that the Saint Malo initiative was worthy of being followed in its own right but that the unwillingness to join the single currency had made the political atmosphere more permissive and therefore more conducive for such suggestions (Interview I 2002; Robertson 2004).

The principle reason for the focus on defence as an area in which Britain could play a leading role was a result of the MoD being the only Department to answer the call for areas of policy that could be 'Europeanized' (Interview A 2002; Interview

---

6 Michael White said this was made clear to him on a lobby journalist basis.

7 The best information this research could find on the membership of (E)DOP was that the membership was the Prime Minister, the Foreign Secretary, Peter Mandelson, Colin Budd, Brian Bender, and Stephen Wall from The Permanent Representation to the EU. It should be noted that interviewees were not keen to reveal the membership of this committee.

I 2002). It also reflects British strategic thinking in the context of the crisis in the Balkans where military dependency on the US was seen as a contributing factor to an ineffective European response to the civil war. Pan-European political embarrassment about the response to Yugoslavia has channelled itself into an accepted discourse that the Union should do more to engage in military and quasi-military activities that promotes and enforces peace in its near-abroad and wider.

The centralized account of the Europeanization of domestic policy formulation runs contrary to the liberal intergovernmentalist account which prefaces the important of domestic interest groups exerting pressure on government to pursue policies that they support. This is partly because the interest groups engaged in this issue did not include the arms manufacturers (see Chapter 7), and only included advisory interest groups. The leverage these interest groups hold against the government are in the electoral and media pressure they can exert. In the Saint Malo case study such groups have fed into the policy formulation process with varying degrees of success. Groups who have influenced the Europeanization of British defence or who are considered to have done so by informed commentators have been very closely linked with the Labour party. This is particularly true of the Centre for European Reform and The Foreign Policy Centre who, despite being officially apolitical are given regular access to high level officials and politicians and are routinely included in Cabinet Office policy committees (Interview A 2002; Grant 2003).[8]

Some analysts argued that the Centre for European Reform, headed by Charles Grant, had initially suggested the pro-European defence policy (Spear 2001). Grant puts his role more modestly as having given external validation to a policy already under consideration (Grant 2003). The role of consultative bodies like the European Institute for Security Studies (part of the now defunct WEU), RIIA, RUSI and other research organizations is to provide the government with a means to consult widely on defence issues. The effect meetings and seminars by these organizations had on policy making are difficult to discern but what is clear is that the advisory output followed on rather than preceded the Saint Malo decision, and therefore cannot be said to have triggered it. Moreover, whilst officials attending these seminars can test whether certain policy initiatives are acceptable to key domestic producer groups no officials interviewed were able to quantify how much influence these events have on UK government policy making (Interview D 2003; Interview G 2002; Interview M 2002).[9]

The Armed Forces are a key interest group in defence policy formulation and thereby in the Europeanization debate; significant opposition from the Forces would have had a serious impact on the government's ability to pursue this policy (Menon 2000, 139; Interview C 2002; Garden 2003; Interview I 2003). Of further significance

---

8   Interview A sat on several Cabinet Office committees exploring EU issues. These committees included think-tank analysts like Charles Grant and Heather Grabbe and academics, for example, Anand Menon.

9   Interview M and Interview E argued that it was useful to test ideas on groups of informed commentators but that decisions were not made by a committee of the knowledgeable. Interview D argued that informal discussions held under the 'Chatham House rule' often produced the most fruitful results in terms of policy ideas.

is the position and role of the Chief of the Defence Staff who advises the PM directly – it would be, similarly, politically difficult for the PM to proceed in the face of vociferous opposition from the Chief of the Defence Staff. Lord Guthrie's role in the formulation process was therefore important, and between October-December 1998 the Prime Minister was in close contact with him concerning the Saint Malo initiative. Guthrie felt that it was in the best interests of the Services to be engaged in this process, so long as NATO was not undermined, in order that they could help shape the policy to best reflect the Services interests (Interview A 2002; Interview C 2002). Those close to Guthrie say he gave his support to the Saint Malo process having come to the opinion that a restructuring of the British armed forces was necessary to better reflect the operational capability of Britain and in securing better value defence forces across Europe (Interview C 2002; Interview D 2003; Interview I 2002). The support Guthrie provided demonstrated a level of acceptance within the UK defence establishment, including from groups that might have been expected to have reservations about the Europeanization initiative.

The Saint Malo initiative was, in terms of competency and responsibility, an area of interest for both the MoD and FCO. The interdepartmental relationship between the MoD and FCO is interesting in terms of the bureaucratic politics surrounding such developments and is also a key area of contested opinion within the history of the Saint Malo initiative. The balance of the available evidence is that the Europeanization of this policy was 'centralized', which suggests that the Saint Malo process was driven by officials within Downing Street and the Cabinet Office who finalized the details of the policy and then sought agreement amongst domestic interest groups. Further, that the fortunate positioning of and good working relations between Richard Hatfield and Emyr Jones-Parry, as Policy Directors of the MoD and FCO respectively, enhanced the development and negotiation of the ESDP provisions into the Nice Treaty (Grant 2003; Interview D 2003; Interview G 2003). Following the Prime Minister's declaration at Pörtschach in October 1998 the debate between the FCO and MoD ended with both accepting the substance of the initiatives (Interview A 2002; Robertson, 2004). The collaborative work of Hatfield and Jones-Parry focussed on crucial issues and negotiating strategies. Where one might normally expect there to be institutional roadblocks erected to halt or divert proposals, the personal relationship between these two officials ensured that the departments worked to a relatively unified agenda (Interview A 2002; Interview M 2002). This key inter-departmental relationship helped to inform a wider bureaucratic context, determined by civil servants, where a common goal was established and institutional interests were put to one side, or negotiated with a presumption for the agreed policy.

To try and argue that the Saint Malo initiative fits into a standard policy formulation approach means to highlight the historical continuation of certain practices to emphasize the absence of radicalism in British defence policy. Further, it suggests that the stimulation for the Saint Malo initiative should have come from within the MoD where defence policy is an area where decisions are made by a small number of individuals, often in the light of incomplete information and as such decisions are made more by accretion than by selection. Moreover, that the MoD should have come to a position of agreement with the FCO towards a joint approach in policy making in recognition of the FCO's pre-eminent role in European policy negotiation. There is not significant evidence for either of these positions within the domestic policy formulation of the Saint Malo initiative; but substantial evidence that the UK European defence policy was pursued from the core executive with its leading advocates being Tony Blair, George Robertson (and subsequently Geoffrey Hoon who became Secretary of State for Defence on 11 October 1999) and their respective political and Civil Service advisors (Interview D 2003; Interview M 2002). This lends weight to a core argument advanced in this chapter that the core executive determines the formal Europeanization of British defence policy but that in other areas of defence Europeanization, interest groups gain a much larger influence over the process.

Perhaps somewhat surprisingly, given the sensitivity of defence issues within Parliament, the scrutiny function of both Houses was given a low profile during the formulation of the Saint Malo initiative. The House of Commons Parliamentary Select Committee on Defence and the House of Lords Committee on European Affairs, did try to scrutinize the initiative, but these efforts were largely lost on both public and political audiences. The political focus at the time was on EU tax harmonization and other public service debates, rather than on defence. Parliament, via the European and Defence Select Committees, both heavily atlanticist in membership, contributed to the Europeanization debate through seventeen reports between 1998 and 2001 (George 2003). In particular, the '*Report on the ESDP*' by the House of Lords Committee on the European Union demonstrated the depth and reach of Parliamentary scrutiny on the emerging European security and defence policy (House of Lords 15th Report 2000). The leverage the Committees had on the Prime Minister and the core executive during the development of defence policy between 1997 and 2000 was muted because of the extent of the government's Commons majority (George 2003; Rifkind 2004).[10]

The evidence from the Saint Malo initiative is that the core executive was able to effectively bypass Parliament through use of several consultation meetings targeted at government backbenchers with the aim of countering fears of the PLP that Saint Malo would undermine NATO. Such a meeting was held of the PLP on 2 December 1998, hosted by the PM and the Secretaries of State for Defence and Foreign and Commonwealth Affairs to launch the initiative within the Party and met with broad agreement (Palmer 2002; George 2003).[11] In short, Parliament had neither a significant effect on holding the government to account on this initiative, because it was not as politically significant as public service reforms in 1998, nor did it play a significant role in the formulation of the policy. Furthermore, opposition to the policy from

---

10 From the Defence Select Committee's perspective they aimed to exert media, public and political pressure through the production of reports. Former Defence Secretary Rifkind said that the Committee has influence to a limited degree. Questioning by the Committee could be awkward but would never be enough to dissuade the adoption of any particular policy.

11 Both interviewees stated that the Prime Minister and Secretaries of State took as many questions as there were from the PLP members who were given reassurances that this did not undermine NATO.

PLP and Conservative party members was subdued because of the government's 'honeymoon' period and because the PLP were content to allow the government to proceed on trust whilst the Conservative opposition were attempting to regroup following their very heavy electoral loss in 1997. Parliament, insofar as it can be seen as an interest group, scrutinized – rather than initiated – defence policy, through Parliamentary debates, the routine scrutiny of the SDR legislation and the Reports of both the House of Commons and House of Lords Defence Select Committees, further supporting a conclusion that policy formulation was concentrated in the core executive to the exclusion of Parliamentary processes.

The absence of Parliamentary initiation and scrutiny of defence policy has a large impact on what can be learnt from the phenomenon of Europeanization, and is a trait factored across the Iraqi and arms trade case studies as well. Europeanization appears to take place, politically, in the realms of the core executive and in public discourse – which is fuelled by a predominantly 'eurosceptic' media, and commercially, through the globalization of capital and culture, and bureaucratically, through developments within government departments and in the relationship between Whitehall and EU institutions. What this tells us about Europeanization is that it is a technocratic process, with public policy outputs. It is controlled at a policy level that is one step removed from what the public might consider 'democratic' and therefore has a wide ranging and important implications for the public to consider.

The Departmental debate between the MoD and FCO, in which a large number of issues – including those on the impact this would have on the transatlantic relationship, was ended by the PM's announcement at Pörtschach. The way this legitimate departmental debate was handled was akin to the 'Napoleonic' style of government that White and Hennessy claim Blair adopted after the 1997 general election (White 2003; Hennessy 2001). The term 'Napoleonic' was coined by the Prime Minister's advisor Jonathan Powell, informed by a classical education, rather than one accepted by the Prime Minister himself – although this term was disclosed via a private lobby briefing at which White and Hennessy were present. The 'Napoleonic' system meant that the Prime Minister and the core executive steered the strategic direction of the policy and then officials resolved the details of this policy. The policy process gave MoD Policy Director Richard Hatfield a great deal of influence over the direction of the policy – once the Secretary of State for Defence George Robertson had persuaded Tony Blair of the wisdom of the policy it took on an enhanced credibility. The resolution of an interdepartmental debate by the PM and the core executive is not exceptional, particularly in the context of Blair's government. This adds further weight to the argument that the Europeanization of British defence policy that occurred at Saint Malo was not a shift in core government preferences but was a tactical shift in defence policy.

The Centrality of the Prime Minister to the Saint Malo Initiative

Tony Blair was, to put it baldly, central to the development of the Saint Malo initiative and the formal Europeanization of British defence policy between 1997- 2000, and that this policy is indicative of the method of governance pursued by the

PM. It was the PM, rather than the Secretary of State for Defence, George Robertson who announced the Saint Malo initiative. Interviewees from the FCO and Cabinet Office argue that this demonstrates the centrality of the PM and Cabinet Office in the process and the temporary marginalization of the MoD and FCO (Interview A 2002; Interview B 2002; Interview M 2002). Even within the first four years of the Labour government the Good Friday Agreement, and public private finance initiative schemes (PFI) are further examples of where the PM has got closely involved with driving key policies through and shows a general trend towards a central role in a diverse range of policies (Forster and Blair 2002, 68-9).

An examination of the informal conference at Pörtschach (21 October 1998), which was effectively the public introduction to the Saint Malo Accords, adds some important context to Blair's public announcement. The PM's aircraft was delayed, reducing the time available to discuss strategy for the informal meeting with key officials, whilst the debate between the MoD and FCO was unresolved (Interview C 2002; Robertson 2004). Surrounding the Pörtschach meeting was the Prime Minister's desire to make a pro-EU statement at the conference to signal the difference between his and the previous Conservative government but on the single policy area identified for entrepreneurship, defence, he appeared to be hampered by a prolonged debate between the lead departments. On the advice of Stephen Wall, and from a presentational perspective, the Prime Minister's communications advisor Alistair Campbell, the PM decided to override the interdepartmental debate and make an announcement signalling the UK's decision to be positive on EU defence capabilities (Interview A 2002; Robertson 2004). This set in train a change of policy without seeking full agreement between the two departments (Robertson 2004). Blair's announcement at Pörtschach was deliberately underplayed to the UK media by the Prime Minister's communications officers, a strategy that ensured that the subtle change in the official emphasis in UK defence policy was not subject to a wider debate in the UK media and thus potential revisions.

The Prime Minister's role, in this instance, is indicative of the extent to which this policy was a crucial early element of the government's first term programme. Moreover, by remaining so closely involved and associated with the initiative Blair invested a great deal of his most valuable asset, his personal credibility, in a policy with very easily measurable successes and failures. By pursuing this policy, he also took a number of political risks. The first of these was with the transatlantic alliance itself. If the policy had been perceived by the US State Department or key NATO allies in a negative way there is a possibility that ESDP could have destabilized NATO. From the perspective of the Conservative opposition and transatlanticist sections of the Parliamentary Labour Party, the Labour government seemed to be reversing a long history of British defence preferences being vested exclusively in the NATO transatlantic alliance (Freedman 1999, ii; Robertson 2004; Redwood 2002; Key 2003; George 2003; Interview D 2003). The previous Conservative government had believed that NATO was more than a military organization also containing a political dimension, through 'Partnership for Peace' that assisted defence transformation in ex-communist Central Eastern European states. In contrast, the Labour party position under Blair, who notably was without a great deal of personal experience of defence issues, seems to have provided a division of labour whereby security issues are vested in NATO and political competencies concentrated in the EU (Portillo 1996, 3).

Whilst Blair may have provided the political motivation and impetus for the Saint Malo initiative he did not involve himself with resolving the fine detail of the policy (Hague 2002, 3; Interview D 2003; Interview M 2002). This task was left to those pro-European policy advisors and politicians employed within Number 10 and the Cabinet Office following the 1997 General Election which included George Robertson to Secretary of State for Defence,[12] Sir Stephen Wall who was moved from UKREP to Head of the European Secretariat in the Cabinet Office, Peter Mandelson to the rank of Cabinet Minister without Portfolio and Roger Liddle as the PM's personal political advisor (Robertson, 2004; Ahmed and Hinscliff 2000, 4; Groom 2001, 23). The Prime Minister's use of his power of patronage was contextually significant to the extent that European policy expertise was predominantly in favour of further European integration and likely to drive this agenda focussed through Labour's first term of office. Furthermore, the close involvement of the Prime Minister marks this policy out as a significant initiative in the first term of the Blair government but does not mark it out as being unusual.

Lowest Common Denominator Agreements

The presentation of the pro-EU defence policy used 'successive limited comparisons' to try and convince external actors of the UK position and to negotiate around this position. The presentation of this policy to the Clinton and Bush Administrations, the US State Department, the US Department of Defense, the French government, and the domestic British audience was more akin to finding lowest common denominator positions. For example, the policy was presented to the US State Department, at desk officer level, as strengthening NATO, to the French President as a genuine advance towards a more closely integrated EU and to the domestic audience as a policy that did not mean a loss of core national sovereignty nor one that would see UK armed personnel being forced into a European army controlled by a supranational EU organization (Tweedie 2002, 2; Interview A 2002; Interview E 2003; de Witte 2004).

The process of attaining lowest common denominator agreement allowed the headline goal of the policy – the improvement of EU co-operation on defence issues – was to be advanced whilst not resolving the minutiae of policy detail. Indeed, it is notable that the minutiae of the policy detail was entrusted to the two Policy Directors of the MoD and FCO, Richard Hatfield and Emyr Jones-Parry, to negotiate with European governments within the confines of a framework established by the Prime Minister and his Secretaries of State (Interview D 2003; Interview G 2003). Whilst the pro-EU UK defence policy arose partly in the absence of alternatives to meet the UK government's short-term EU strategy and longer term UK defence ambitions in 1999 and 2000, the government invested a great deal of effort through

---

12 Robertson was a leading figure in the pro-EU section of the Labour party. He was also a member of the Royal Institute of International Affairs, and a Labour Party spokesman on Defence and Foreign Affairs, 1982-93.

bilateral negotiations with all EU government in ensuring that the integration of defence policy was a success (Interview D 2003; Interview E 2002; Interview G 2003). These efforts concentrated on securing agreement on operational and institutional arrangements and similarly ensuring that the smaller countries within the EU were fully involved in the development of ESDP in the lead up to the Nice IGC. (Interview A 2002; Interview E 2003; Jonson 2003). Gaining agreement on the Berlin Plus provisions, which ensured EU access to NATO assets, and ensuring that smaller member governments remain actively involved in the process was described by a Cabinet Office official as being the only measure of success or failure the UK government holds for the Saint Malo initiatives (Interview M 2002; Interview A 2002). The official added that the importance for the UK government was that the ESDP became operationally credible once the Berlin Plus provisions were signed (Interview M 2002; Interview A 2002).

By using careful diplomatic presentation skills and avoiding negotiating on precise policy details UK government officials were then able to negotiate with a wide range of internal and external actors to reach a lowest common denomination agreement that allowed the Saint Malo initiative to progress. In this respect a liberal intergovernmentalist framework accurately accounts for the process by which, in this instance agreement is reached.

Conclusion: The Dominance of the Core Executive

The Saint Malo and Pörtschach examples, examined in this chapter demonstrate that the Prime Minister and his close advisors, on the basis of a desire to make a positive statement of intent at Pörtschach, implied an aggregation of domestic policy pressures. The formulation of defence policy in the 1997-2000 period was completed on a narrow reading of national interests as defined by this small group of politicians and officials, within the core executive, who were motivated to achieve a particular aim and did so in a manner reminiscent of Lindblom's 'successive limited comparisons' (Lindblom 1959).

The Saint Malo initiative amounted to a tactical shift of UK defence policy within established core preferences. This tactical shift aimed to meet a series of short-term EU policy goals, the need to become engaged in European integration and to a far lesser extent maximize budgetary efficiencies within UK defence policy to focus finance on core government preferences. Furthermore, these initiatives aimed to meet long term defence policy goals of improving UK and EU capabilities to meet military crises in the near abroad like the Balkans, but also to confront the long term problem of keeping the United States involved in EU security whilst still bearing the brunt of the burden of European security.

In terms of bureaucratic processes, this chapter has highlighted the extent to which the domestic formulation of the Saint Malo process is similar to the 'success limited comparisons' model and therefore shows up a weakness in the liberal intergovernmental model. The 'routine' policy formulation processes were bypassed by the PM and the core executive to expedite the development of a Europeanized defence policy. Blair's adoption, explicitly, of the 'Presidential' style of government meant that the policy was directed by the PM and the core executive rather than being managed by the respective Whitehall departments. Similarly, the PM ended the debate within Whitehall – that between the MoD and FCO – with the announcement at Pörtschach, demonstrating, above all else, the influence of the PM on this particular policy. The detail of the policy and managing negotiations with other EU governments were then entrusted to key officials particularly the Policy Directors of the FCO and MoD, the Security Policy Directors of the FCO and MoD and Cabinet Office officials.

The Saint Malo process is also an example of the presentation-focussed politics that the Blair government is said to pursue (Allen 2002, 6: Shrivesley 2002, 20). Whilst Alastair Campbell was central in co-ordinating the presentation of the Saint Malo initiative to the media at Pörtschach and Saint Malo, he was not, importantly key to the development of the policy itself. The presentation of the European UK defence policy to the MoD/FCO post-Pörtschach, to the French government and US President, State Department and Department of Defense, all focussed on lowest common denominator aspects of the policy that would result in broad agreement. This presentation technique aimed to advance the Europeanization of defence to a 'near finished stage' where differences of policy objectives could be managed within the confines of new institutional structures.

Interview evidence showed that important impacts of the Saint Malo initiative were not considered by the Prime Minister and Cabinet Office officials, before announcing the policy shift at Pörtschach, and then, latterly Saint Malo. UK policy makers did not consider the strong manpower, equipment and budgetary efficiency arguments that could be made to justify Europeanization. Such an omission highlights several weaknesses in LI's explanations of domestic policy making. The first of these weaknesses was that the decision to adopt a pro-European defence policy was principally taken by the PM in the absence of domestic interest group pressure. Moreover, domestic interest groups merely provided support for this policy after the decision had been taken. Second, LI does not attribute priorities to influencing factors like budgetary efficiencies versus international positive or negative externalities. Yet, the balance of evidence in respect of Pörtschach and Saint Malo is that positive externalities (geopolitical considerations and the desire to appear pro-European) were the principal motivations for a tactical change in policy.

Thus, the balance of evidence is not that domestic policy formulation is based upon the aggregation of interest group preferences by the government, but that the MoD responded to a call from the PM to look for policy areas that the government could be effective with on the European stage. The PM's desire was based on ideological motivation and the influence of positive and negative externalities. In contrast, the MoD's motivations were geopolitical. Thus, while LI provides a useful framework to explore domestic policy formulation – it highlights the value of interest groups and the role of governments in aggregating these interests – it provides an inaccurate explanation of domestic policy formulation in this example. What this chapter also highlights is the utility of Lindblom's 'successive limited comparisons' framework – which emphasizes the atomized nature of intra and inter-departmental negotiations, an important dynamic in this policy area.

In sum, this chapter has demonstrated that the formal Europeanization of British defence policy formulation by the 'new' Labour government was done by a very small number of officials within the 'core executive' and at great speed to satisfy the twin short-term political needs of the government's EU policy and to improve the EU's autonomous military capabilities. Importantly the chapter has highlighted the salience of personal relationships within the core executive on UK defence policy formulation and its speed, and offers this as a contrast to the somewhat ponderous pace of much defence policy reform. The vital difference in this case was that defence policy was adopted as a Prime Ministerial project and became subject to extra political pressure and opportunism by key officials. As will be shown in Chapter 7, the rapid Europeanization of the arms trade has resulted from very different drivers, which are just as salient within Europeanization as the pre-eminence of the core executive in deriving Europeanized domestic policy.

Chapter 3

Intergovernmental Bargains: Concepts and Preparations

The next two chapters explore what this book terms 'formal Europeanization' as it occurs at the intergovernmental level – more precisely the codification of supranational provisions that entrench Europeanized policies. This chapter focuses on the example of the negotiation of the ESDP at the Nice IGC (February-December 2000) and particularly the role of officials and politicians. Nineteen elite interviews with the UK and French IGC negotiating teams as well as officials from the European Commission provide the basis upon which patterns of negotiation are drawn out as well as their implications for Europeanization.

This research demonstrates that British government negotiators effectively managed the ESDP negotiations and therefore ensured the Europeanization of defence occurred with the maximum number of British preferences uploaded into the European level. The British government's success in uploading its defence preferences goes against much of the Europeanization literature that suggests that preferences are downloaded from the supranational to national level. Moreover, the government's success in locking in British preferences to the European level demonstrates the UK's relative strength over defence and security policy. Moreover it shows the effectiveness of the British government's co-ordinating machinery within the FCO and Cabinet Office to ensure that British preferences prevailed. This chapter further highlights the extent to which diplomatic effort and issue-specific negotiations was done outside of the formal IGC structures; specifically in terms of the bilateral meetings between government delegations to agree 'win-set' positions before the formal IGC process. The chapter further argues that negotiations on issues that can be construed as forming part of a Europeanization agenda are a process of 'successive limited comparisons' between negotiators who were trying to secure a position that met with all their respective lowest common denominator aspirations. In providing evidence for this the chapter examines the tactics that were used and the positions that were conceded to reach consensus between the states parties.

Liberal intergovernmentalist explanations of intergovernmental negotiating are particularly helpful to examining the Nice IGC's codification of ESDP. This analysis progresses through a liberal intergovernmentalist framework and examines seven factors, namely: governments are the principal units in the international system; negotiations are dominated by governments who have intense issue-specific preferences and capabilities; effective international bargaining is only viable if there is preference convergence; geopolitical and exogenous factors were significant in the negotiations; governments act as 'gate-keepers' between domestic electorates and international negotiators; negotiated outcomes are lowest common denominator agreements; and the EU is an international regime for the co-ordination of national policies. These seven factors are used to provide a framework for the chapter and for the analysis of this set of negotiations.

This chapter argues that liberal intergovernmentalist explanations of international bargaining are convincing. It further argues that national governments were the principal actors in the negotiations, to the exclusion of the EU's supranational institutions – this being partly a facet of the nature of defence policy, and partly a feature of structural position of governments in the EU. Furthermore, a number of governments who held strong issue-specific preferences and capabilities dominated the negotiations and the final outcome reflected a convergence of these governments' preferences. This chapter also argues that negotiators retain a 'gatekeeper' role between domestic public and political audiences and other member government negotiators and, furthermore, that the EU's primary function is to serve as a co-ordinating forum for national policies.

International Bargaining

By way of a review, liberal intergovernmentalist explanations of international bargaining revolve around the following central elements. That lobbying from domestic interest groups creates pressures on the government to change domestic policy. Then, if governments decide that a collaborative EU policy is in the national interest it then tries to coordinate the policy through international negotiations. Moreover, governments enter international negotiations with the aim of achieving a more favourable outcome than if they had continued to pursue an independent national policy. International negotiations provide a supply side solution to member governments' demands for international policy solutions and further LI assumes that negotiations pose practical challenges in the need to 'create' and 'claim' value (Lax and Sebenius 1992, 50).

The optimum negotiating position remains un-theorized – all that existing European integration theories are prepared to do is assert that a negotiated outcome will be optimal. The ability to pinpoint the settlement area would be an important aspect of creating a formal theory of Europeanization. However, what we are left with is a hypothesis that IGCs resulting in Treaty amendments produce better outcomes than could be achieved by the government acting unilaterally. To 'create value' negotiators must reach a mutually beneficial consensus and to claim it they must reach an agreement. The outcome might not conclude at the most optimal point for the government, because of strategic decisions taken during negotiations to concede particular issues on tactical or ideological grounds or to change policy proposals during those negotiations but it must produce a benefit for them.

The distributional outcomes of the negotiations are the principal focus of negotiators when they attempt to 'claim value'. This assumes that the political costs of failing to reach an agreed outcome outweigh the distributional costs of agreeing to a disadvantageous agreement. Logically then, this means that the analytical focus is on the problem of claiming rather than creating value. However, on issues of 'high' politics, like defence and security, where governments hold intense preferences, there may be a demand for compromise but governments are likely to be more sensitive to their interests and therefore be more willing to resist when they perceive that a negative sum game exists. So, there is a general principle that negotiations try to claim value in negotiations; but with the substantial caveat that if the policy under negotiation touches upon issues of 'high-politics' and core sovereignty governments are more likely to choose to end negotiations without agreement than to agree to a suboptimal conclusion.

There is a further assumption that IGC negotiations are non-coercive and therefore negotiators can veto or 'opt out' of agreements and are not forced to comply (Forster and Blair 2002, 108). Moreover, IGC negotiators are aided by an information-rich system. Negotiators in EU bargaining are aware of the preferences and constraints of other negotiators, and are also aware of the technical implications of enforcing any particular outcome – this set of information is made available by the Commission, in particular. The free flow of information between negotiators is further assisted by the Permanent Representations (COREPER) and European Council that bring negotiators within close everyday working proximity of each other (Forster and Blair 2002, 108).[1] The value of these interactions is often disregarded by EU studies scholars. The interaction between the Permanent Representatives, the Commission and the European Council is important however, as a part of the process of intergovernmental bargaining that codifies the salient element of informal integration that occurs on an everyday basis (Moravcsik 1998, 490).

Moravcsik argues that the transaction costs within intergovernmental bargaining are relatively low because of the efficiencies that are generated through the IGC infrastructure, which facilitate flows of information between negotiating parties (Moravcsik 1998, 479). Transaction costs are similarly reduced by lengthy negotiations and therefore the flow of information through regularized channels, rather than channels created specifically for that set of negotiations.

The Nice IGC lasted ten months (19 February to 11 December 2000), during which negotiators were able to table numerous proposals and counter-proposals with few attached costs. Indeed, this chapter argues that a great deal of ESDP negotiations were conducted outside of the formal IGC frameworks. Conversely proposals made in the last four days of the IGC, 7-11 December 2000, regarding institutional reform imposed costs on negotiating time and entailed opportunity costs, because of the

---

1 COREPER (Comité des Représentants Permanents) is based on Article 207 of the Treaty of Rome. Every Member State has a Permanent Representative in the EU with the rank of ambassador. The fifteen Permanent Representatives together form the Committee of Permanent Representatives, better known as COREPER. When the ambassadors meet, this happens in COREPER II. COREPER I consists of fifteen deputy Permanent Representatives. Under COREPER, there are numerous functional working groups with officials who prepare the subjects in the various policy fields. The Permanent Representatives prepare the activities of the Council and carry out the assignments given by the Council (Article 207). COREPER makes its decisions on the basis of the findings of the functional working groups. In these matters, the Permanent Representatives have a certain margin of negotiation granted them by their governments, with which they also continually hold consultation in the course of the negotiations. Pieter Jan Boon (information specialist, European Documentation Centre based at the Tilburg University Library).

finite time to analyse and respond to these proposals. Side-payments and issue linkages (both of which are negotiating strategies that tie one set of negotiations to another) are similarly tools used by negotiators to facilitate agreement during IGC bargaining, although there is little evidence that these tools were used in the ESDP negotiations. These negotiations were left in isolation precisely because the British government, in particular, tried to secure agreements on key terms before the December round of the IGC. The importance of being the first negotiator to move, sequencing, strategic misinterpretation, the use of coercive threats, and unilateral commitments are negated as important factors by the assumptions liberal intergovernmentalist explanations make.[2]

The operating assumptions outlined above limit the scope for negotiators to conclude radical and path-breaking deals. Therefore the cost of not ratifying an agreement provides a focal point for predicting negotiations. Moravcsik notes this pressure as '...the simple but credible threat of non-agreement provides rational governments with their most fundamental form of bargaining power' (Moravcsik 1998, 65). This can be reduced to a cost-benefit analysis of whether advantage lies in co-ordinating national policies into EU policy or retaining national policies.

Domestic pressures and the size of potential domestic 'win-sets' informs judgements about whether to pursue a co-ordinated EU policy or an independent policy.[3] Moreover, international bargains can influence the views of domestic interest groups. These groups can change their preferences in the light of international negotiations to create a greater opportunity to effective ratification of the negotiated output (Putnam 1992, 457-8). Thus the process of bargaining is not a static process of international negotiations followed by a process of seeking a domestic win-set, but is conceptualized as a process of reactions to negotiations that have effects at the domestic level which in turn re-informs the government's negotiators as to whether they can secure domestic support for the negotiated outcome (Putnam 1992, 457-8).

The assumption that governments behave rationally leads to a position that these governments will not accept collective EU policies that they perceive to be inferior to autonomous national policies. A further and somewhat reductive assumption that follows on from this is that collective policies that are subject to negotiation are already deemed to be to the advantage of those EU governments willing to negotiate subject to the output meeting the win-sets of all negotiators; if policies were not part of a positive sum analysis they would not have made it to the negotiating table (Moravcsik 1998, 492). Thus, because IGC negotiations must conclude with

---

2   Side payments are payments or benefits in kind to achieve a mutually acceptable balancing of benefits between negotiators. Side payments are used by those governments with intense preferences to overcome the objections or reservations the reluctant negotiating party might have about the particular issue under negotiation. Issue linkage is the connection of multiple issues within a negotiation to broaden the bargaining so that a greater range of issues and, therefore, a higher percentage of the total bargain. By broadening negotiations to incorporate multiple issues, the negotiating parties find it more problematic to reject a linked negotiation over multiple issues than on a single-issue basis.

3   Win-sets are achieved when policies meet the approval of relevant constituencies and form an essential part of Putnam's two level game analysis.

unanimous support from the member governments, IGC outcomes can only be driven beyond the lowest common denominator through the construction of coalitions, the use of 'opt-outs' and the threat of exclusion from the bargain.

A dominant view within European studies is that IGCs are the turning points of EU history. This rationale leads to the conclusion that Europeanization and European integration are intergovernmental, and negotiations are liberal to the extent that governments have no uniform national interests (Moravcsik 1993, 480). Placing governments at the centre of Europeanization develops limits their role to that of a conduit through which domestic actors influence domestic government policy rather than directly influencing international bargaining. The separation of domestic producer and interest groups from international bargaining is crucial to an understanding of how negotiations proceed and why governments retain primacy in the formal Europeanization of policy. Thus, in the formal policy area governments are able to perform a gate-keeper role between domestic politics, producer group pressure and international bargaining.

The analogy of a gate-keeper role is strong in the context of an intergovernmental negotiation – politicians and officials from national governments are the lead actors in any bargaining round. Where this account begins to lose some of its strength is in placing the negotiations, the experience of officials and recent nation to nation diplomacy in context. To situate EU intergovernmental negotiations within these contexts immediately throws open the prospect that informal routes of Europeanization that are arguably formed from the continental European experiences of officials having embassy placements in the early stages of their careers, working alongside continental colleagues on EU related problems and issues, right up to nationally instituted structural frameworks that promote a Europeanized way of thinking and working. Whilst it can be said that all of these informal routes are to a greater and lesser extent informed by formal methods of integration; there is considerable analytical value in exploring them separately.

If one views international bargains as the product of a convergence of member governments' interests and are often the expression of the lowest common denominator between governments, then possible linkages between issue areas dramatically effects what a government will view to be in its core interests. This links back to the previous discussion about where negotiators view the optimum bargaining outcome occurs. In particular, linking multiple issues makes it far more difficult to accurately plot where a negotiations settlement area will fall. However, all of this analysis leads to the conclusion that the EU is an international regime that facilitates the co-ordination of national policies, rather than providing a political system – a higher level of government, which is undermined by the conclusions of Chapter Seven that the EU has adopted state-like attributes in formulating policies about the European defence industrial base.

States are the Principal Units in the International System

Moravcsik's liberal intergovernmentalist framework suggests that governments are the principal units in the international system, international negotiations and specifically the EU. In the latter two cases this is because the EU and its institutions derive their legal framework and legitimacy from the member governments. Moreover, significant developments to institutions and constitutional treaties are also determined by the member governments. The superiority of member governments in the EU is contested because of the developing role of supranational institutions (Moravsik 1998, 491; cf Arnold 2002; Boswold and Oppermann 2006). These institutions add a layer of decision-making and authority that some, including Jeremy Richardson, argue undermine the primacy of member governments (Richardson 1999, 5). However, as Moravcsik argues, governments are the principal actors in treaty negotiations, giving them primary significance over the EU and EU integration.

The EU is founded on international treaty bargains in which the member governments are the sole signatories. IGCs are conducted in a political system in which governments are able to veto the entire package of deals being negotiated (Putnam 1992, 457). Indeed vetoing a single element of the package has the effect of vetoing the entire package unless provision is made for a government to 'opt out' as the UK government did at Maastricht, with the social chapter provisions (Forster 1999, 351-2). The ability to 'opt out' offers a substantial challenge to the conception that the most compelling reason to negotiate is the fear of not agreeing as they effectively insulate negotiators from these effects. Thus, the main consideration for discontented governments is a cost benefit analysis of vetoing the entire package, versus the cost of accepting a disadvantageous policy.

The ESDP negotiations were almost the sole preserve of governments. The negotiations were dominated by the member governments from the Saint Malo Accords, through the Cologne and Helsinki Councils in 3-4 June and 10-11 December 1999 and then through to the Nice IGC, 7-11 December 2000. The European Parliament and WEU through debates, research and public pronouncements tried to exert pressure and influence on the member governments between the Saint Malo Accords and the IGC (European Council Regulation 2000; European Parliament 1999).

European Parliament (EP)

MEPs find themselves unable to strongly influence the British government's policies and preferences through an institutional exclusion from domestic politics. The links between UK MEPs and their domestic political parties are not as close as UK MPs with their party political machineries. MEPs do not have a right of access to the Houses of Parliament or their research facilities and are not included in the consultation processes of the three major UK political parties (Newton-Dunn 2002; Clegg 2002; White 2004). The EP was restricted to a lobbying role between Saint Malo and the final stages of the Nice IGC, 7-11 December 2000. The EP lobbied extensively with government negotiators to enhance the communautaire elements of ESDP, and to give a greater role to the EP in initiating foreign policies that might necessitate a military element (Newton-Dunn 2002; Clegg 2002).

The EP was, as an institution, excluded from the negotiations at Nice, sending instead two official observers, Elmar Brok and Dmitris Tsatos. At previous IGCs

EP observers had no formal voting powers, but were consulted by negotiators.[4] The unwritten understanding of this arrangement is that whilst the EP cannot formally negotiate, if the observers express a very strong disagreement on an issue this will have a bearing on the negotiations (Interview M; Interview H; Interview D; Interview G). The EP has to ratify new treaties and as a result retains some generalized leverage over the integration process, although the consequences of an EP veto would have far reaching consequences for the EU (Evans-Pritchard and Jones, 2000). Agence Europe reported that the EP observers at the Nice IGC, particularly Elmar Brok, were 'upset' at the lack of consultation but with little practical effect (Bulletin Quotidien 7863, 2000).

The European Commission voluntarily played a limited role in the negotiations of the ESDP. Former Vice-President of the Commission Lord Brittan noted that there was an institutional taboo surrounding the Commission discussing or promoting greater integration in the security or defence spheres as this is a policy area in which governments have exclusive control (Lord Brittan 2002). According to Lord Brittan the Commissioners are conscious of their supplicant position to governments because the Commission derives its legitimacy, role and function from treaties agreed between member governments (Cini 1999, 20-1 and 224; Christiansen 2000, 11; Lord Brittan 2002).

Between 1998 and 2000 the Commission was sceptical about whether the EU member governments would provide a credible security and defence policy with associated capabilities (Lord Brittan 2002; Lord Garden 2002). During the IGC Agence Europe reported that the Commission publicly expressed preferences concerning ESDP (Bulletin Quotidien 7865, 2000). Further evidence from negotiators suggests that the ESDP was negotiated and shaped through ministerial meetings in addition to regular meetings between Foreign and Defence ministries, not as a response to European Commission pronouncements (Interview E; Interview F).[5]

The strength of evidence is that supranational institutions like the EP and the Commission playing a highly marginalized role – in the case of the former because of its structural position and in the latter because it opted to remain a supplicant party to the intergovernmental bargaining. However, the EP and European Commission did play a role in forming the wider, informed debate on the subject. Interviewees like Lord Robertson and Lord Brittan argued from different positions that these institutions had raised the profile of the ESDP debate (Lord Robertson 2004; Lord Brittan 2002).[6]

---

4   Both Interview M and Bill Newton-Dunn have previously been closely involved with IGC negotiations.

5   Interview E came to this view from the perspective of having worked on the Saint Malo initiative and the bilateral negotiations with the French and other EU governments from 1998. He viewed this more in terms of a routine exchange of policy ideas. Interview F was particularly involved in the IGC negotiations and thus was able to point to the relative exceptionalism of conducting an entire policy negotiation outside of the formal IGC framework.

6   Lord Robertson said they had raised the profile of the debate but were often wide of the mark in addressing key issues whilst Lord Brittan felt that they brought positive contributions to the debates.

One observation that results from the role of the Commission and the Parliament is that not only do the supranational institutions not help in advancing European integration in areas that they intervene in, but that they can also serve to slow or reverse processes of formal Europeanization. However, the two institutions did play a role in shaping an informed debate amongst the policy community about ESDP and European integration. Key UK officials argue that this did not have significant effects on the direction and outcome of their negotiations with other EU governments, although the real effect of this intervention is very hard to measure. The hypothesis that governments were the principal actors in the ESDP negotiations is highly persuasive. Furthermore, the existing literature on EU bargaining under-specifies the extent to which the flow of information between supranational institutions and negotiators impacts on the negotiations, and as this relates to the example of Nice the flow of information between the European Commission, EP and the bargaining governments had a very limited impact on ESDP negotiations. However, as Chapter Seven will show the European Commission and European Parliament can generate the effect of rapidly deepening and widening Europeanization given conducive circumstances and pre-existing agreement that establish an exploitable policy framework.

International Structural Factors do not Shape National Interests. National Interests and Preferences are Shaped Through the Domestic Policy Process

In asserting that governments are the leading actors in the international system, one must then conclude that domestic political processes, rather than international systemic pressures, drive national interests. This section explores the domestic and international pressures on the British government to pursue a Europeanized defence policy.

There are three broad contentions concerning the domestic pressure on the British government to pursue a pro-European defence policy. The pre-determinist argument is that the Labour party's 1997 manifesto informed its desire to show leadership in a European policy area (Key 2002; Redwood 2002). The Conservative Party politician John Redwood is a leading advocate of this argument:

> My view, in general, is that the Government wrongly offered defence an area where it thought it could lead, and divert attention away from its failure to join the Euro, as part of its posturing over EU policy (Redwood 2002).

This position is supported by, former Conservative Party Leader and Opposition Defence spokesman, Iain Duncan Smith in testimony to the House of Lords Select Committee on European Issues Sub-Committee concerning Defence (Gourlay 2002; House of Lords Select Committee on the EU 2000; George 2002; Key 2002). In addition to these politically motivated opponents who are naturally keen to be critical of government policy there was also media commentary claiming that the Saint Malo initiative was linked to the government's reticence to be positive on the single currency (Livingstone 1998; Daily Telegraph 2000). The pre-determinist view is not only held by members of the Conservative and Liberal Democrat parties, but also some members of the Parliamentary Labour Party (PLP) who were a quiet and acquiescent minority to the PM and the core executive. These MPs believe that the government pursued the policy as an end in its own right but that this also saved the government from having to take a politically dangerous decision regarding the single currency (George 2002; Palmer 2002; White 2004). The government's plans for Europeanizing British defence did not face substantial opposition within the PLP beyond a desire to secure guarantees that the Saint Malo initiative would not undermine NATO.

International pressure on the UK's domestic policy can be seen, for example, through the scepticism that exists about how reliable the United States' commitment to European security is. This discourse states that to retain America's involvement in European security Britain has to persuade European allies to bolster their military capabilities to 'share the burden' of European security (Daily Telegraph 2000; White 1998; Eastham 2000; Berger 1999). The concern over US Presidential and State Department's attitudes towards the EU ran parallel to the UK government arguing for military action in Kosovo (Parker 2003; Peel 2003; Brogan 2000). The Prime Minister was convinced by George Robertson and his European Policy Advisor, Stephen Wall that the government could act to bolster the transatlantic Alliance and also fulfil the Labour party's election manifesto pledge to become a 'force for good' in the world (Robertson 2004; George 2002; Interview M).[7] Saint Malo was a timely initiative as it extended the Anglo-French co-operation that had operated in Kosovo (Wallace 2002; Interview C). Military collaboration provided the context in which the UK MoD felt confident in promoting closer a Europeanized defence policy (Andreani, Bertram and Grant 2001; Grant 1998; Interview I).

Charles Grant, Director of the Centre for European Reform, spent a great deal of time discussing these issues with FCO, MoD and Cabinet Office officials, particularly with the Policy Units of the MoD and FCO and the European Secretariat of the Cabinet Office as well as with Tony Blair's personal political advisor Roger Liddle (Grant 2002). The evidence is that Liddle was impressed by Grant's case for European defence integration and similarly that Liddle conveyed these arguments to the Prime Minister. The fact that the policy was taken forward is strong evidence of the persuasiveness of these views (Wallace 2002; Interview I; Interview M).[8] Grant supported the idea of EU based defence as a means to strengthen the NATO alliance whilst promoting a serious French defence contribution in the eyes of the Alliance through the Saint Malo initiative (Schake, Block-Laine and Grant 1999). Grant's

---

7 The balance of the evidence suggests that Hatfield and his Policy Unit created drew up the Saint Malo initiative and potential impacts and presented it to George Robertson. Hatfield convinced Robertson of the merits of the policy who then brought it forward to the Prime Minister. Robertson's divergence from this view comes from his account that he instructed Hatfield to produce this policy. It is not clear from the evidence which of these views is the strongest. Officials were not keen to suggest explicitly that they had worked on this without instruction although they were happy to strongly infer this.

8 This point is linked to a broader issue about how Tony Blair has conducted his Premiership. Lord Wallace and Interview M argued that Blair was keen to seek views outside of the confines of Whitehall but with the caveat that these views came from 'trusted' sources – hence the relative importance of Roger Liddle and Charles Grant who are informed European commentators with the confidence of the PM.

role is perceived to be a strong external validating influence on Blair's opinions on this policy, although as discussed in Chapter 2 a multitude of actors and institutions were included in the consultation process to provide validation for a policy direction already settled by Downing Street (White 2004; Black 2003).[9]

Those who view Saint Malo as a 'unique opportunity' argue that negotiations took place in the context of converging disparate motivations that culminated in the Saint Malo Accords (Gnesotto 2002; Lord Wallace 2002; Lord Garden 2003). These converging motivations were that the pro-European preferences of the Labour government resulted in government departments developing policy areas that could be Europeanized and that pro-EU defence policies were linked to UK government intransigence on the single currency. The linkage of these two motivations implies the co-ordination of domestic policies within a European framework that all EU member governments engage in (Lord Brittan 2002; Lord Wallace 2002).[10]

The unique opportunity argument also suggests that the Labour government made a step-change in thinking from previous governments in deciding there were tangible benefits in Europeanizing a policy issue from inception rather than joining once the framework of the policy had been established as they had done with every other significant EU project including the inception of the Union itself (Interview D; Interview G; Interview M; Sowemimo 1999, 349). Furthermore, the development of NATO, coupled with the increasing reticence of the United States to intervene in so-called 'out-of-area' operations and the reluctance of America to intervene in the case of the Kosovo Albanians contributed to the 'unique opportunity' of Saint Malo (Dunn 2001, 151; Clarke and Cornish 2002, 777-8).

Richard Hatfield convened a working group within the MoD from December 1997 to June 1998, to develop policy proposals around EU based solutions for European security and defence issues. Detail of the membership of the working group is restricted information.[11] This working group concluded that European security and defence could be strengthened to the benefit of both the UK and NATO (Interview B; Interview D). The rationale for this conclusion was that the US is more likely to want to act in conjunction with a militarily strengthened EU (Grant 2002; Lord Garden 2002; Interview C). ESDP should militarily strengthen the EU because it provides a framework through which to engage in a multilateral defence initiative and also to share the US' burden of European security (Dunn 2001, 146). This line of thinking was successfully promoted by Richard Hatfield to both George Robertson, the Secretary of State for Defence and then onto the Prime Minister, core executive and the Cabinet.

---

9 Michael White described Grant as being part of Blair's inner circle and confirmed that rumours around Westminster at the time were that Saint Malo had been inspired by him. Ian Black also supported this view.

10 Although this concept was expressly rejected by the Prime Minister's personal political advisor Roger Liddle who maintained that each policy area was taken and negotiated on its own merits to the exclusion of any potential linkages, this is a minority view of the 23 relevant interviewees in this book.

11 The author was refused information as to the membership of this working party.

The policy work completed by Richard Hatfield's working group was exceptional in its range and scope, taking in possible outcomes and scenarios as a response to the Prime Minister's request for departments to find areas in which the UK government could be pro-active in Europeanizing. The exceptionalism of this group comes from the extent to which Hatfield drove this work forward and was able to present the Secretary of State with a very well developed set of proposals (Hopkinson 2002; Garden 2002).[12] William Hopkinson (former Assistant Under Secretary of State in the MoD) argues that it is not necessarily exceptional to have working parties examining areas of policy, but it is exceptional for that working party to devise a marketing strategy for the policy as well as scoping all possible counter proposals and obstacles that might be made by negotiating parties and the United States (Hopkinson 2002). Hopkinson argues that the particularly enthusiastic work of the Hatfield working party was because of Hatfield's personal view that Europeanized solutions should be sought (Interview C; Interview D, Hopkinson 2002). This MoD working group was also one part of a federation of competing bureaucratic interests that were distilled by the Prime Minister and his close advisers – an aggregation of domestic interest groups akin to the liberal intergovernmentalist conception of policy formulation.

Those close to Lord Guthrie argue that towards June and July of 1998 senior military officials, including Guthrie himself, viewed the UK's Strategic Defence Review (SDR) as facilitating closer collaboration with other EU governments by gearing the British armed forces to the 'small and flexible' roles of peace enforcement and humanitarian missions which were to become part of the ESDP (Nice Treaty 2000, Annex II to VI). Moreover, the SDR made clear that the British government was taking the potential of the EU's CFSP seriously as a useful tool of foreign policy (House of Commons Select Committee 1999). The SDR established a change in UK strategic preferences that would allow a more effective use of the defence budget (Interview D; Interview G; HM Treasury 2002; Rogers 1998; Clarke 1998a; House of Commons Defence Select Committee Evidence 1998). Moreover, despite hostility towards policies that might undermine the transatlantic Alliance, senior military officials were broadly in favour of policies that would encourage European allies to increase their domestic defence spending and improve capabilities (Interview C; Hopkinson 2002). Indeed, one interviewee believes that the Petersberg tasks and ESDP provides a more realistic range of tasks for the British military in the twenty first century (Interview C). Despite reticence towards a policy that might undermine NATO the Chief of the Defence Staff steered the Services into a position of constructive engagement with the government offering conditional acceptances to their policy proposals (Interview C; Interview D). Thus, evidence suggests that the national interests that guided Britain's approach and negotiating strategies for a Europeanized defence policy were derived from domestic pressures, but there are several notable counter-factual arguments to this view.

Howarth suggests three key exogenous factors that shaped the development of ESDP: the degree of political will generated in the EU from the Saint Malo conference

---

12 Hopkinson and Garden as former senior MoD officials argued that the prominence of a single individual in this process was unusual. A more usual route would be that the consideration of the policy be widened to a greater number of MoD officials.

in December 1998; the emergence of a military industrial base, which occurred outside of any British government entrepreneurship; and transatlantic consensus on NATO and the British commitment to the ESDP project (Howarth 2000, 93). Elizabeth Pond argues that the EU's impotence in the Kosovo crisis was the key driver in the ESDP negotiations (Pond 1999, 77). The UK government's position on the Saint Malo initiatives and ESDP can be attributed to exogenous factors and the belief that ESDP strengthens transatlantic relations (Interview D; Interview G; Lord Robertson 2004). This was the position of the government before, during and after the Saint Malo negotiations and indeed this book argues was an innovative response by the government to the problem of retaining NATO and US interests in European security.

A further intergovernmental negotiation that assisted the development of ESDP was a parallel development in NATO. The NATO framework document of 24 April 1999 produced a new defence role for the European members of NATO. The announcement produced a formal link between EU military initiatives and internal NATO restructuring (Rutten 2001, 29). This link aimed to modernize the Alliances military forces for 'out of area' and 'peace enforcement' tasks but was a modest and unsuccessful endeavour (Rutten 2001, 29 and 54-59). At the NATO summit, the British government representatives praised '...the determination of both EU members and other European allies to make the necessary steps to strengthen their defence capabilities' (Rutten 2001, 26).

The NATO summit, 23 and 24 April 1999, produced agreement amongst the Heads of State and government on NATO conducting 'out of area' operations (Hura et al 2000, 1). American officials were keen that NATO could conduct out of area operations without the need for a United Nations mandate. Despite military operations in Kosovo having a formal UN Security Council resolution mandate European governments refused to agree to the new Strategic Concept practice of conducting 'peace-enforcement' operations without UN approval (Rutten 2001, 24-25). NATO members acknowledged ESDP developments and particularly the EU governments' enthusiasm for being able to conduct autonomous actions (Rutten 2001, 22). The EU negotiators, principally the UK and German government officials, secured agreement from America on access to NATO capabilities, based on the following principles:

a. assured EU access to NATO planning capabilities able to contribute to military planning for EU-led operations.
b. The presumption of the availability to the EU of pre-identified NATO capabilities and common assets for use in EU-led operations.
c. Identification of a range of European command options for EU-led operations, further developing the role of DSACEUR in order for him to assume fully and effectively his European responsibilities.
d. The further adaptation of Nato's defence planning system to incorporate more comprehensively the availability of forces for EU-led operations (Rutten 2001, 22).

Pressure for the UK government's initiative on European defence might at least in part have stemmed from the reform in NATO during the 1990s (Grant 2002; Rifkind

2004).[13] If this is the case it leaves interest formulation in a conceptually problematic position, as it would suggest that developments within international institutions can drive both domestic policy formulation and the creation of negotiating strategies. However, the evidence suggests that UK government preferences within NATO and the EU were determined by the pressure exerted by policy groups within the MoD and 'new' Labour's wider policy circle whose views were informed by a conducive political agenda and the experiences in the Balkans during the 1990s.

The EU is an International Regime for National Policy Co-ordination

Moravcsik argues that the EU is an international regime for national policy co-ordination (Moravcsik 1998, 20-21). His analysis is that as governments are the principal actors in international negotiations, as a result of the pre-eminence of intergovernmental bargaining in Europeanization and this leads to the position that the EU's institutions are merely co-ordinating and regulating institutions (Moravcsik 1998, 19-21). The ECJ and Commission's outputs in terms of legal judgments and regulations and directives are cited as counter-factual arguments to this view. The ECJ, in certain key judicial decisions, has extended the policy remit of the EU beyond the point where the EU co-ordinates domestic policies determined by member governments. The 'Factortame' series of cases both in the House of Lords and the ECJ extended the judicial principle established in the so-called 'Costa' (1967) case that the ECJ was the superior court to the UK's House of Lords (Factortame 1990-2001). The importance of these examples is central to the debate about what the European Union is and how it treats Europeanized policies. LI's view of the EU, is that it is a regime for coordinating and regulating the transfer of fifteen and now twenty-five governments' sovereignty, reducing transaction costs and preserving governmental sovereignty on an issue specific area.

The federalist view of the EU is that it provides a higher form of government than national governments and thus on policies in which it has competencies it behaves as a replacement for national governments. However, in a policy area like ESDP, where governments dominate, the institutional framework of the EU as a way of coordinating government policies. Security and defence are areas of core national sovereignty – the importance of this case study to Europeanization as a political phenomenon is in its symbolism as an area in which many commentators argued competency would remain outside of EU frameworks.

The ESDP negotiations and treaty articles provide strong evidence of the EU as a co-ordinating forum for domestic policies. The tight constraints on the direction of ESDP, through negotiations by the UK and three other governments, partly explains why the EU is limited as an actor in the case of ESDP. To ensure parliamentary ratification would be forthcoming after the negotiations had concluded, UK government negotiators judged that they had to ensure that any operational element

---

13 Charles Grant argued that the discussions in NATO about ESDI and the following reforms had provided an additional motivation for the Saint Malo initiative. Malcolm Rifkind countered this with his opinion that greater efforts should have been sought to keep Europeanized defence within a strictly NATO framework.

of ESDP remained under the control of governments rather than providing the EU with the ability to take decisions under delegated authority (Interview D; Interview E; Interview G).[14] In the example of ESDP, the EU has been used as a means by which to coordinate national policies without the need to recourse to individual bilateral agreements, which would bring considerable transaction costs.

The ESDP negotiations provided UK officials with a forum and framework for advancing their preferences for enhanced co-operation on security and defence within the EU, which they could coordinate through close liaison with the other negotiating parties prior to the formal negotiations at Nice. The framework provided by the EU allowed UK officials to advance an agenda of security preferences that provided for the transfer of modest amounts of sovereignty to the EU on security and defence. This would be a transfer that did not undermine the EU's NATO maintained security provision. ESDP established an innovative way of using NATO capabilities when the Alliance as a whole is not involved in the proposed military action.

Conceptually, this chapter has highlighted the dynamics within 'formal Europeanization' and the processes at work behind the preparation for intergovernmental negotiations, processes that are unique to the formal Europeanization of defence, but not necessarily to other Europeanization processes. The next chapter advances these themes through the Nice negotiations to explore the exceptional way ESDP negotiations were kept separate and distinct from other issues areas and the patterns of negotiation that occurred there.

---

14 This was never really a danger in ESDP negotiations as the issues as had been thoroughly rehearsed through all the intervening summits between Saint Malo and the European Council at Nice. Interview H argued that the only danger of supranational control being suggested came from the French government trying to exert control over negotiations; however he argues that the UK government would have threatened the other negotiators that they would not sign the treaty articles if this had been seriously proposed.

Chapter 4

Saint Malo and Nice: The Machinery of Negotiating

This chapter examines the negotiations at Saint Malo and at the Nice Intergovernmental Conference (IGC). Building on the previous chapter, which focused on the conceptual elements of international bargaining, this chapter explores the who, the how and the why of the formal Europeanization of British defence policy. In doing so this chapter advances the argument that 'major' governments, with intense issue-specific preferences and capabilities, dominate the formal Europeanization of policies.

The main driver for including the ESDP provisions in the Nice Treaty came from the Anglo-French meeting on 4-6 December 1998 that produced the Saint Malo Accords (Rutten 2001). UK and French government officials were also heavily involved in the conferences that followed on from Saint Malo and further clarified and extended the principles established at Cologne (3-4 June 1999), Helsinki (10-11 December 1999) and Sintra (28 February 2000), and where for example capabilities were prioritized as an area of focus for negotiations (Interview E; Interview Swedish MoD Official 2003).[1]

EU defence co-operation had been suggested as far back as 1954 but had become a lower priority for European integration following the creation of NATO. The Maastricht negotiations had reignited the issue of a common defence policy, through the framing of the CFSP, but it was the UK government in 1998 at Pörtschach (October) and Saint Malo (December) that provided the political impetus to this initiative. A considerable number of bilateral meetings were held between the UK and French MoD and Foreign Office officials between 25 October and 4 December 1998 to ensure that the two governments were able to find a common policy that met win-sets in both countries domestic political systems (Interview D; Interview G).[2]

The Policy Directors of the MoD and FCO, Richard Hatfield and Emyr Jones-Parry were the lead negotiators of the Saint Malo Accords. Hatfield and Jones-Parry simultaneously negotiated with the French Foreign Office negotiator, Phillipe

---

1   Interview E revealed that the UK negotiators had written the 'toolbox paper' document that had been adopted at the meeting in Sintra. A Swedish MoD official also reports that the UK government's role in creating this paper had caused some friction between the UK government and the Finnish government who felt that they had been prevented from making the level of contribution they should have been making as hosts.

2   Many of these meetings were routine meetings between EU governments on defence and foreign policy issues. However, because of the public announcement of the Saint Malo Accords greater credence was given to the detail of the Accords and how these might develop.

Errera, mindful of what might be acceptable to him, whilst also being mindful of the need to secure agreement in the domestic constituencies of the FCO, MoD and Cabinet Office. The British negotiators had been given clear instructions of where the UK government's red-lines existed and Hatfield and Jones-Parry were very well aware of these red-lines having been so closely involved in the development of the initiative (Interview D; Interview G). Hatfield and Jones-Parry were given a great deal of freedom to negotiate the detail of the policy with French government negotiators, within a broad framework of 'red-lines' established by the PM, and the Secretaries of State for Foreign and Commonwealth Affairs and Defence, Robin Cook and George Robertson. They told Hatfield and Jones-Parry that negotiations should not conclude at a point where the EU would seek to replicate or undermine NATO's role in European security nor seek to decouple the EU from NATO.[3] George Robertson and other interviewees noted that the negotiated agreements at Saint Malo and the Nice Treaty output on ESDP were remarkably similar (Interview D; Lord Robertson 2004). One of the key UK government negotiators argued that the Saint Malo Accords were not substantively changed between 6 December 1998 and the final signatures on the Nice Treaty on 11 December 2000: the language had been refined whilst the concepts had remained stable (Interview D).

The Saint Malo Accords gave ESDP a significant momentum because of the perception that the UK and French governments had diametrically opposed views on European security. This meant that agreement between these two on closer defence ties within Europe was highly significant. Similarly, the Saint Malo Accords provided the scope and a framework for the further negotiations at Sintra, Cologne, and Helsinki culminating in ESDP provisions being included in the Nice Treaty (Interview D; Interview H).

It is a widely held received truth that the UK and French governments hold intense and opposing preferences on security and defence. As a consequence UK officials felt that gaining French government agreement for a Europeanized defence policy ensured that a critical mass of militarily strong governments in the EU were in support of this initiative and therefore would be difficult for less influential governments to oppose, from a purely practical negotiating position (Interview H; Interview M). Moreover, the agreement between UK and French governments on issues of principles and substance before putting security and defence proposals to the other EU governments was key to ensuring that ESDP would remain within UK and French red-lines.

There were also practical advantages for UK officials in negotiating with French officials before the Nice IGC (7-11 December 2000). These advantages lay in ensuring that French government preferences were stable and secured before the

---

3 The 'red-lines' system establishes constraints on negotiators. The red-lines are placed at the point of the last acceptable policy outcome and should not be breached by British negotiators. Negotiators can strike a deal anywhere within these 'red-lines'. At complex negotiations where multiple issues are being negotiated the 'red-lines' system offers a unique opportunity for British negotiators to move within several policy areas to give ground to foreign negotiators on certain issues to ensure the largest win-set possible on an area of particular interest or importance to the British government.

IGC negotiating took place so that the French government would not seek to use its political leverage over the policy against the UK government's interests (Interview E; Interview M).[4] The close working relationship between UK and French officials continued throughout the preparation for and during the Nice IGC with close coordination between UK and French foreign and defence ministries by COREPER (Interview A; Interview F; Interview M). The British and French negotiators also coordinated the responses to the UK / French government view in the negotiations, enabling challenges to this view to be managed.

The British and French governments held intense defence-specific preferences and capabilities that they sought to enshrine at the European level. The Saint Malo Accords were important to the development and negotiation of ESDP as they established an agreed framework through which the UK and French officials could develop the policy with other EU partners, and ultimately in IGC negotiations. What the liberal intergovernmentalist approach fails to appreciate is the importance of negotiations that occur outside of the IGC structures. The evidence from the ESDP negotiations is that the Saint Malo Accords provided the basis for ESDP and were where the 'real' negotiations took place. Viewed, in this light an emphasis on IGC negotiating in isolation is, on its own terms, reductive and under-specifies a key part of the process.

Formal Europeanization is a Product of National Convergence

From the assumption that governments are rational, it follows that these governments only pursue common policies if these initiatives secure greater opportunities than independent approaches (Moravcsik 1998, 3&8). Defence is a paradoxical policy area in this respect. Defence strikes at the heart of the autonomy of a government because of sensitivities to territorial defence and committing national human resources and national identity. However, defence is also an area of international cooperation, albeit intergovernmental in nature, where the Article V provisions of the Washington Treaty that established NATO confers responsibilities on signatory governments (Washington Declaration 1949).

Defence and security policy has been long established as an intergovernmental area in which policy is ultimately guided by autonomous governments but subject to co-ordination to achieve agreed ends. The convergence of EU governments' defence interests to form ESDP was ultimately codified at the Nice IGC, but can also be seen to have emerged through a series of political and military developments from the 1990 Maastricht negotiations onwards. This bargaining reactivated the issue of defence as a reaction to the EU's inability to react to the conflict in the Balkans and the increasing insularity of the United States government which led to demand for an EU defence and security policy (Duff 1997; Dover 2005).

The first meeting where there was a convergence of views between the French and German governments occurred at Potsdam (1 December 1998). At this meeting

---

4 The French government tabled amendments to the ESDP provisions on the evening of 3 December 2000 that were rebuffed by the UK government as being outside of their red-lines and would provide a justification for UK government to not sign the Nice Treaty.

the governments announced they were working together to try and define the CFSP more closely and to include a defence dimension (Rutten 2001, 4-6). The French President and German Chancellor also stated that the WEU should be integrated into the EU and emphasized the importance of capabilities in driving EU external relations policy (Rutten 2001, 4-6). EU capabilities should be developed using existing national capabilities or by calling on pre-existing NATO capabilities identified for this use, something that was subsequently enshrined at Nice (Rutten 2001, 4-6). The Potsdam declaration states that both countries believe that the EU's conflict prevention measures ought to be improved (Rutten 2001, 4-6). This meeting was significant in establishing common positions between two of the three major EU states took the work at Pörtschach forward by a couple of short steps providing a small measure of momentum to the process.

The second event that saw a publicly announced convergence of government interests was the Saint Malo Accords (3-4 December 1998) that added a credible agreement to Prime Minister Blair's Pörtschach announcement two months earlier.[5] The convergence announced at Saint Malo had been extensively negotiated, in preparation for the meeting, by British and French officials. The British delegation consisted of the Prime Minister, Richard Hatfield (Policy Director, MoD), Emyr Jones-Parry (Policy Director, FCO), Paul Johnston (Director of the FCO Political-Security Department) and the Prime Minister's communications advisor Alastair Campbell, who met with their French equivalents. The British delegation brought several texts to Saint Malo, one of which they knew would not find support amongst French officials. This document proposed dividing NATO into two sections, the first section would transform the EU into the political wing of NATO and the second section would form the military wing extended to incorporate tasks from the Petersburg list (Interview D; Interview G).[6] This document was not put to the French officials partly because they felt it would politically untenable for the French President, who was concerned about 'Anglo-Saxon' dominance of NATO, and also because negotiators quickly agreed that there was too little common ground between governments to try and revise proposals leading them to negotiate from first principles (Interview D). French proposals included greater levels of military autonomy for the EU, in line with the historical Gaullist position (Interview D; Interview G).[7] This proposal was not accepted by the UK government because the fear of US withdrawal and the potential damage to NATO were overriding priorities for the UK government (Johnson 2001; Lord Robertson 2004).

The gap between the negotiating positions of the UK and French governments left the lead UK negotiators Hatfield and Jones-Parry with tighter constraints on

---

5   Interviewees argued that this was the next logical stage for the initiative, a phased integration of more details gaining momentum across EU governments, or a means to end a debate concerning EU defence between the FCO and MoD whilst Saint Malo was the public announcement of an Anglo-French initiative.

6   This document is not currently in the public domain.

7   As with the UK government's positioning papers brought to Saint Malo the French government's papers are not in the public domain either. The only evidence for their existence or content comes from elite interview evidence.

'claiming value' at the negotiations. The UK PM and the core executive were committed to a more positive stance on European defence. They had invested a great deal of time, through routine meetings, convincing the French government that an initiative to be launched at Saint Malo was credible and worthwhile (Interview D; Interview E; Interview G). The Saint Malo meeting represented the last politically viable chance for either the UK or French governments to withdraw from negotiations of collaborative defence initiatives. A statement had been prepared, as is standard practice, by the European Secretariat of the Cabinet Office in recognition of the prospect that the negotiations might fail (Interview D; Interview M).

Instead of announcing failure, officials agreed to a final attempt to draft the agreement from fresh throughout the evening, having withdrawn from the formalities of the summit dinner on 3 December. The dynamics of the negotiations between Policy Directors was particularly important. The lead UK negotiator Richard Hatfield worked with Emyr Jones-Parry on the British side of the negotiations, whereas the French MoD negotiator barred the French Foreign Office Policy Director from the negotiations, underlining the difference between British and French policy making styles and bureaucratic interaction (Interview D; Interview G). The absence of planning for the negotiations that did occur meant that the negotiators had to provide their own secretarial skills and even a computer to type the agreed text (Interview D; Interview G).

The authority for these negotiations was tenuous; neither the MoD nor the FCO had authorized them, nor had they planned or discussed any supplementary positions.[8] The authority for the negotiations came from the Prime Minister, but there was a considerable risk to Hatfield and Jones-Parry if they strayed too far from the originally agreed 'red-line' positions of their departments. Cabinet Office officials periodically observed the proceedings and were able to report to the Prime Minister how the negotiations were progressing and officials from the French President's Office did likewise (Interview D; Interview G). The final document was produced at around 3am on the morning of 4 December and was 'written in a strange Franglais' that allowed an acceptable agreement to be struck on broad principles whilst carefully side-stepping the problematic issues of human resources and procurement, the detail of which could not be resolved in one evening's negotiations (Interview D). The first principles of collaborative EU security and defence were potentially the most problematic area for UK and French officials to reach agreement. In doing so, and particularly in one evening, represented a significant advance.

The UK and French government negotiators then slipped the single sheet of A4 paper that contained the proposed Joint Declaration under the doors of the UK Prime Minister, Foreign Secretary, Defence Secretary and French President, who had only

---

8 The personal risks inherent in proceeding from this standpoint were obvious but both negotiators believed that they knew their respective Departmental views well enough to be able to continue without referring back. Moreover, the Prime Minister was providing the authority for these negotiations, further insulating them.

a very short time in the morning to agree or reject its content.[9] As one interviewee put it

> Very considerable risks were taken by both the British Prime Minister and French President in accepting a document that went to the heart of national sovereignty with only five or ten minutes consideration. No doubt there were many moments over the next two years when they wondered whether they'd done the right thing that morning (Interview D).

Despite the different interpretations placed on key phrases by the UK and French governments at that stage and then during the next two years, the text agreed at Saint Malo was fully understood in terms of its scope and its implications by the negotiators who had drafted it on 3 December. The different interpretations placed on the text by the two governments were motivated by political positioning by both governments appealing to domestic audiences (Grant 2002; Lord Robertson 2004). The agreed document was, between Saint Malo and Nice summits, continually used to bring both the UK and French governments back to the agreed line when their individual interpretations threatened to take the debate beyond the agreed boundaries (Interview D). Overall the Saint Malo declaration was made in order to ensure that the EU could '..take decisions and approve military action where the Alliance as a whole is not engaged' and shows a tangible step towards the Europeanization of defence policy (Rutten 2001, 8).

The outcome of the Saint Malo negotiation is significant because of the absence of detail in the Accords that established the ESDP process. Finding common interests between the UK and French governments on European defence policy was not as problematic as some have asserted, but it was challenging (Walker 1999). The French government had a long history of support for the notion of creating a European defence capability and were also motivated by the need to address the perception of Anglo-Saxon imbalances in the leadership of NATO (Howarth 1995, 17-40). The reform and then break up of the Soviet Union gave further impetus to analysts who had envisaged a distinct European military capability. However, discussing an autonomous EU defence capability was still taboo, which provided for a renewed focus on the Anglo-Saxon dominance of NATO (Asmus et al 1996, 79-101). The majority of EU governments prefer to ensure European security through NATO largely because such reliance is financially and operationally expedient for many of them. The reluctance to improve military capabilities was evident from the Maastricht and Amsterdam negotiations where foreign and security outcomes were 'exceedingly modest' (Heisburg 2000, 5). Thus Maastricht and Amsterdam created a pressure on the British government to become entrepreneurial on EU defence. This is a pressure that the Major government resisted but that George Robertson maintained was an important one for the Labour government to respond to. The rationale for this position was that minimized the opportunity for other EU governments to take the lead on this issue and entrench their preferences at the supranational level (Robert Key 2002; Interview M).

---

9 Interviewees argued that this was not a satisfactory situation but that there was a positive atmosphere to try and get a positive result from the summit, which is why such circumstances were permitted.

The French government's continued desire to rebalance NATO away from the perceived control of the UK and American governments was clear in the June 1999 Cologne Council and the December 1999 Helsinki Council which implied a rebalancing towards control of NATO by European member governments (Rutten 2001, 82). Richard Hatfield argued that the removal of the UK veto on defence and security within the EU had 'let the genie out of the bottle' and automatically prompted discussions on more ambitious plans for EU defence structures (Hatfield 2000). For agreement to be reached between the French and UK governments on defence policy, convergence was needed between the UK's preference for NATO's security guarantee and the French government's preference for greater EU autonomy. The compromise reached at Saint Malo of greater EU capabilities but within a NATO context was, according to Lord Robertson and Malcolm Rifkind, an attempt to satisfy both governments (Lord Robertson 2004; Rifkind 2004).

The extent to which the French government is keen on pursuing policies that might lead to an autonomous EU defence and security structure as a replacement for NATO was disputed amongst interviewees (Bruce George 2002; Interview C; Interview M). This was a subject that drew very strongly worded responses from interviewees for this research. For example, Bruce George MP and Sir Malcolm Rifkind stated that there was no debate to be had on this issue – the French government clearly supported the Saint Malo initiatives as a means by which to advance a decoupling agenda from NATO. More moderate views came from Whitehall interviewees who argued that the French government did hold such preferences but were constrained by the realities of the pre-eminence of NATO and limited European defence budgets. FCO and MoD officials argued that the French government was broadly supportive of the transatlantic Alliance but were unable to overtly support it because of domestic political considerations. Two key UK government negotiators at the Nice IGC strongly argue that the French MoD and Foreign Office were in full agreement with a process that reinforces rather than undermines NATO (Interview D; Interview H).

The presentational focus on autonomy from NATO was purely a device to appeal to a Gaullist domestic audience (Interview E; Interview H). As noted above other commentators are more sceptical about French intentions. Bruce George MP, longstanding Chairman of the House of Commons Defence Select Committee and Robert Key MP, former Shadow Defence Minister, believe that the French government is actively seeking in the medium term to create an autonomous EU force that undermines NATO (George 2002; Key 2002; Rifkind 2004). Lord Brittan, former Vice-President of the Commission, and Lord Garden offer some support to this view by arguing that it was the absence of support across the EU for such a move prevented the French government pursuing this policy seriously (Lord Brittan 2002). The Saint Malo accords provided a compromise where both positions were acknowledged and put to one side for the sake of efficient policy making and to improve EU defence capabilities (Interview D; Interview M).

The UK and French governments' divergent views concerning defence policy highlight the dynamics of issue convergence within the EU. The two governments showed common interests in preserving the NATO security guarantee, independent defence policies and improved capabilities for EU external relations policy sphere (Froehly 2000). The election of the Labour party in 1997 on a manifesto that encouraged Europeanization provided an important catalyst to the UK government becoming entrepreneurial on EU policy making. In particular, the Labour government wanted to position the UK at the 'heart of Europe' and in doing so sought to improve European capabilities outside of strictly NATO frameworks, unthinkable under the previous Conservative government (Key 2002; Rifkind 2004).

If one follows the liberal intergovernmentalist view that Europeanization only occurs when rational governments agree to collaborative policies when these offer tangible benefits to the national interest over and above independent policies, then the ESDP negotiations are an interesting case in point. This and Chapter 2 have outlined the budgetary, equipment and strategic reasons why ESDP would be more beneficial to the UK than an autonomous policy. The task for government negotiators was to 'claim value' in finalising a collective policy, whilst retaining national independence and the transatlantic security guarantee. The Saint Malo Accords achieved agreement amongst government negotiators and did, therefore, produce a convergence of national interests.

The Gate Keeper Role

Part of the liberal intergovernmentalist conception of Europeanization is that governments act as 'gate-keepers' between the domestic political system and the international bargaining table (Mbaye 2001). The gatekeeper metaphor is drawn from Putnam's account of bargaining behaviour that is cited in '*The Choice for Europe*' (Moravcsik 1998, 65). Both Moravcsik and Putnam agree that domestic interest groups lobby governments in pursuit of their own interests (Moravcsik 1998, 473; Putnam 1992, 436-7). They also agree that political parties seek electoral victories through constructing coalitions between interest groups and foster continued interest group support through meeting these groups' expectations once in government (Putnam 1992, 434).

The formal Europeanization of policies occurs when governments take the aggregated preferences of domestic interest groups, which they adopt as policy, forward to international negotiations. Putnam asserts that the government's negotiators must seek to maximize the satisfaction of domestic interest groups whilst minimising the adverse consequences that might result from the absence of negotiated output between governments (Putnam 1992, 457). The tension that Putnam's work adds to the business of negotiating at the intergovernmental level is that he believes government negotiators are conscious of domestic developments and of attaining agreements that meet a 'win-set' within the domestic system (Putnam 1992, 456-7). On the liberal intergovernmentalist reading of Europeanization once the domestic pressures have been aggregated into government policy and preferences, the 'win-set' has already been established. Government negotiators must remain within this 'win-set' without reference back to the domestic interest groups for ratification (Putnam 1992, 450-1). This tension is further borne out by the process by which international agreements are ratified. Each government's negotiating officials brings the agreed bargain back to the domestic political system to seek ratification; in the case of the

UK government the Treaty of Nice was ratified by both Houses of Parliament.[10] Not all governments will requite votes in their respective Parliaments to gain ratification, although the method of ratification affects the size of the potential available 'win-set'. For instance, a requirement for a two-thirds Parliamentary majority for ratification necessarily require a broader agreement than if a simple majority is required, and therefore affects the behaviour of negotiators.

Putnam argues that the ability of the negotiators to achieve domestic ratification determines the extent to which the negotiator can manoeuvre to 'claim value'. Negotiator's judgments are not captured at one moment in time but are subject to a continual iterative process of review during the negotiations. Negotiators therefore have to make judgments during the entire negotiations about whether an individual measure will be ratified by the UK Parliament and accepted by key domestic groups. An inability to secure approval from key groups in the domestic political system, and a resultant inability to guarantee ratification, gives negotiators some freedom to try and secure concessions from the other negotiating teams (Moravcsik 1998, 441-6). In this respect international negotiations are iterative, rather than sequential, and whilst ultimately treaty negotiations are ratified post-facto, the negotiators have to be aware of the effect various negotiated permutations have on the ability to secure both Parliamentary ratification and domestic acceptance.

In the case of the Treaty on European Union, in 1992, the UK Conservative Government had a majority of seventeen in the House of Commons and nine MPs who were willing to vote against the Government on ratifying the Treaty and who went on to lose the Government whip in 1994 because of continued rebellious behaviour (Cowley and Norton 1999, 88-9).[11] Prime Minister John Major could legitimately claim at the IGC negotiations that he was constrained by the size of the possible 'win-set' in Parliament.[12] If Prime Minister Major and his officials did not negotiate a treaty at Maastricht acceptable to the majority of his MPs and Peers then the treaty would not have been ratified in the UK Parliament. In practice, John Major was reliant on the work of his officials to negotiate within agreed red-lines and he provided the authority within which they were able to do this. The Prime Minister argued strongly with his negotiating partners that the UK government would be unable to ratify the treaty without several key concessions from them including social chapter opt-outs (Forster 1999, 352). This reinforces the liberal intergovernmentalist view that one of the key motivators for bargaining officials is the fear of not reaching a positive negotiated outcome. Moreover, it demonstrates the leverage governments, who struggle, for whatever reason, to ratify the agreement in their domestic system, have over negotiations, thus jeopardising the entire treaty.

---

10 European Communities Amendment Act was passed in the House of Commons on 18 July 2001. A treaty can be made law by Crown prerogative and therefore does not need a vote in Parliament unless it changes domestic law, as was the case with the Nice Treaty, though not the defence clauses.

11 The relevant MPs were: Sir Richard Body, Theresa Gorman, Iain Duncan Smith, Richard Shepherd, Sir Trevor Sheet, Toby Jessel, Christopher Gill, Ann Winterton, Sir Teddy Taylor.

12 The Conservative government's majority in 1992 was 21.

EU governments do, therefore, act as gate-keepers between the domestic political system and international negotiators during formal Europeanization. The government's negotiating team is the only group empowered to make offers and counter offers at the intergovernmental bargaining table, and government ministers are the only actors that can agree to proposals they feel that the government will get ratified in parliament. The gate-keeper role is further entrenched by the absence of supranational negotiators at the international level. This role allows negotiators to assess domestic win-sets without the domestic audience being affected by international influences and also to extract concessions from other government negotiators. In ESDP negotiations the Labour government had a large potential win-set, through its Parliamentary majority, but maintained self-imposed constraints – managed through careful coordination by COREPER, the European Secretariat of the Cabinet Office and the FCO.

Lowest Common Denominator Outcomes

To reach agreement across fifteen autonomous governments, all of whom wield a veto over the whole package of negotiated agreements, requires the agreement of even the most reluctant negotiator. Moravcsik argues that the number of EU negotiations, its political system and the consequences of the member governments failing to agree lend themselves to the production of lowest common denominator Europeanized policies (Moravcsik 1998, 482-3). This section explores the substance of negotiations to assess the extent to which the Presidency conclusions at the Nice IGC were merely the lowest common denominator policies or whether the Anglo-French coalition, log-rolling, side payments or threats of exclusion took the ESDP beyond this point.[13]

Between December 1998 and December 2000 the UK, French and German governments attempted to advance ESDP negotiations with independent policy initiatives. The German government used its Presidency of the EU (January to July 1999) to try and advance the ESDP agenda in accordance with its own preferences. The German government initiative became a formal EU process embodied by the Cologne Council June 1999 (Rutten 2001, 41). The German government's EU Presidency produced a set of guiding principles for the Council that incorporated a desire for CFSP and ESDP to be credible policies, and for the EU not just to have military capabilities, but also a decision making structure to authorize actions across the full range of conflict prevention, crisis management tasks and the Petersburg tasks as defined in the Treaty of European Union (Rutten 2001, 14-19). Moreover, the NATO Council Communiqué (24-25 April 1999), stated that the Alliance

---

13 Bargaining seldom involves a single issue at a time. Politicians, diplomats and the like are forced to balance their preferences on some issues against their preferences on others, given that they probably won't get their way on all of them. A concession may be made to another party on a less important topic in exchange for that other party's support on a more vital issue. This process is known as log rolling. Side payments can be typified as distributing the benefit of a policy to all partners, whilst threat of exclusion is effectively a promise to be excluded from the benefits of any negotiation.

supported the development of ESDP and shared the aspirations of the UK and French governments that ESDP should provide the EU with the capability to act autonomously, when the Alliance as a whole is not engaged. It also stated that there should be a formalization of EU rights to NATO planning facilities and that the availability of pre-identified NATO assets for use in EU led operations should be similarly codified (Rutten 2001, 20).

The Cologne Council (3-4 June 1999) occurred in the context of the Kosovo crisis. The effect of the crisis on ESDP negotiations is a keenly contested issue. Alyson Bailes, former Political Director at the WEU and former Deputy Head of the Policy Planning Unit in the FCO (1984-1986), claims that the Kosovo conflict played a leading role in galvanising EU Member governments to support the measures outlined at the Cologne Council (Bailes 2000). Bailes contends that the Kosovo conflict brought the French and UK governments together in agreeing that they should be active in persuading the EU into a more effective foreign and defence policy and similarly that the EU should be endowed with greater military capabilities (Bailes 2000). This view is supported by NATO publications concerning Kosovo, and the work of informed security commentators who have argued strongly in favour of the catalysing role played by Kosovo (NATO 2000; Roth 2000). This view also builds on those discussed in Chapter 2 that the experience of the Balkans in the 1990s had convinced the British and French governments that they could work profitably together in the defence sphere. The literature also suggests that Kosovo played a motivating role in the creation of ESDP and also fed into a debate about how enhanced capabilities would have been used by the UK in the Kosovo theatre (Bailes 1998; Hoogland 2001).

While Kosovo polarized the debates about autonomous EU defence capabilities and whether collaborative policies were more advantageous than unilateral actions, it did not resolve the debates concerning how this military role should be developed (Moens 1998). The division of opinion concerning the approach towards Kosovo is that on the one hand the French and Italian governments viewed the military action in Kosovo as an Anglo-American venture that was saved from disaster by extensive diplomatic efforts made during the bombing raids (Bulletin Quiotidien April 1999). On the other hand the US President made the bombing strategy a condition of the US military's involvement to minimize casualties and to try and avoid a ground campaign completely (Fisk 2002; Harries 1999; Lewis 2000).

The development of planning capabilities and assets, essential to the Europeanization of defence, was advanced by the French and German governments in consultation with NATO (Rutten 2001, 40). In Toulouse on 29 March 1999 the French and German governments agreed to reform the 'Eurocorps' into a rapid reaction force capable of 'out-of-area' operations and with headquarters capable of being used for international peacekeeping and peace support operations (PSO) (Rutten 2001, 40). Parallel to this Spain, Belgium and Luxembourg also agreed to restructure their military forces to make them more mobile and rapidly deployable too (Pond 1999). These developments show how Europeanization can occur outside of formal IGC structures, and through the entrepreneurial behaviour of individual governments and even further down, through the behaviour of Chiefs of Defence Staff. The Cologne meeting (3-4 June 1999) was dominated by efforts to define ESDP more closely. The summit reaffirmed that the EU should be given the capacity for autonomous action, backed by credible military forces and established a precise timetable for action (Rutten 2001, 41). This timetable consisted of the heads of government deciding that by the end of 2000 the WEU would have completed its function and would be subsumed into the EU. They also agreed that governments should have regular and ad hoc meetings of the General Affairs Council which would incorporate Defence Ministers, to create a permanent EU Political and Security Committee (PSC), and that an EU military committee should make recommendations to the PSC as should an EU military staff.

The PSC is based in Brussels and is composed of national representatives at Senior Official / Ambassador level. The PSC deals with all issues concerning CFSP and ESDP in according with treaty provisions and without prejudice to the Commission. In cases of military crisis management operations the PSC ensures under the authority of the Council, political control and strategic direction of all operations, by evaluating options for response. The PSC also provides guidance to the military committee. The Military Committee is composed of member governments Chiefs of Defence staffs as represented by their military delegates and only at the most senior level when it is absolutely necessary. It provides a military consultancy function and makes recommendations for the PSC as well as ensuring the military direction of all EU related military activities. The Military Staff are situated within the Council and provides advice and support for the ESDP in the military sector including EU-led crisis management operations. The Military Staff provide assessments of military situations and also strategic planning services within the framework of the Petersburg Tasks including the identification of appropriate forces (Dover 2007a).

The Cologne Council also concluded that WEU assets should be transferred to the EU and that Javier Solana should be designated as High Representative for CFSP in line with the decisions taken at the Amsterdam IGC (Rutten 2001, 40-45). The meeting gave the EU a military capability, but did not define the political or military doctrine that underpinned the policy. This failure to agree was caused by divergent agendas between the UK and French governments who wanted the EU to be given more autonomy to act when NATO was not involved and the Italian and German governments who were concerned about the consequences of greater EU powers (Wilson 1999; Bennett 1999). This highlights the assessments governments make about the utility of collaborative versus unitary policies. German Foreign Minister Joschka Fischer attributed a lack of progress in the ongoing action in Kosovo to the different views between member governments; the UK government was in favour of continued military action, the German government was against and the Italian government had requested a pause (Walker 1999). Without agreement on even the strategic response a lowest common denominator agreement was highly unlikely.

This evidence reinforces LI's analysis that formal Europeanization is often a facet of lowest common denominator outputs although it might equally be said that the ongoing action in Kosovo made it impossible for governments to agree on institutional and operational military issues. This further shows the precarious nature of formal Europeanization in the foreign, security and defence spheres where the intergovernmental nature of the policy means that independent positions from States can undermine European cohesion. From this perspective, and one held by the German Foreign Minister, Joschka Fischer, the most important output from Cologne was to secure agreements in principle rather than agreements of minutiae – a distinction that helps to qualify the extent to which this evidence validates LI (Interview E; Interview F).

The Saint Malo Accords were adopted at the European Council at Helsinki on 11-12 December 1999. The Helsinki Council added details to the Saint Malo Accords by establishing the PSC from 1 March, 2000 the Military Committee and Military Staff, establishing 'headline goals' by 2003 that would commit the governments to commit 60,000 troops capable of executing the full range of Petersburg tasks (Rutten 2001, 82-3). These forces would be capable of being deployed in 60 days and sustainable for up to a year. The post 'neutral' EU Member States, most notably Sweden, insisted on improving the non-military crisis management of the European Union, a position that affected what is the lowest common denominator position (Interview Swedish MoD Official 2002).[14] The main outcome of the Helsinki Council, the progression from a general commitment to a defined process with a specific set of objectives aimed at providing capabilities and institutional underpinnings to the policy. These outcomes did not cover the precise details of how European capabilities would be improved nor signalled the objectives of the military and political committees that had been established. As a result EU external relations negotiators, NATO delegates and the fifteen national Chiefs of Defence Staff still had to negotiate these details after the conclusion of the Cologne Council (Interview F; Interview H).

Many of the gaps in operational and institutional details left over from Cologne were bridged at a meeting of the EU defence ministers on 28 February 2000 in Sintra. The shape of ESDP doctrine was tackled by the 'Toolbox paper' drafted by the UK FCO (Interview D; Interview E). The 'Toolbox paper' gave weight to the UK Prime Minister's desire for the ESDP to be a capability driven policy to make collaboration more attractive than unilateral policies (Interview D; Interview E). The 'Toolbox paper' argued that the Helsinki Headline Goals should be adopted as a part of ESDP. It omitted military planning issues, geographical operational scope and the constitution of ESDP forces (Rutten 2001, 94-111). To counteract deficiencies emanating from the Helsinki goals the 'Toolbox Paper' proposed some key planning assumptions e.g. '(EU governments) will carry out tasks in and around Europe but have to be able to respond to crisis world-wide.... (the EU should also be involved in executing) complex peace enforcement tasks in a joint environment in or around Europe' with a timetable leading to a Capabilities Conference that should meet by the end of 2000 (Rutten 2001, 94-111). The British involvement in drafting the 'toolbox paper' points strongly towards a log-rolling strategy though the UK government tried to ensure the success of the ESDP negotiations by creating a significant momentum towards the policy, and also to ensure that British preferences were fully reflected in the Europeanized policy (Interview E; Interview M).

---

14 The reason why the Swedish Government were so keen to push the softer, policing aspects of the ESDP was due to the domestic political situation which gave the views of the Communist and Green Parties great credence and produced a scepticism about the wisdom of potentially undermining Sweden's independence and neutrality in the defence sphere.

The significance of the 'toolbox paper' was that it allowed UK MoD officials to agree the political framework for the defence initiative and planning elements of ESDP. However, by December 2000 the relationship between NATO and the EU's ESDP had not been resolved by member government negotiators. The British government argued that NATO should remain the mainstay of European security with ESDP acting as a means by which the EU could share the burden of the security effort. After intense lobbying of the Pentagon and State Department this position was supported by the American administration (Interview E; Interview I).[15]

The French government rejected the need to formally link ESDP with NATO until such time as the capabilities and institutional shape of the ESDP were finalized, and this was eventually done in 2003 (Rutten 2001, 94-111; Vulic 2004)[16] The French government's position was that ESDP should be free from American involvement to avoid the ESDP pursuing American foreign policy aims (La Guardia and Smith 2000; Acquantine 2002). The US State Department rejected the French government's characterization of America's influence in Europe and viewed this as further evidence of the French government's desire to 'de-couple' from NATO (CNN 2000; Maples 1999; Tisdall 2000). These concerns echoed those of Madeline Albright in 1998 when she raised three concerns about closer EU cooperation on defence which were the need to avoid 'de-coupling, duplication and discrimination' against non-EU members of NATO within a potential autonomous EU defence capability (Albright 1998).

Albright's concerns particularly focussed on the prospect of the EU duplicating NATO tasks, structures and capabilities and which might lead the EU to discriminate against non-EU NATO members like Turkey (Sloan 1997). The potential reaction of the US administration was an important factor in the ESDP negotiations. Whilst the American administration was not an official negotiator at the Nice IGC, the UK negotiators placed great credence in the policy preferences of the US (Interview E; Rifkind 2004). The presence of US administration preferences in the negotiations, albeit tacitly, made the ESDP more likely to conform to a lowest common denominator policy.

The 'Toolbox Paper' suggested that NATO's Deputy Supreme Commander Europe (DSACEUR) should participate when appropriate in the EU Military Committee although not as a full member which met US State Department concerns (Rutten 2001, 102-106). Similarly, the paper suggested that the EU Military Staff would not act as a military headquarters but would

> ...[C]o-ordinate and stimulate the development of European military capabilities, developing an appropriate relationship with NATO's force planning process... organise and co-ordinate operating procedures with national, multinational and NATO HQs

---

15 Johnston, Hatfield and Jones-Parry were all involved in the negotiations and meetings with the US State Department whilst Liddle advised the PM on how the Saint Malo initiative should be advanced in the light of US views.

16 Alexandre Vulic did, however, say that the French government's acceptance of NATO as the central security institution was a large concession and one that demonstrated their commitment to ESDP.

available to the EU; liase with national HQs, European multinational force HQs and NATO (Rutten 2001, 102-106).

These measures moulded the ESDP to fit within the NATO paradigm (Interview E; Interview H; International Herald Tribune 1999). However, the UK government's negotiators although having written the 'toolbox' paper did make a number of concessions, notably by not specifying too closely the levels of capabilities expected by each contributing member government and avoiding formalising the relationship between ESDP and NATO (Interview E; Interview F).[17] The intense negotiations between national defence officials led to the establishment of four ad-hoc working groups that were established to examine capabilities and the permanent arrangements between the EU and NATO, spreading Europeanization across institutions (Rutten 2001, 120-139). The ad-hoc working groups covered security issues, capability goals, modalities for EU access to NATO assets, and the definition of permanent consultation arrangements (Rutten 2001, 120-139). At this Council progress was made were key concessions to gain support of the Irish and Swedish governments for the agreement (Rutten 2001, 120-139; Interview E).

To resolve the issues surrounding the capabilities dimension of the ESDP defence ministers met informally on 22 September 2000 at Ecouen where the 'Capabilities Catalogue' was discussed. Prior to this meeting the defence ministers and chiefs of defence staff drafted a more complete version of the catalogue but excluded '...tasks of combat forces in crisis management, including peacemaking' (Rutten 2001, 143-146). The catalogue included four types of Petersburg operations that the EU might engage in. These were: 1) separation by force of the belligerent parties; 2) prevention of conflicts; 3) delivery of humanitarian aid; and 4) evacuation of nationals (Rutten 2001, 143-146). The development of the Petersburg tasks into the four operational hypotheses provides clear evidence of negotiators manoeuvring to meet win-sets across the fifteen governments. This reappraisal of the ESDP tasks allowed the UK government to stay within its negotiating 'red-lines' which excluded ESDP being engaged in 'hard-security' issues (Interview D; Interview G; Interview M).[18] The purpose of these negotiations were, therefore, to find the lowest common denominator positions between negotiating parties and to draft an acceptable agreement that took this into account.

The defence ministers agreed that a conference on Capability Commitment would take place on 20 November, 2000. At the Capabilities Conference governments voluntarily committed themselves to making national contributions that corresponded to the capabilities required for the Helsinki Headline Goals. The member governments confirmed that they would be able to meet the Headline Goals and went further to pledge a pool of 100,000 persons and approximately 400 combat aircraft and 100 vessels (Rutten 2001, 158-163). The UK's contribution to the Headline Goal figures were 12,500 land component personnel, 18 warships and 72

---

17 The FCO and COREPER would have liked to have made this link clear but could not do so within the confines of the negotiations and French government preferences.

18 The UK government perceived the need to more tightly define the range of capabilities that could be performed by the EU under ESDP, this meant gradually writing out roles that breached UK preferences.

combat aircraft (MoD 2001). The voluntary aspect of the commitment was a direct consequence of unwillingness amongst EU governments to advance the process and policy beyond the lowest common outcome (Centre for Defence Studies 2001; House of Lords 2000). Indeed, the Capabilities Conference provided an important context to the Nice IGC negotiations adding important details to the ESDP. Evidence from the UK government negotiators is that ESDP negotiations were finalized before the last few days of the IGC at Nice and thus avoided the somewhat frenetic negotiating reported from the final days negotiating at Nice (Norman 2000; Peel 2000; Graham and Groom 2000).

The culmination of the IGC was the European Council meeting, held at Nice 7-11 December 2000. This dealt with institutional reforms, preparations for the enlargement of the EU and ESDP provisions (Secretary of State for the Foreign and Commonwealth Office 2000). The negotiations concerning institutional reform had, in the context of the pre-IGC negotiations, deliberately been under-discussed (Bulletin Quotidien 7854, 7855, 7856 2000). In contrast to ESDP which had been fully negotiated by December 2000, institutional reform had been ignored although a considerable number of governmental positions were made public before the negotiations began (Peel 2000; Groom and Norman 2000). Despite this, many governmental negotiators came to the international negotiations without sufficient knowledge about the preferences of the other negotiators or where win-sets could be achieved (Interview F; Interview H). The main pressure to reach agreement was the threat of the treaty failing through an inability to agree; which provided negotiators with a choice of accepting an imperfect treaty or getting no agreement at all (Bulletin Quotidien 7854 2000). UK government negotiators argue that the timing of the French government's Presidency was fortunate in this respect, since the prospect of a treaty not being signed at Nice was the largest political motivation for the French government's negotiators to ensure that institutional reform was secured (Interview E; Interview H; Vulic 2004).[19]

The negotiations concerning ESDP were markedly different to those concerning institutional reform because ESDP clauses had been negotiated in successive forums from December 1998, whereas the negotiations concerning institutional reform were largely conducted in the last four days of the IGC (Interview E; Interview F; Interview H). As this chapter shows, much of the ESDP negotiations and formalization of this Europeanized policy, were conducted in bilateral meetings before Nice leading to agreement well in advance of the final reading of the 'Presidency Report on ESDP' that was ratified at Nice. The protracted negotiations and paragraph by paragraph intergovernmental agreement ensured the ESDP articles could find support in all 15 member states. As a result the Presidency report was agreed on the first day of the Nice IGC (7 December 2000) without any further negotiations (Interview F; Interview H).[20]

---

19 Alexandre Vulic argued that this was the case for the French government because they felt that such significant advances had been made a Saint Malo.

20 Interviewees noted that the ESDP provisions were the first to be signed and that this reflected the advanced state of completion resulting from the number of bilateral meetings between UK officials and other EU government officials.

One of the main areas of contention in ESDP negotiations was the relationship between the EU Military Committee (EUMC) and NATO. Three issues dominated this debate: first, whether NATO has the right of first refusal on crises; second, how far the EU could act autonomously with NATO assets; and third, the extent to which the EU should build its own military planning institutions or use NATO facilities. None of these issues were conclusively resolved during negotiation (Interview F; Interview H). The operational provisions negotiated at Nice established a close working relationship between the EU and NATO (Rutten 2001, 168). For example, one provision establishes extensive meetings at the PSC level and between NATO and EUMC biannually whilst another states that in a time of possible deployment liaisons between the EU and NATO would be increased (Rutten 2001, 174).[21] The negotiations clarified the autonomous capability of the EU and access for EU governments to pre-identified NATO assets (Rutten 2001, 168). Whilst the creation of an autonomous EU capability seems radical, the lack of military planning facilities or assets means that the EU is unable to act without NATO's assistance. UK officials would have preferred to have formalized NATO as the institution of first choice for all EU security issues. Richard Hatfield said, in evidence to the House of Commons Select Committee on Defence,

> The key thing that is autonomous is the ability to take political decisions. The only independent input that the EU will have in terms of machinery is a small-ish military staff, about the same size the WEU had which has been abolished, which can frame the questions that will be sent off to the NATO planning staffs for preparing options for them to consider. Beyond that, it will depend on drawing on capabilities either from NATO or from the EU nations, so there will not be anything else independent being created for the EU as such (Oakes 2001).

The British emphasis on the EU developing closer relations with NATO is indicated by the amount of detail devoted to the subject in the Annexes of the Presidency Report on ESDP (Rutten 2001, 168-209). The Annexes outline the procedure to be followed when the PSC consults the EUMS with a view to determining whether military options should be produced and how the EU then consults with NATO's planning capabilities (Oakes 2001).[22] Leading on from this the automatic right of

---

21 Closer working provisions also included creating ad hoc EU / NATO working groups on capabilities issues and less regular groups focussing on particular areas of expertise. NATO representatives are also invited to meetings of Defence Ministers. Regularized contacts between the secretaries-general, Secretariats and Military Staffs of the EU and NATO and exchanges of information are also planned.

22 In this instance the following procedures would be followed: On the recommendations of the EUMC assisted by the EUMS, the PSC will send the designated operation commander, via the EUMC, strategic directives enabling him to draw up the necessary planning documents for the operation, making use of the guaranteed access to NATO planning capabilities. These plans will then be submitted to the PSC for approval. Experts from the two organizations, in liaison with DSACEUR as strategic co-ordinator will meet to specify the predetermined NATO assets and capabilities concerned with this option. Once the assets and capabilities to be used in the operation are specified, the EU will forward a request to NATO. The handover of predetermined assets and capabilities used in the EU operation together with the

access to NATO capabilities was fiercely negotiated outside of the confines of the IGC (Hunter 2003, 73). The Turkish government, as a non-EU NATO member, raised considerable objections to the provision of an automatic right of access to NATO assets. Turkish officials argued that non-EU NATO members would be excluded from the decision making process on the range and scope of any operations involving NATO assets (Hunter 2003, 113). They were also concerned that the EU might use NATO assets to act in the Eastern Mediterranean area (Rutten 2001, 164). British and American negotiators concluded an agreement with Turkey on 16 December 2001 that provided guarantees over the geographical scope of EU operations and also gave Turkey the right to be consulted, but not to veto operations (Joshi 2002).

George Robertson invested a great deal of his own time, as NATO's General Secretary, on this issue in bilateral meetings with the Turkish Prime Minister persuading the PM and his officials that this would not compromise Turkish national security (Lord Robertson 2004). Robertson's role is interesting – as a former British government Minister and the Defence Secretary who brought the Europeanization of defence forward, he was then engaged in persuading a NATO member to allow a credible policy to be formed. The role of important bureaucratic actors in formal Europeanization has been highlighted through the domestic policy formulation and IGC chapters of this study and is a profitable avenue for future research.

The Nice Treaty modified the CFSP sections in the Amsterdam Treaty and added annexes relating to the ESDP. The Presidency Conclusions stated that the result of the Saint Malo initiative was:

> To give the European Union the means of playing its role fully on the international stage and of assuming its responsibilities in the face of crises by adding to the range of instruments already at its disposal an autonomous capacity to take decisions and action in the security and defence field (Rutten 2001, 168).

The practical implications of the Nice Treaty were to subsume the WEU and its defence competencies into the EU (Treaty of Amsterdam 1998; Treaty of Nice 2001). The amalgamation of WEU functions into the EU has created new institutions.

---

arrangements for making them available and any recall conditions will be identified at a PSC / NAC meeting. Throughout the operation the Alliance will be kept informed of the use of NATO assets and capabilities, if necessary by convening a meeting of the PSC and NAC. The commander of the operation will be invited to the EUMC meetings to report on the progress of the operation The Presidency may invite him to attend meetings of the PSC and GAC. Having first informed the NAC, the PSC will propose to the Council that operation be terminated. The EU will terminate the use of NATO assets and capabilities.

These are the Political Security Committee (PSC)[23], the EUMC and the EUMS.[24] In addition to new institutions the negotiations codified the pledge at the Helsinki Council to develop an EU military force of up to 60,000 troops able to be deployed within 60 days and for up to a year conducting a large number of tasks ranging from peace-keeping to peace-making (Rutten 2001, 176).

Enhanced co-operation was included into Article 27(a-e) of the Nice Treaty. These provisions describe how enhanced co-operation can be used in relation to ESDP (Treaty of Nice 2001). Enhanced co-operation allows groups of states the right to carry out a policy without the consensus of all EU governments. A majority of governments had to be in favour of an initiative under the Treaty of Amsterdam whilst Article 24 modifications at Nice means that only eight member governments have to be in favour of an initiative (Treaty of Amsterdam 1998; Treaty of Nice 2001). Prior to the enlargement of the EU to 25 governments, a majority of nations will still need to be in favour of an initiative for it to become an EU policy. After enlargement less than a simple majority of governments now need to support the initiative, thus

---

23 The PSC is the lead institution in decision making on CFSP and ESDP. The PSC also acts as a crisis monitoring and crisis management organization. In practice this means that the PSC will keep track of the General Affairs Council, provide guidelines to departments and committees with interests that spread into the CFSP and ESDP sphere and also deals with crisis situations. In crisis situations the PSC is able to take soundings and exercise 'political control and strategic direction of the EU's military response to the crisis' meaning that the PSC has overall political authority. The PSC will also evaluate the opinions and recommendations of the Military Committee specifically the strategic military options, chain of command, operational concepts and plans that will be submitted to the Council. If a crisis were to occur the Secretary General or High Representative would chair the PSC. The Nice Treaty lays out that to maintain full control over a military-crisis situation, a procedure is followed: the PSC would send a recommendation to Council based on the opinion of the Military Committee. The Council might then decide to launch a military operation within the framework of a joint action. The joint action would contain a clause defining the role of the High Representative / Secretary-General. Once the operation had begun the Council would be kept informed through PSC reports presented by the High Representative or Secretary-General in their capacity as Chairman of the PSC (Rutten 2001).

24 EUMC is the highest military institution within the EU. It is staffed by the Chiefs of Defence (CHODs) and represented daily by their military representatives. (MILREPS). The EUMC exercises military direction of all military activities within the EU framework. The EUMC provides military advice and recommended courses of action to the PSC on military matters within the EU when requested. The EUMC also works on military doctrine and costings for all military operations within the EU's remit. 'Upon the PSCs request it issues an Initiating Directive to the Director General of the EUMS to draw up and present strategic military options. It evaluates the strategic military options developed by EUMS and forwards them to the PSC together with its evaluation and military advice. On the basis of the military option selected by the Council it authorizes an Initial Planning Directive for the Operation Commander. Based on the EUMS evaluation, it provides advice and recommendations to the PSC:- on the Concept of Operations (CONOPS) developed by the Operation Commander on the draft Operation Plan (OPLAN) drawn up by the Operation Commander. It gives advice to the PSC on the termination option for an operation.' Presidency Report on the ESDP, Annex IV. Presidency Report on the ESDP, Part II.

only a third of EU governments are required to support a proposal under enhanced co-operation. This has potential impacts on the ESDP and could allow ad-hoc coalitions of governments to advance integration against UK government preferences.

The French Foreign Minister attributed the success of ESDP negotiations to '...the EU's political will and the will to gather all the military and civilian capabilities necessary to ensure the credibility of the defence policy' (Bulletin Quotidien 7855 2000). This only partly addresses the question of whether ESDP negotiations produced lowest common denominator outputs. IGC negotiations are guided by the principle of unanimity and thus to gain agreement across fifteen governments for an issue area there must necessarily be a convergence of core interests and agreement to exclude aspects of proposed policies that fall outside of some negotiating parties acceptable limits – hence negotiated outputs will always be lowest common denominator agreements.

In the case of ESDP negotiations the evidence shows that there are four governments who had intense issue specific preferences; namely the UK, French, German, and Swedish governments. The remaining governments, whilst playing a full role in negotiations, did not possess the same range and depth of institutional red-lines on ESDP that provided greater latitude for the four governments with intense preferences to negotiate and as a result this section has argued that EU intergovernmental negotiations can produce a positive sum-game, and therefore go beyond lowest common denominator agreements. The ESDP case study provides considerable evidence that governments are highly sophisticated in the way they select issues on which they feel core issues of sovereignty, autonomy and key policy interests are affected. In addition, by identifying governments with intense issue specific preferences, agreements can be struck with those governments, creating a positive sum output.

Summary

The liberal intergovernmentalist explanation of IGC negotiations is very strong. The fundamental tenets of the theory are validated by the Nice negotiations. British government negotiators bargained rationally to try and maximize the benefits to the UK's national interest which was defined by the PM and the core executive. Negotiations concerning ESDP were not explicitly linked to other issues being negotiated at the Nice IGC. However, there was evidence of a very close co-ordination of UK negotiators across all the issue areas – COREPER and the European Secretariat of the Cabinet Office kept a close and evolving note of all the negotiations as they progressed. This gave these co-ordinating institutions a broad view of the negotiations which allowed them to suggest areas in which concessions could be demanded or given as necessary. Many of the interviewees for this thesis argued that this gave the UK government negotiators a slight advantage over their fellow negotiators, and that the UK government was exceptionally well co-ordinated. In essence, whilst there was overall Cabinet Office co-ordination on the process of negotiating this staging did not affect the subject specific preferences demonstrated by the British government.

A notable element of the ESDP negotiations was that defence was kept distinct from different issues at the IGC (like voting rights in the Council and numbers of MEPs) being linked to ESDP negotiations. The crucial issue for negotiators was how strongly committed the government was to the ESDP policy within the iterative parameters they perceived from domestic 'win-set' providers like Parliament, interest groups and the armed forces. Moreover, post-agreement ratification in Parliament and securing domestic political support from interest groups are too simplistic to explain negotiating behaviour in IGCs. The assumptions made by negotiations about domestic political support for a measure provides the context in which negotiators can propose any changes to the proposals or make concessions to other negotiators. By this rationale the government's large House of Commons majority should have afforded it a great deal of negotiating latitude and win-set on ESDP because even with a large rebellion from Labour MPs the bill ratifying the Nice Treaty would have been won. The evidence from officials and negotiators involved in the development and negotiation of ESDP was, however, that the Prime Minister and his core officials took particular care to control and manage the development of ESDP from the Saint Malo Accords in December 1998. For example, they authored the 'Toolbox Paper' presented at Sintra in February 2000 and demanded that the 'Capabilities Catalogue' was given renewed prominence ten days before the Nice IGC.

UK government negotiators argued that the government's strong preference on ESDP produced an identifiable pattern of Europeanizing behaviour. The UK government decided to use the considerable political leverage it possessed through military and economic strength to frame the ESDP debate, to suit British preferences, and drive the policy towards the intergovernmental negotiations at Nice. This was particularly true in the example of the Sintra 'Toolbox Paper' and the bilateral meetings between the Policy Directors of the FCO and MoD Emyr Jones-Parry, Richard Hatfield and their respective opposite numbers in fellow EU governments (Interview D; Interview E; Interview G). This behaviour demonstrates that domestic win-sets are not solely determined by Parliamentary majority, which would have given the government considerable negotiating latitude. Domestic win-sets were therefore built from a complex picture of perceived agreements from the armed forces, the media, a notion of public opinion, and a similarly iterative sense of what is in the UK's national interest.

An important element from these negotiations is that there was a point before the final agreement of the Treaty where the PM and his close advisors had to make a decision about whether the outcome would find sufficient domestic support. However, they did not just discuss this once, it was part of a continual iterative discourse in the negotiating team about whether proposals would achieve domestic or intergovernmental win-sets. This chapter has argued that the government's negotiators controlled the development of ESDP to ensure that the policy reflected core UK preferences and provided the largest win-set possible on a policy issue on which the Labour government was wary for historical reasons. UK negotiators were able to manage and strongly influence ESDP negotiations through authoring key positioning papers and in the number of bilateral negotiations they held with fellow EU government officials. Indeed, this chapter argues that most of the ESDP negotiations occurred outside of formal EU frameworks, including the Saint Malo

Accords in December 1998. The large number of bilateral negotiations between UK negotiations and other EU government negotiators developed ESDP to a largely completed stage by the European Council at Nice.

LI makes the hypothesis that external factors and the fear of not reaching an agreement are the principle motivations within the international bargaining (Moravcsik 1998, 64). This chapter found that the fear of not reaching an agreement was one of the dynamics in the negotiations but not the primary motivation; and one that was only triggered once the Saint Malo Accords had been signed. Furthermore, this chapter has advanced the argument that enhanced co-operation between the French and UK governments in December 1998 at Saint Malo, and subsequent bilateral negotiations outside the formal IGC framework, brought the bargaining beyond a point where a fear of failure dominated, to a discussion about how the policy would operate and whether it would have full capabilities.

This chapter has presented strong evidence that governments act as 'gatekeepers' between domestic politics and pressure groups and the other EU negotiators. Evidence of this came from the weak link between negotiators and domestic parliamentarians and other interest groups and also by the effective exclusion of the European Parliament and European Commission from the negotiations. Furthermore, governments who had intense issue specific preferences and capabilities were the influential actors in the negotiations. In ESDP bargaining these included the UK, French and German governments and the effectiveness of international co-operation and these negotiations resulted from preference convergence. Less influential governments were able to add policies to ESDP through offering their conditional support for the policies. These governments including the Swedish and Danish government had less intense preferences and therefore could offer agreement more easily than UK, French and German governments.

In the example of Nice IGC negotiations outcomes were not the product of preference convergence across the 15 EU governments but convergence amongst governments with intense preferences and acquiescence from governments with less intense preferences. In ESDP negotiations the EU was a co-ordinating forum for national policies reducing transaction costs between governments rather than extending an EU political system. This research has shown that formal Europeanization frequently occurs outside of formal IGC frameworks through the interactions of officials, initiatives taken at a national level, right through for former Secretaries of State promoting a Europeanized policy in their supranational roles. The formal Europeanization of policies occurs at Treaty amending conferences, and in the example of defence policy is still dominated by governments, producing an inherent instability in this policy sphere, and making intergovernmental analyses perennially relevant.

Chapter 5

Why Governments Transfer Sovereignty: Formal Europeanization

The final element of formal Europeanization, which occurs through intergovernmental conferences, is the transfer or pooling of sovereignty by governments to the supranational level. The motivational aspects for these transfers are particularly important to those seeking to make sense of Europeanization as a political phenomenon. Discursively, these transfers lend themselves to analyses that only rational governments seek to transfer sovereignty when it is in their interests to do so when it provides a better option than continued unitary action and when it adds value to their independent policy. This chapter critically explores why the British government took the decision to formally Europeanize its defence policy and thus transfer elements of its defence and security competencies to the EU under ESDP. In doing so it analyses the choices available to governments in these ESDP negotiations and the distribution of benefits amongst governments transferring sovereignty. Furthermore, it explores whether the EU constitutes a co-ordinating forum for governmental preferences and analyses the balances of power inherent in the EU, especially between the UK, French and German governments.

As discussed in Chapter 3, formal Europeanization is only possible when the collective policy holds greater benefits for the negotiating parties than continuing to pursue a unilateral policy. In the case of a Europeanized defence policy, a key motivation has been to improve the EU's defence capabilities through co-ordination and a streamlining of capabilities and command structures, as well as to see a Union better able to project itself on the world stage. Furthermore, transferring sovereignty to the EU has helped the UK government to negate the 'anarchy' problem of fellow EU governments' preferences taking EU security structures in a direction that would not meet UK defence preferences, as highlighted in Chapters Two and Three. The co-ordination of defence and security policy through the EU, in a policy that met core UK government redlines, effectively locked other EU governments into UK preferences. The transfer of governmental sovereignty to the EU adds credibility to the Saint Malo initiative and similarly reduces the future transaction costs of developing pan-European collaborative defence ventures. Transferring defence sovereignty is therefore an efficient way for British government preferences to be expressed and realized. Moreover, within the IGC structure the decision to transfer sovereignty is a deliberate one. The transfer of defence sovereignty to the EU was not the product of institutional spillover – competencies acquired over time – but was a process managed by the British government who had rationally concluded that a collaborative ESDP was in their interests.

Explaining Sovereignty Transfer

Formal Europeanization and, by inference, the EU serve as instruments to overcome the constitutional bars to binding one legislature to an external legislature (Moravcsik 1998, 3-4). Moreover, these institutional arrangements enable controls to be placed to regulate a transfer of sovereignty and monitor governments' defections from agreements once the transfer of sovereignty has occurred. This analysis has been explored in great depth by Simon Hix and Alberta Sbragia who argue that the EU is a political system in its own right exerting a governmental role over and above that of national governments, a position that is radically different from liberal intergovernmentalist explanations of the integration project, which suggests that governments are pre-eminent in the EU and the international system more widely (Hix 1999, 1-17; Sbragia 1992, 258 and 292).

Competing explanations of sovereignty transfer highlight the different types of benefit governments can derive in terms of securing credible commitments from other governments for collective policy solutions (Allen 1996, 290; Gordon 1997, 74-100; Rummel and Wessels 1983, 34). These accounts also suggest that intergovernmental bargains are the first step in an ever deepening cooperative arrangement between European states on that particular issue area, and across the full range of European policy areas (Majone 2000, 2). Even on these terms Europeanization can occur within and outside of formal IGC structures. The IGC route merely provides the most obvious route through which the formal Europeanization of policies occurs; whilst domestic policies, and patterns of official and bureaucratic behaviour can be tracked to suggest the extent to which policies are Europeanized.

There are other factors, identified in the extant literature, that inform the analysis of why governments decide to delegate sovereignty to the EU. The argument that vulnerabilities on a specific issue drive the degrees to which governments are prepared to delegate sovereignty – and thus protect their position – is a key concept employed within this chapter. The smaller governments of the EU are dependent – sometimes directly – on the financial strength and political credibility of the larger EU governments like the UK, France and Germany. These smaller governments seek to cement influence, and thus secure their domestic preferences, over these larger countries through collaborative policies managed within EU institutions (Moravcsik 1998, 475; Walker, 2004; Economist 2004; Grabbe and Guerot 2004). The disadvantages smaller governments feel in terms of economics, institutional votes and military power and therefore a lack of influence and inability to effectively formulate political coalitions within the EU, leads them to be more prepared to transfer elements of their sovereignty to EU institutions.

In Ben Tonra's study of government conduct within the CFSP frameworks he argues that smaller states benefit considerably from working with larger states: 'Minor states usually lack significant intelligence or espionage capabilities and, as a general rule, have smaller diplomatic staffs from which to gather and analyse data' (Tonra 1997, 183). Similarly, Moravcsik draws a comparison between the effectiveness of domestic foreign policy capacity and governmental preferences on foreign policy co-operation (Moravcsik and Nicolaidis 1998, 64). As a consequence LI argues that '..geopolitical concerns would dominate [....] positions [...] in those areas without clear and certain economic implications, such as [...] foreign policy cooperation' (Moravcsik 1998, 402). The evidence presented in Chapter 2 suggests that the British government's decision to become a policy entrepreneur on ESDP was partly a consequence of geopolitical and strategic circumstances that aimed to maximize British influence at the 'heart of Europe'.

The liberal intergovernmentalist approach suggests that a government's capacity to act unilaterally is conditional on its position within the existing balances of power in the EU (Moravcsik and Nicolaidis 1998, 64). Institutionally and militarily capable governments have a larger capacity for an effective unilateral foreign policy than those governments without these capabilities and moreover, a government's power position within the EU is a product of two factors, first, the number of highly influential governments in the EU, termed polarity and secondly, the governments' share of key material resources (Krasner 1993, 21-42). These factors weigh heavily on the strategic direction of a government's foreign policy. Stephen Krasner argues that,

> The behaviour of individual states, regardless of their domestic political characteristics, is constrained by their own capabilities and the distribution of power in the system as a whole (...). The external environment will inevitably pressure states to move toward congruity between commitments and capabilities (Krasner 1993, 21).

The British and other EU governments seem to have internalized this view. British negotiators were able to exert influence on the development and negotiations of ESDP because, relative to other EU governments, the UK has extensive military capabilities and a senior position within NATO and the UN, the key institutions in the European security sector (Nicola Butler, 2004). The extent to which the UK government is an authoritative voice on security affairs in the EU provides it with a freedom and flexibility in negotiating positions that other European governments do not share. The added negotiating flexibility of the British government was also the result of the additional personnel deployed to co-ordinate the UK's approach towards ESDP negotiations across the Cabinet Office, MoD and FCO (Interview E; Interview M).[1] British officials also tried to co-ordinate the bargaining positions of the other respective governments during the negotiations, through holding many bilateral liaison meetings (Interview E; Interview M). The deployment of additional diplomatic resources to policy co-ordination allowed the British government to strongly influence the path and progress of the ESDP negotiations (Interview F; Interview H).[2]

---

1 Interview E highlighted the additional diplomatic resources, particularly Officials time, that went into ESDP negotiations. Interview M argued that this was standard practice where issues might become part of the bargaining at a European Council.

2 It might be expected that UK officials involved in the Nice European Council would argue that they had considerable influence on the direction of ESDP negotiations. However, there is strong textual evidence from examining the Saint Malo Accords and Presidency Conclusions from Nice that the initial proposal was largely unchanged throughout the entire negotiating period which strongly validates this position.

A government's position within the European balance of power is determined by its share of certain decisive capabilities. These capabilities are seen as transferable, and can be used in unrelated policy areas, and furthermore that the utility of a particular capability contributes to the government's influence within the EU (Waltz 1986, 333). Economic strength (size of economy and GDP) are important state-based capabilities in the EU. Countries with strong economies can be expected to possess a high level of technology that may be used, transferably, for military purposes as well as private industry. In the case of ESDP, the salient capabilities were military assets, financial capabilities, institutional affiliation and roles within these institutions and influence over the foreign and security policy of other member governments. In ESDP bargaining the British government's military strength – and ability to project force, provided it with a great deal of influence over the ESDP.[3] In short, therefore, in military and security spheres the UK government had considerable scope within existing preferences to innovate, because of its position within EU and European security structures (Interview F; Interview G; Interview H).[4]

Britain's membership of, and position within, relevant security-related institutions like the UN, NATO and G8 adds to Britain's position within the international system. Exclusion from these international institutions diminishes the opportunity to influence international responses to events and forms an element of the discourse regarding the maintenance of the UK's nuclear deterrent; that is ensuring that the British government is not marginalized in the international system. The British government is particularly privileged in holding a veto power in the UN Security Council, a large number of European Parliament seats and EU Council votes, although this is being steadily diluted through ever expanding enlargement of the EU. In addition to the UK's institutional strengths it enjoys an enhanced and privileged access to American officials in the Whitehouse, State Department, Pentagon and the CIA. Privileged access to US policy makers and policy shapers is said to allow the UK to be the conduit between the US and the EU, and helps place the UK as the pre-eminent authority within the development of the ESDP, although Michael Noonan argues that the US State Department and Pentagon's support for this initiative was conditional on ESDP not using NATO funds for replicating NATO in the EU (Williams 2004; Noonan 2004; Interview A; Interview M).

Interviewees from the key foreign and defence policy departments in the British government argued strongly that the close day-to-day relationship between British and American officials in the State Department and Pentagon gave the British government a key advantage over fellow European governments in dealing with defence and security issues, including in technology transfers. William Hopkinson

---

3 All the UK based interviewees in this research argued that Britain's military strength was a compelling reason why it was able to lead on ESDP. Notably though Charles Grant argued that Blair's strongly pro-European views assisted in making this case in Europe and Lord Wallace and William Hopkinson added that the UK's prominent roles in NATO and the UN further assisted this position.

4 The principle ESDP negotiating team argue that they had considerable room to manoeuvre in comparison to some of their fellow negotiators because of the UK's prominent position as a leading defence actor in Europe but were confined by self-imposed red-line constraints.

argued further that the American view was always considered very favourably by British officials whilst a Foreign Office official noted that his interaction with US officials revolved around explaining UK positions and reassuring American officials about intended actions. John Allen Williams, Chair of the Academic Advisory Council of the National Strategy Forum and senior academic commentator, argued that the 'privileged relationship' is very real and serves to advance an Anglo-Saxon security perspective on the globe (Rifkind 2004; Hopkinson 2003; Interview E; Williams 2004). The enduring quality of Britain and America's 'special relationship' will be explored in Chapter 6 and particularly for the effects it has had on Europeanization across all areas of deepening Europeanization.

Realist scholars have referred to the influence of 'national morale', 'quality of diplomacy' as well as 'prestige' in international relations (Gilpin 1981, 13 and 30). Joseph Nye refers to these factors as the 'second face of power' (Nye 1990, 29). According to Nye a government's indirect influence is based on the '...attraction of (their) ideas or on the ability to set the political agenda in a way that shapes the preferences that others express' (Nye 1990, 31). Indirect influence is more difficult to measure than direct influence, but the available evidence suggests that the British government's unique experience and capabilities in defence and security policy, as well as economic power, its strong links with key American government departments and prestigious military history meant that Britain was able to shape the pre Saint Malo debate and then the formulation of ESDP (Nye 1990, 32; Interview C; Robertson 2004). Influence over the speed and direction of formal Europeanization, particularly in the defence and security spheres, therefore seems to be dependent on standard conceptions of balances of power within the international system. Further comparativist research is required to assess whether states with high capabilities have greater sway over the direction of formal Europeanization in other fields; the evidence available on defence, foreign and security policies certainly suggest that this is the case.

Through liberal intergovernmentalist lenses the EU is an institutional framework for the pursuit of governmental policy preferences (Moravcsik 1998, 8). Locating defence and security policy preferences within the EU brings about 'costs', namely constraints on government's autonomy. By inference, the EU will continue to retain and expand its competencies only where it provides more 'benefits' than 'costs' to national governments (Moravcsik 1998, 482; Ginsberg 1989, 2; cf Jorgensen 1997, 167-180; Jorgensen 1999, 78-96; Smith 1998, 304-333; Glarbo 1999, 634-651). The nature of these benefits range across the financial, social, political and practical outcomes and are contested by integration scholars, notably 'functionalist regime theory' critiques (Waltz 1979, 96). Within this latter view international institutions help governments to overcome problems in formulating collective actions (Hasenclever, Mayer and Rittenberger 1997, 616). The EU reduces transaction costs and, by being an efficient conduit of information between governments, uncertainty (Axelrod and Keohane 1996, 250). Thus, where as international treaties, like the Kyoto environmental treaty have to be negotiated at an international forum outside of the remit and scope of a regularized institutional framework, and therefore entail high costs, the EU provides a stable institutional framework through which agreements can be reached, managed and enforced (Regelsberger et al 1997, 183; Bulmer and

Edwards 1992, 150). The EU also acts in a managerial role adding operational detail and interpretation to policies within the issue area to negate the need to create separate agreements on smaller operational issues within the headline agreement. However, neorealist critiques would suggest that there is a missing balance of power structure that underpins the EU (Mearsheimar 1994, 5-49). This perspective accepts a limited independent role for the EU and consequently argue that the Union can be an instrument of government policy (Mearsheimar 1994, 5-49).

By marked contrast functionalist regime theory, holds that the EU may be used as an instrument of government to exert power and influence (Krasner 1982, 506; Krasner 1991, 336-366). The question of what the EU is and how it serves to advance or hinder the work and role of national governments is crucial to an analysis or formal Europeanization. The EU as a co-ordinating institution is markedly different from an international organization that acts as a dominant partner in a federal political system. Within the formal Europeanization of defence policy, the EU firmly falls into the category of a co-ordinating organization, directly along the lines that liberal intergovernmentalism outlines (Moravcsik 1998, 485-6).

All European member governments seek to create coalitions of supportive governments to shape the policy agenda and negotiations of EU policy. However, as Chapters 3 and 4 argued the evidence suggests that governments with strong issue specific preferences and capabilities are particularly active in ensuring their preferences prevail and in doing so seek to achieve a convergence of preferences with other governments at the negotiations. This provides part of the explanation as to why British government officials were so active in conducting a large number of bilateral meetings with the other EU government officials, to try and secure the most advantageous set of agreements for the British government.

The influence and ability of governments to create persuasive coalitions in European Council negotiations is dependent on the issue area, the strength of the respective governments' policy preferences, and the influence of external actors (like the US) or domestic circumstances on the negotiations. Members of these influential coalitions gain what Joseph Grieco calls 'voice-opportunities' (Grieco 1996, 261-306). Voice-opportunities are 'institutional characteristics whereby the views of partners (including partners) are not just expressed but have a material impact on the operation of a collaborative arrangement' (Greico 1996). Becoming a constructive member of a negotiating coalition affords a government the opportunity to shape elements of the policy to suit their own preferences, whilst also allowing the major governments in the coalition, in this case the UK and French governments, to advance a policy agenda in a way that suits their core preferences. The rationale for this is that the junior coalition partners gain a greater measure of influence over the precise detail of the policies remaining within the coalition than they would if they were outside of the coalition altogether. This was a point notably grasped by the Swedish government who sought to use their role as a 'critical friend' to ESDP to add further 'soft security' roles to the negotiated outcome (Jonson 2003; Interview E).

Finally, liberal scholars have noted that a commitment to the EU can offer an opportunity for governments to enhance their autonomy from domestic pressure (Moravcsik 1994, 1; Wolf 1999, 333-363). This can be a particularly useful tool for governments. It provides a media and discourse driven separation from responsibility for certain policy issues, although because of the core sovereignty concerns about defence policy it is unlikely a government would use the EU in this way. Governments have strived to retain control of their defence policy, and by inference their competency over territorial defence, thus this sort of displacement activity would serve to undermine the standing of the government.

By transferring issues from the domestic level to European intergovernmental negotiations, governments are able to increase their leverage over domestic actors (such as Parliament and interest groups) in various ways (Moravcsik 1994, 7). Through the 'gate-keeper' role governments gain a privileged access to information from other negotiating governments and thus can shape the domestic debate through managing the dissemination of this information (Flagaard and Moravcsik 1993, 282-285). The government's monopoly over the flow of information is coupled with the role of the UK parliament in the ratification of the negotiated output, limited as it is to a retrospective ratification, rather than take an active role in negotiations. British parliamentarians are able to vote for or against the entire treaty package without being afforded the opportunity to amend any of the negotiated outputs. Parliamentary scrutiny of IGC output and negotiations comes from the ability of parliamentarians, as a whole, to either vote to ratify or turn down the government legislation that enshrines the Treaty in British law and through the Standing Committees on the Intergovernmental Conference.[5]

The Standing Committee is empowered to study the issues of the IGC in close detail and is able to suggest and lobby the relevant government ministers and Prime Minister about how they think negotiations should proceed. This scrutiny reduces, however, to a simple vote to accept or reject the negotiated package, this being particularly true in the case of the ratification of the Maastricht Treaty in July 1993 where the issue became a matter of confidence in John Major's Conservative government (Stephens 1997, 332). The Labour government, enjoying a majority of 179 in the House of Commons, between 1997 and 2001, allowed a great deal more room for the government to manoeuvre to achieve Parliamentary ratification of the output from the Nice European Council (Palmer 2002; Clegg 2002).[6] However, the Prime Minister and his core executive introduced self-imposed tight restrictions on their negotiating leverage to ensure that the government's core defence and security preferences were not breached.

Alan Milward argues that governments seek to transfer sovereignty to the EU to effectively lock other EU governments into their preferences, thus having the effect of increasing the influence of the proposing government (Milward 2001, 16-17; MacCormick 1999, 123-126). Milward describes this as the 'European rescue of the nation-state' – that governments manoeuvre on the European stage to ensure that their policy preferences are reflected through the collective policies of the EU-15,

---

5   This is primarily the work of the European Scrutiny Committee which also then forms an IGC standing committee before treaty approving European Councils.

6   Indeed Nick Palmer, and Nicholas Clegg, commented that it would have been exceptional for Parliament to have blocked the treaty legislation given the realities of British Parliamentary politics at the time.

and since his book was published the EU-25 and now EU-27. Certainly for the British government the case for stronger EU capabilities, as a key motivator in the ESDP negotiations and process, was strong (Liddle 2003; Wallace 2003).[7] For the British political executive ESDP was seen as a means by which governments can 'add-value' to their security and defence policies by providing an enhanced international intervention capability when NATO as a whole does not wish to be engaged (George 2003; Interview C).

The ability of the EU to effectively co-ordinate defence and security issues is, however, contested. Foreign policy issues that potentially lend themselves to the military solutions are a great source of disagreement, negotiation and particular sensitivities in the EU, particularly around the issue of national sovereignty. There are further sensitivities about which European security organization should be given institutional responsibility for any deployment. These debates centre on accusations that the French government is seeking to undermine the transatlantic alliance or that NATO control of a particular operation offers the United States too great an influence over any policy. There are also difficult questions about the political legitimacy and funding of European defence. Funding is a particularly troublesome area within the EU's role in defence and security sphere (Garden 2003a, 2; WEU Assembly 2003). The Netherlands is the only EU Member currently to have a dedicated budget for ESDP activities, and even this budget is restricted so that it covers only Dutch activities within the ESDP framework (Newton-Dunn 2002; Grant 2002).

Some of the political sensitivities around EU military issues are advanced by Christopher Hill, Martin Holland and this author who argue, through respectively analysing the EU's response to the Balkans crisis and political upheaval in South Africa, that the EU and its external relations apparatus is punching below its weight in international affairs (Hill 1993; 305-328; Holland 1995; Dover 2005). In the context of the EU's involvement in international affairs through the EPC mechanisms, and latterly the CFSP, which attempts to co-ordinate EU foreign and security policies, have only registered marginal success in gaining closer EU voting patterns in the UN and in coordinating lowest common denominator responses to elements of the Yugoslavian civil war (Bruckner 1990, 187). Indeed, the EU's ability to operate in the foreign and security policy sector have been hindered by the need to gain agreements based on unanimity, and the absence of political will to advance solutions that are not based around economic diplomacy and technical support. The EU has been effective in establishing general policy principles, but the policy instruments to reinforce these first principles agreements have been slow to follow. Similar stumbling blocks include the preference for EU security and European military interventions to be conducted under either the NATO or UN banner, and that an EU defence presence has been viewed as a direct threat to the NATO alliance and one that should therefore not be pursued. This was a position held by the Major Government and one publicly expounded by the Blair government in the first year of its term in office, which led to UK officials shaping the debate to ensure that ESDP could not be viewed as being

---

7   Liddle argued that the Prime Minister was very robust in asserting this as his primary aim. Lord Wallace similarly believed that the experience of the Balkans and the need to act positively in Europe's near abroad were significant motivations.

a threat to NATO. The position of the Benelux countries and Germany, Italy and Spain was that ESDP should not remove the NATO security guarantee over Europe. The progress of the negotiations made it plain that the ESDP was complementary to NATO rather than a threat (Ruane 2000).

Though the basis of the NATO Alliance has been the overwhelming presence of the United States, eleven of the EU-15 of 1997-2001 are members of NATO (Robertson 2003; Department of Defense 2000, Chapter Two).[8] As a result eleven EU governments have considerable experience of collaborative defence initiatives in which national sovereignty is both pooled and preserved. The EU has not organized its security and defence in isolation and indeed several leading EU security commentators, such as Anthony Forster and William Wallace, have argued that the EU Members of NATO have used the American security guarantee to effectively under-finance European security, and therefore 'free-ride' (Wallace 2002). The defence budgets of many Members of the EU are well below that of America and indeed Britain and France (Military Balance 2004, 335).[9] The EU members have the collective experience of collaborative defence ventures, joint operations and training experience and the experience of this joint working should serve to reduce the initial costs of running the ESDP, indeed the deepening integration on a narrow range of activities after 2001 provides some evidence for this. All of this should add strength to the argument that ESDP serves to provide additional value to national defence budgets and capabilities. In turn, this leads to a follow-on conclusion that ESDP negotiations were a means to co-ordinate national policies and further reduce the transaction costs of reaching agreements and institutionalizing British and French government preferences.

The strength of the liberal and rationalist literatures can be found in trying to locate the British government's aims in defence policy and European affairs more generally (Moravcsik 1998, 476).[10] The British government's motivations for Europeanization as set out in the opening chapters were to improve the autonomous defence and security capabilities of the EU, so that the EU could intervene militarily in situations where it felt appropriate to do so and where NATO, as a whole, did not wish to be involved. This initiative would also serve to secure the medium term future of NATO through European governments sharing the burden of European security with the US, and only activating a military response through the EU when NATO chooses not to act.

---

8 EU member governments who are also members of NATO are Belgium, Denmark, France, Germany, Greece, Italy, Luxembourg, Netherlands, Portugal, Spain and the United Kingdom.

9 All 2001 in US $. US – 299,917m, France – 32,438m, Germany – 26,279m, Italy – 21,528m, Netherlands – 6,083m, Luxembourg – 156m, Portugal – 2,277m, Spain – 7,007m, UK – 33,967m. EU members of NATO contribute 164,564m.

10 Moravcsik notes that in his words 'exceptional circumstances' geopolitical circumstances have played a role in governments aims for collaborative policies. This is certainly the case for ESDP where part of the motivation for the policy was in the side-benefits for improving European military capabilities.

Institutional Choice – Delegation and Pooling

When the British government made the decision to transfer elements of its defence and security sovereignty to the EU it did so in the context of the type of institution and range of functions within the host institution. This was important as the main potential cost of transferring sovereignty is that the host institution gains further post-agreement policy competencies through institutional creep rather than government agreements. Further, that if the institutions created did not have sufficient experience and capabilities to effectively manage ESDP the agreement would almost certainly be less advantageous than a unilateral policy solution and therefore formal Europeanization would not occur (Andreani, Bertram and Grant 2001; Forster 2001, 15-33).

Rational theories of institutional choice places an emphasis on functionality. For example rationalists; '..explain institutional choices in terms of the functions a given institution is expected to perform and the effects on policy outcomes it is expected to produce, subject to the uncertainty in any institutional design' (Pollack 1997, 102). Institutional choice theories, however, emphasize their applicability to the development of the EU and the range of institutions created in its name (Pollack 1997). Compared to other international institutions, like NATO and the UN, Europeanization has produced a large number of different types of institution – from co-ordinating institutions in external relations to supranational governing institutions, like the European Court of Justice. EU institutions can limit member governments' autonomy in two ways: through either pooling or delegating authoritative decision-making.

> Sovereignty is pooled when governments agree to decide future matters by voting procedures other than unanimity. [...] Sovereignty is delegated when supranational actors are permitted to take certain autonomous decisions, without intervening interstate vote or unilateral veto (Moravcsik 1998, 67).

Pooling sovereignty provides a solution to the problem of incomplete IGC contracts; namely those which require additional intergovernmental agreements to bring them to fruition (Winkler 1999, 39-40). Qualified majority voting (QMV) provides a simpler route to gaining intergovernmental agreement because fewer governments are required to endorse a proposal. Under QMV fewer votes are taken in the Council because intransigent governments can be quickly isolated and the threat of a vote often leads to compromise. QMV also ensures that the national permanent representations have to seek negotiated settlements rather than exercise the right to veto, thus encouraging a collegiate rather than confrontational approach to negotiations (Moravcsik 1998, 73; Interview F; Interview H).

Mark Pollack lists four functions that delegated sovereignty might achieve (Pollack 1997, 103). Delegation increases the credibility of commitments, which is crucial in policy areas where core national sovereignty is seen to be at issue, like with the single currency and ESDP (Sandholtz 1993, 1-39). Furthermore, there are governmental incentives to delegate the right to initiate proposals to European institutions. One reason being that, from a negotiating standpoint, initiating a policy weakens a government's ability to manoeuvre and bargain at the intergovernmental level because it has already outlined to its fellow negotiators the collective policy that best reflects its core preferences. Research in Chapter 4 suggested that the UK government had significantly benefited from its position as the initiating government. In gaining a negotiated bilateral agreement with the French government at Saint Malo British officials created a highly influential coalition to advance this initiative into the European Council at Nice. The evidence suggested that, in doing so the British government effectively protected its core defence preferences during the ESDP negotiations.

In sum, the pooling rather than delegation of sovereignty in the ESDP negotiations was the only realistic option for the British government. This is because the government did not wish to transfer significant amounts of its defence and security autonomy to the EU. Furthermore, the shape and roles of proposed institutions is a very large consideration for negotiators during European Council negotiations and those governments formulate their negotiating positions partly as a response to institutional proposals.

Balances of Power Within the EU

Governments face potential 'costs' from transferring security and defence sovereignty to the EU, not least in disrupting existing balances of power. The fact that the EU accepts transferred security and defence sovereignty inevitably results in some disruption, however minor, to relationships between governments and international organizations like NATO and the UN (Pol de Witte 2004). This is partly because of the emergence of another competent organization in this field and also because of potential conflicts of interest in membership and capabilities but also a question mark over how the new institution might impact on international affairs, whether it will hold a contrary strategic vision to existing institutions. Pol de Witte argues that these potential shocks are limited by the transparency between EU and NATO governments and the central institutions.

Between 1997 and 2001 several factors shaped EU governments position within the EU balance of power. The end of the Cold War left the United States as the only credible superpower. Moreover, German unification signified an increase in German government capabilities and drastically changed the distribution of capabilities within the EU. More importantly, perhaps, the collapse of the Soviet Union ended European bipolarity leaving in its wake a unipolar post-cold war international system (Waltz 1993, 44-79; Mearsheimar 1990; Layne 2001; Wilkinson 1999). The latitude for EU governments in this system to innovate on policy issues, like ESDP, has consequently increased because the confines of cold war strategic thinking have lifted. However, the importance placed on retaining, the existing balances of power and not creating 'shocks' remained a priority of the FCO, according to two high ranking officials (Interview E; Interview G).

To avoid the potential pitfalls of altering balances of power within the EU, the British government, through its officials at the FCO, MoD and Cabinet Office, dedicated the time between Pörtschach, 25 October 1998, and Saint Malo, 4 December 1998 to managing the development of the Saint Malo initiatives. The balances of power, on this issue in particular, lay between the UK and French governments, UK and EU governments and between the British government and US Administration. Similarly, between the Saint Malo summit and the European Council at Nice UK officials conducted a large number of meetings with officials from other European governments and the US State Department (Interview E; Interview H). This was to ensure that ESDP did not disrupt good working relations between UK government and its European and American allies (Interview D; Interview E; Interview F). The care and attention devoted to maintaining pan-European and trans-Atlantic harmony through finding a formal outlet for a Europeanized defence policy was not matched by a similar level of care in the case of the 2003 war on Iraq, as will be seen in the next chapter.

So called 'shocks' to the international system can overcome problems with disruptions to the balance of power, like the end of the Cold War, and are also a key supply side factor in the creation of new EU institutions (JDCC 2003, Para 12).[11] The collapse of the Warsaw Pact and the problems associated with the Kosovo crisis (1999) are two of the many contributing factors between the Cold War and the eventual decision in 2000 of the EU to codify a common defence and security policy (Wallace 2002). 'Shocks' provide a supply side solution to the problem of delegating sovereignty to the EU in three ways: first, 'shocks' help to shift existing balances of power and institutions, like NATO, that exist to retain the pre-'shock' status quo; second, 'shocks' discredit old ideologies and working practices that leads to a political climate where new ideas and working practices are acceptable (Interview C; Interview D; Lord Brittan 2002).[12] Third, that these 'shocks' create a general sense of shared opportunity for institutional reform (Lord Brittan 2002). For British policy makers, particularly those in Downing Street, the Cabinet Office, and the Policy Director's staff in the FCO, key concerns centred around how the development of a UK European defence policy would affect the relationship between the UK and EU, the UK and France/Germany and most pertinently the relationship between the UK and United States, and therefore the focus was on adding value without creating 'shocks' (Interview D; Interview E; Interview I; Wallace 2002).

The German government's influential role within the EU and the possible 'shocks' that could have been created by German disagreement, and with it the effect on Europeanization across the board, made consultations between national Foreign and Defence offices very important (Interview E; Interview F).[13] During the 1970s and

---

11 The UK Ministry of Defence's definition of 'shocks', in the strategic context, are high impact, low probability events that have an immediate primary impact but then produce consequential impacts. These high impact events are also capable of triggering an escalation of circumstances to produce a sustained shift of international circumstances. The example the MoD use is the fall of the Berlin Wall in 1989.

12 Interview D and Brittan argued that upheavals in the international system often created permissive environments in which officials and politicians could advance policies that would have been impossible to advance previously. Interview C thought that 'shocks' like the Cold War produced new scenarios that the military had to react to rather than this being a pure opportunity for entrepreneurship.

13 This was the very strong opinion of these interviewees who spent a great of their time managing the expectations and responses of fellow EU governments including the German

80s the German government's influence within the EU increased due to its continued economic success and involvement in the UN and Eastern Europe, although it failed to exercise similar levels of foreign policy entrepreneurship (Rummel and Wessels 1983, 39). In particular, Germany's position on the frontline of any East-West conflict meant that unilateral German government foreign policies might lead to shifts in the EU balance of power and would '…lead to negative reactions, thereby reducing the Federal Republic's influence and room for manoeuvre' (Rummel and Wessels 1983, 40).

The end of the Cold War provided a permissive environment in which prohibitions on the German government to formulate unilateral foreign policy were lifted and they could take a more active role in international relations – even though successive German governments have shown a reluctance to do this. This is changing however, with German troops engaging in peacekeeping operations since the turn of the century in the Balkans.

Post-unification Germany has placed a greater emphasis on its ability to develop unilateral policies (Bulmer, Jeffery and Paterson, 1997). The political-cultural and historical barriers on the German government to formulate effective unilateral foreign and defence policies means that there is added motivation for them to take a full role in CFSP and ESDP, as a key means to engage in external relations. For example, Anne-Marie Le Gloannec notes that post-unification German preferences changed 'from a champion of federalism into an advocate of intergovernmentalism, from a Musterknabe of Europe into a convert to British policies' (Le Gloannec 1999, 21). This is partly demonstrated by the German government's engagement with, and enthusiasm for, ESDP as a continuation of the policy of seeking European security efficiencies through collaborative defence ventures (Interview C; Hopkinson 2002).

Evidence from British government negotiators suggests that German government officials did not have preferences that were as intense as British and French government preferences (Interview D; Interview G; Interview M). The German government was however engaged in shaping the ESDP to reflect its transatlantic security preferences, in the 1990s the Germans were arguably closer to the US Administration than the British, and in having recognized the need for the EU to be able to act in its near-abroad (Interview E; Interview F; Interview H).[14]

The post-World War II preference in Downing Street, the FCO and MoD is that the so called 'special-relationship' between the UK and the US supersedes all other foreign policy considerations (Short and Rifkind 2003, 24; Massie 2003, 21; Massingberd 2002, 1). Contemporary explanations of the pre-eminence of the 'Special Relationship' have centred on the notion of the 'Anglo-sphere', an inherent trust of English speaking countries with Anglicized traditions (Sullivan 2003; Bennett 2002, Bennett 2003). However, the balance of power issue concerning ESDP is in whether the perception of French government preferences for EU security to be

---

government to avoid causing these very disruptions.

14 Evidence from the UK's ESDP negotiating team was that the German government negotiators had fully accepted the need to improve EU capabilities whilst retaining US involvement. Which was not to say that they accepted the need for Germany to improve its military capabilities.

managed separately from NATO is merely rhetoric or is the official French MoD or Ministry of Foreign Affairs position. In short, the balance of interview evidence is that the French government held a preference for security structures outside of NATO but do not wish to make these preferences a reality before the EU committed to realistic defence spending plans and has the political motivation for an effective defence structure. Francois Heisbourg argues that the French MFA saw ESDP as a distinct process separate from NATO whilst UK officials argued that the two were inevitably linked (Heisbourg 2004).

A media-based interpretation of the Saint Malo Accords was that it would undermine NATO – America's preferred institutional structure for managing European security and to establish a separate locus of power away from the US (Layne 2001; Schake 2001). However, interview evidence strongly suggests that the British government's red-lines make it clear that NATO was the continued security institution of choice and that British negotiators were prepared not to come to a disadvantageous agreement on ESDP rather than undermine this fundamental aspect of their preferences.

The British government was careful to avoid causing a shift in the balance of power between the US and the EU on this sensitive issue. As part of this approach the strategy adopted by the key officials within the UK MoD and FCO was to keep US officials fully informed of the working parties and moves towards greater levels of activity concerning the ESDP (Interview D; Interview E; Interview F; Interview G). According to key officials this was a standard strategy for ensuring that the US State Department remained supportive of UK policy and also ensured that Britain remained a beneficiary of 'solid' diplomatic relations with the US (Interview C; Interview D). With a privileged link to the US, British negotiators were therefore able to openly discuss their intentions, red-lines and analysis of progress in the ESDP negotiations with confidence that this discourse would remain private (Interview E; Interview M).[15]

Through extensive daily consultation, UK officials attempted to allay White House, State Department and Pentagon fears about an EU split from NATO, French motivations and the UK government's ability to manage change in EU security within the transatlantic preference (Interview D; Interview E; Interview M). The closeness of the UK-US trans-Atlantic relationship has had both positive and negative effects on the formal Europeanization of defence policy. On the positive side the closeness between the two governments helped facilitate a set of policy proposals that did not threaten trans-Atlantic security structures. Indeed officials were able to confirm in the minds of the security advisors in the Pentagon and Whitehouse, Samuel Berger and Anthony Lake that an ESDP of Britain's making would promote the idea that European governments should take greater steps to underwrite European security (Interview G; Interview E). On the negative side it reinforced a perception amongst the UK's European partners that the UK saw its allegiances lying with the US Administration and not the EU. This would have dire consequences for formal

---

15 This was a particularly important reciprocal element to the relationship with the US. UK officials felt confident that there analysis would not be passed to the other EU governments by America, thus preserving an important control of the flow of information.

and informal European political cohesion in the run-up and aftermath of the Iraq campaign as highlighted in Chapter 6.

The relationship between France, Germany and the UK was a key consideration in the debate about balances of power for policy makers within the FCO, Downing Street and MoD. The negotiation and development of the ESDP did not significantly alter the balance of power between the British and French foreign and defence ministries. This is because of a long recent history of joint operations and policy development throughout the Bosnian civil war and the peacekeeping operations that followed (Interview C; Wallace 2002).

Despite a strong recent history of collaborative efforts in military interventions key British defence and military personnel were reluctant to state a preference for dealing with the French military and government above working with the US military, Pentagon and State Department even though these operations had become a matter of routine and success. As Chapters 2 and 3 suggested the key hurdle British foreign policy officials faced was in persuading officials from the French Ministry of Foreign Affairs that UK entrepreneurship on ESDP was a genuine effort in this field as opposed to short-term rhetoric. The balance of power between the UK and France was not adversely affected by the moves towards the ESDP, but a new spirit of co-operation between the French and British foreign and defence ministries continued throughout the negotiations spurred on by the Saint Malo meeting (Interview D; Interview E). The relatively limited nature of the Europeanization of foreign and defence policy co-operation imposes few costs on the British government and thus is attractive as it has allowed the UK to develop, support and influence policy in areas of the world relatively free from British influence (Bulmer and Edwards 1992, 150; Richardson 1993, 150; Taylor 1991, 145).

Making Agreements Credible

The transfer of national sovereignty to the EU may serve to prevent governments from defecting from agreements and to provide a political tool that obviates the need for governments to blame each other from such defections (Putnam 1992, 445). The 'costs' of negotiators blaming each other for defections are considerable and can be measured in terms of a reduction in the flow of information and exchange of bargaining information during negotiations making it harder to reach future agreements (Putnam 1992, 445). Part of the initial diplomatic exchange in early and mid-1998 between the UK and French Ministries of Defence was to gauge the commitment of each government to the ESDP proposals. This was crucial to the construction of trust between the two sets of officials to develop these proposals and bring them into a European fora (Interview E; Interview G). Once the Saint Malo Accords had been signed, it was politically untenable for either government to defect or accuse the other of defecting as this would make further co-operation on ESDP more problematic (Interview D; Interview E; Interview F; Interview M).[16]

---

16 The interviewees that provided this information all came to this view from having considering experience of these issues at a European level. Interview M noted, however, that

The problems such breaches of trust cause in international relations are shown by the evidence presented in Chapter 6 about the breakdown in trust in 2003 between the UK and French governments regarding the Iraq conflict and the 2005 EU budget negotiations concerning the Common Agricultural Policy. The disagreement between the two governments on both these issues had a direct result on the continued piecemeal development of ESDP, in this instance via French President Chirac initiating informal ESDP summits without inviting UK officials and similarly issuing instructions to French government officials not to engage in discussions with UK government officials about ESDP (Grant 2002; Black 2004).[17]

The transfer of sovereignty to the EU through pooling or delegation, provides solutions to the problems of incomplete contracting, but it impacts differently on the actions and influence of member governments. Delegation of sovereignty does not enhance one government's control over other governments because the sovereignty is transferred to a supranational coordinating institution. The independence of a supranational actor to which sovereignty has been transferred is variable, but the potential cost for governments trying to control these institutions is large (Moravcsik 1993a, 15).

When sovereignty is pooled, however, it 'is not transferred to a supranational body because the crucial decision-making role is taken by an interstate body' (Keohane and Hoffmann 1991, 8). Thus, when sovereignty is pooled, governments can exert pressure on their negotiating partners and as a result can potentially extract further policy concessions (Putnam 1992, 452). In some circumstances, therefore, the pooling of sovereignty can actually increase a member government's influence and presents a key attraction of formal Europeanization to the British government. They see Britain's pre-eminent place in the European security system secured by Europeanization. This means that the ESDP provisions and pooled sovereignty serves to make the UK a disproportionately stronger actor in the international security system, if ESDP works as it was originally designed to do in 1998.

Governments with effective unilateral policies benefit mostly from an un-Europeanized policy regime and have little to gain from international co-operation. This poses an interesting set of questions to those advocating a deeper Europeanization of British defence policy. Prima facie, Britain has maintained an effective unilateral defence and security policy, within many intergovernmental structures, and has no pressing need to delegate this sovereignty to the EU (Interview C; Hopkinson 2002). Yet, as Chapter 2 suggested, the main benefits to the UK from delegating sovereignty on defence and security were to improve EU defence capabilities, to strengthen the transatlantic Alliance, and to eventually produce budgetary efficiencies through collaborative research and development, procurement and training budgets. The benefits of this delegation are supplementary to the idea that negotiators bargain towards specific and calculable benefits.

---

such events are very carefully managed so that their significance is down played to the public and parliamentarians.

17 This command from President Chirac went unreported but was brought up independently by both interviewees.

However, it can be strongly argued that the side benefits of British government entrepreneurship on defence policy met short-term political objectives. These were, for example, demonstrating the British government's pro-European credentials and securing continued American involvement in EU security, that aimed to overcome the potential costs associated with provided 'shocks' to the international system. In contrast, smaller EU governments and less effective military actors sought to co-operate on ESDP where they saw that they could have a practical effect on and benefit from the policy (Moravcsik and Nicolaidis 1998, 61). A case in point is the negotiating position of the Nordic countries who universally emphasized the need to improve EU crisis management capabilities. They argued that NATO is primarily focussed on territorial defence and thus EU crisis management ought to be conducted outside of NATO frameworks (Graegar, Larsen and Ojanen 2002, 219-220). The development of ESDP allowed smaller EU governments, in co-operating with the development of the policy to add further elements that did not undermine its fundamental tenets.

Conclusion

The final element of formal Europeanization, the transfer or pooling of sovereignty, proceeds along liberal intergovernmentalist lines. Within the defence context formal Europeanization has occurred through the British government transferring small amounts of defence and security sovereignty to the EU in the belief that this would produce greater benefits than pursuing a unilateral policy. From the British government's perspective the ESDP outcome was an efficient and rational development, securing its pro-European and Atlanticist preferences.

The analysis made by officials advising the Prime Minister and his core executive was that the projected costs of cooperating on defence were much less than the benefits that could be accrued. The potential costs centred around potential future losses of autonomy, risks to existing balances of power within the EU and the risk of institutional spillover within the ESDP taking the policy remit beyond the Nice European Council output; something that has subsequently been negated by the fallout from the Iraq war. The risk of these costs occurring were however low, according to British government officials, not least because of the extent to which they had effectively managed the negotiations and because of the agreed text in the European Council conclusions that ensured that further extension of ESDP would need a unanimous agreement by the EU governments.

The potential costs of pursuing ESDP were also remote because the agreed text clearly marked the policy as intergovernmental in nature and in operation. For example, governments are not compelled to take part in military operations initiated under the ESDP banner and similarly the 'Headline Goals' established at the Helsinki Council in December 1999 are entirely voluntary. The intergovernmental and voluntary nature of ESDP therefore allowed the British government to pursue a formal Europeanized defence policy that similarly met short and medium term political and strategic aims.

The negotiated ESDP also entailed a transfer of small elements of defence and security sovereignty in areas which issues of common agreement already existed but remained un-codified. For example, the ESDP reflects a policy that deals with crisis management and peacekeeping functions that were already areas in which the UK and France had particular experience of in the Balkans. Moreover in research, development and procurement policy, which are predominantly economic issues, the existing EU trade and industry agreements provide the EU with considerable experience and history of effective collaboration. These issues are brought out more fully in Chapter 7 which deals with the Europeanization of the arms trade.

The liberal intergovernmentalist explanation of Europeanization can be located within a significant body of literature that analyses EU external relations from a rationalist perspective (Ginsberg 2003, 1-2: Smith 2003, 3-5). Within these approaches the exact level of co-operation between governments remains unspecified, although it is effective in identifying the costs and benefits of this intergovernmental cooperation (Moravcsik 1998, 479-80). Moreover from this perspective it is clear why QMV in external relations has been controversial. Security, defence and the deployment of military assets are elements of the security policy sector where autonomy is a key indicator of a government's sovereignty, which is why governments have cautiously negotiated the transfer of elements of their security and defence sovereignty. Whilst the EU's external relations policy regime remains non-binding, unanimous and intergovernmental, German, French and British government support for the development of this area can be explained by the few costs they incur for doing so and in terms of the impact the cooperation has on national autonomy.

The evidence suggests that governments transfer elements of their sovereignty to the EU to achieve credibility for government commitments (Moravcsik 1998, 4-8). Establishing multilateral credibility for governmental preferences binds the signatory governments into a framework whereby they cannot change their preferences (Moravcsik 1998, 4-8 and 64). For negotiating governments, therefore, a key element of the cost-benefit analysis they conduct is the extent to which a collaborative policy is in the government's perception of short, medium or long term national interests and similarly the likelihood of their being circumstances where the government's view of ESDP might fundamentally change. In the specific example of ESDP the framing of the policy enshrines the autonomy of governments to decide whether to engage or commit assets to ESDP. The ESDP outcome therefore removed a core element of the 'costs' of agreement, making a negotiated agreement far more explicable.

One of the key problems associated with the British government transferring defence and security sovereignty is characterized as the problem of 'anarchy'. This draws on a realist perspective that governments are keen to avoid exposing themselves to the associated risks of transferring 'sovereignty vulnerability' to external actors. In this instance this vulnerability is partly overcome by the presence of the EU to regulate the behaviour of governments and its ability to make further delegation less costly. Moreover, there are four key supply side factors that militate against the problem of 'anarchy' and make governments more willing to transfer sovereignty: first, the government's prior experience of dealing with the EU builds trust among governments to continue this practice. Second, the EU has supportive constituencies, the Commission, European Parliament and judicial service that pressure governments to strengthen and expand the institutions and their competencies. Third, the presence of existing EU institutions reduces uncertainty and thus makes governments more willing to transfer sovereignty. Fourth, existing institutions reduce transaction costs making it easier for governments to agree the nature of new institutions. As a pre-existing institution in which a great deal of positive experience has been accrued and in which the creation of new agreements, institutions and processes entails low transaction costs, the EU was a low-risk institution in which the British government decided to transfer elements of its defence and security sovereignty.

The transfer of sovereignty in the formal Europeanization of policy occurs is a deliberate and active process of government delegation. Andrew Moravcsik, for instance, rejects the notion that sovereignty transfer can also be a passive process, caused by government inaction that allows the EU institutions to grow unchecked or by the EU acting in a purposive manner to enhance its own powers; the classic example being the European Court of Justice (Shaw 1995, 11; Ward and Marshall 1995, 19). This view is questionable, even in this example which is dominated by intergovernmental negotiating, as there is evidence of Europeanizing factors occurring outside of formal IGC structures. The amount of autonomous power the EU has over any particular policy area is reflected by its ability to influence national decisions or practices or to make decisions that do not reflect the preferences and policies of leading governments. ESDP is an intergovernmental area in which member governments can volunteer capabilities and support to actions without committing themselves to permanent operational arrangements. In this respect, the institutions of the EU retain little control over policies that might affect the autonomy of member governments (Ginsberg 2003, 1-2). This conclusion, as will be shown by Chapter Seven, is limited to formal Europeanization and not to Europeanization in general where, in the specific instance of the arms trade Europeanization can occur without the consent of government.

The transfer of defence sovereignty through the ESDP challenges a liberal intergovernmentalist view that agreements between governments are particularly difficult to achieve and further that voluntary defections from agreement, by governments, are particularly likely because of the permanent nature of international treaties (Moravcsik 1998, 4-8). The case of ESDP challenges these core assumptions; the UK government did believe that their foreign and security goals could be further advanced through ESDP and indeed that the policy would allow the UK to engage in humanitarian and peace support operations with the assistance of EU partners and with pre-identified capabilities and an institutional mechanism for raising additional military assets.

This case study challenges the view that agreements between governments are difficult to achieve. The key hurdle to agreement on ESDP occurred at the Saint Malo summit between the UK and French governments. This obstacle was the perception that the two governments held diametrically opposing views on European security and the UK government's red-line preference that European security should be underwritten by NATO whilst the French Ministry of Foreign Affairs were more ambivalent about a continued role for NATO. Once the two governments published the Saint Malo Accords, which provided a clear blueprint for the development of ESDP, it was clearly demonstrated that these two diametric views had been accommodated in these agreements. Following Saint Malo, agreement amongst the other member governments of the EU was not as difficult to achieve, as a liberal intergovernmentalist approach would assert (Moravcsik 1998, 485).[18] The evidence shows that there is a cost-benefit analysis advanced in the process of negotiations and the transfer of sovereignty – this chapter has argued that the potential costs of this transfer were low and this will be further demonstrated by the next chapter which examines the ESDP following the Nice IGC agreement in a wider context.

---

18 For example, Moravcsik argues that withdrawing defence and security coverage has been historically used in European Council negotiations as a threat by British and French negotiators to secure concessions from other negotiators.

Chapter 6

The Iraq War – The Problem of National Interests for Europeanization

The earlier chapters of this book have focussed on the formal Europeanization of British defence policy through the discrete diplomatic cycle of the Anglo-French Saint-Malo meeting and Nice IGC negotiations. This chapter explores the effect of the war on Iraq on the Europeanization of security, defence and foreign policy and across the EU's non-security policy areas. This war caused a great deal of diplomatic friction between European governments on a subject that a fully formed EU foreign and security policy would have to deal with. The lessons learnt from the Iraq war are, therefore, important to the future Europeanization of defence and security policy. The respective positions of the British, French and German governments and the European Commission prior to and during the war are explored and critically assessed for where they converged and diverged, and how these positions fit within a 'European' concept of security policy.

This chapter is split into two distinct sections; the first section deals with the diplomacy that preceded the war on Iraq between the British, French, German, and American governments as well as the diplomacy that occurred in the EU and UN. The second section places this diplomacy within the context of the internal EU diplomacy, particularly through the example of the British Government's Presidency of the EU in the last six months of 2005. This Presidency was selected because it foregrounds the British government's approach to the EU, negotiations and Europeanization from the institutional position of Chair of the EU.

The Iraq case study brings out several important lessons for formal and informal Europeanization that will be explored and expanded throughout the chapter. These lessons centre on the how the EU, as a security actor and polity, is founded. More specifically that European security and defence policy co-operation and the common positions between governments can be undermined by the behaviour of influential European governments seeking to advance narrow self interests. The example of Iraq highlights the subordinate position of the EU and its institutions in the formulation and operation of a European security, defence and foreign policy – and that the intergovernmental underpinnings of this policy area makes predicting the pace of Europeanization problematic. However, this chapter will also argue that the Iraq war conversely facilitated the deepening Europeanization of soft-security functions, whilst providing a context in which economic and political integration has slowed.

War with Iraq

An enormous quantity of media and analysis on international relations since 2001 has obsessed on the impact of the attack on the World Trade Centre on 11 September 2001 (Gunarantna 2002; Chomsky 2002; Kellner 2003; Daadler and Lindsay 2003; Shepherd 2006, 71). In conducting the research for this chapter it would have been easy to fall into the same pattern of constructing the '9/11' attacks as a, or even 'the', pivotal moment in international affairs (Crawford 2006; Sands 2005; Hutton 2003, 30). The US-led coalition's military action against Iraq cannot be analysed without a small reference to 9/11, because of the links made by both the American President and British government between the loose global network of terrorists known as Al-Qaeda and Saddam Hussein's government in Baghdad, and therefore provided a justification for war (Coughlin 2001, 31; Latham 2002, 22; Sullivan 2002). An interesting aspect of the negotiations leading up to the Iraq war was the sense of futility in the diplomatic efforts – that the war was inevitable from the summer of 2002 and a widespread belief that the Bush Administration was seeking legitimacy for a pre-meditated attack on Iraq. The war also polarized the leading EU governments on an issue of wider relevance than just the Union. The extent to which being a member of the EU confines or modifies government behaviour gives some indication of the extent to which a distinctive EU polity has been created.

The American-led coalition of the US, UK, Australian and Polish armed forces engaged in offensive military actions against Iraq from 19 March to 1 May 2003. As previously suggested, the road to war had seemed inevitable since the attacks on the World Trade Centre in September 2001. The strategic environment changed and with it came an unwillingness on the part of the Bush Administration to countenance rogue states and future threats to US interests at home or abroad. The mood music for Iraq had looked ominous from the end of 2001 and got demonstrably worse when President Bush delivered his now infamous 'axis of evil' State of the Union address (January 2002) that named Iraq, Iran and North Korea as countries with or capable of developing Weapons of Mass Destruction (WMD) with a desire to harm the United States (Borger 2002, Theodoulos 2002). Ironically, North Korea and Iran have shown a willingness to actively develop nuclear weapons but have not faced US military action whereas Saddam Hussein's Iraq has yet to yield any evidence of WMD materials.

In January 2002 the Bush Administration adopted a National Security Strategy that incorporated a notion of pre-emptive strikes against countries they perceived to be a threat to their national security and this has subsequently become known as 'the Bush Doctrine' (The Whitehouse 2002; Watson 2002). This doctrine also allowed the United States to pre-emptively attack perceived enemies without necessarily having a mandate from the United Nations, and on 28 January 2003 President Bush confirmed this by announcing that he was prepared to attack Iraq without such a mandate (Harnden 2003, 1; Borger 2003, 1). This doctrine has some intellectual heritage in the EU. The British government's strategic ambitions announced in 1997 included a commitment to changing the international system by force, if necessary, to promote democracy and liberalism in the world.

The British View of Iraq

The British government's position on Iraq, as with all British interventions in the Middle East, is tainted by an imperial legacy. Having been instrumental in the creation of Iraq in the 1920s and as an important figure in arming both Iran and Iraq during their 1980-1988 war the British government had a myriad of political and economic reasons to be involved in the Iraq campaign (Scott 1996). Having sought to supply Saddam Hussein with high-end military technology in the 1980s the British government now sought to argue that the Iraqi leadership were a danger to international security and that military intervention was required immediately to neutralize the threat. Importantly for the European debate, the British government focussed on the danger of the Iraqi government possessing WMD and stated that its aim was to remove these weapons (Blair 31 January 2003; Blair 3 February 2003; La Guardia and Helm 2002; Grice 2003). Iraqi WMD was said to be peculiarly dangerous to international security because of the perceived links between the ruling Ba'ath Party and international terrorist groups, to whom Saddam Hussein might transfer such technology. The prescience of the debate on WMD between EU governments has been demonstrated by the coalition armed forces failing to find any WMD materials, and the links between Saddam Hussein and terrorist organizations failing to materialize (Ptiffner 2004, 25-46; Phythian 2004). The British Prime Minister, in particular, sought to elide the possession of WMD by countries like Iraq, which were loosely classified as 'rogue', with the developing threat from international terrorists (Milne 2003, 24; Roy 2003, 2; Times Editor 2003, 21). Both the French and the German governments publicly questioned, with strong justification in hindsight, how much of a threat Iraq was to the international order and whether there was any evidence of links between Al-Qaeda and the Iraqi government (Boyes 2003; Harnden and Guardia 2003, 1; Henley 2003, 2). The effect of this dovetailing of threats was that the British government could argue that 'rogue' states and terrorists equally threatened British economic and political interests in the Middle East and at home. This was a classic British foreign policy choice, to seek stability in the international system through a small scale military intervention, a good example of this being Suez in 1956. This point runs contrary to the emerging EU foreign and security policy which is consensual and norms based (Dover 2006).

The officially stated purpose of the war against Iraq was to uphold UN Security Council Resolution 1441 – 8 November 2002 (United Nations Security Council 2002). The focus of the international debates about the war centred on what actions this resolution permitted and, therefore, the legality of the war. Resolution 1441 brought a new round of arms inspections on Iraq and threatened 'serious consequences' if the inspections were impeded and disarmament was not forthcoming and documented. The phrase 'serious consequences' is considered in international politics as variously as permitting armed conflict or limited to diplomatic or economic sanctions. It was around these different interpretations and the legality of the war that European governments vehemently disagreed – this chapter explores this disagreement and the effect it has had on the Europeanization of defence and security policy as well as non-security policy areas.

'Old Europe' vs 'New Europe'

The diplomatic divide in Europe over the war in Iraq began to take shape at the end of 2002 and continued into the first two months of 2003. Despite being in possession of broadly the same intelligence as the British, American and Australian governments, the Russian, French and German governments opposed the potential military action in the strongest diplomatic terms. The German government was domestically hamstrung by the then Chancellor Gerhard Schroeder having promised not to enter a military coalition with the Americans, whilst the French and Russian governments were accused firstly of having signed lucrative oil contracts with the Iraqi government and secondly adopting an anti-American position (Beaumont and Islam 2002; Rennie 2002, 14). Unhelpfully, US Secretary of Defence Donald Rumsfeld described this ad-hoc alliance as 'Old Europe' implying that it represented outdated and outmoded thinking (Rumsfeld 2003; Parris 2003, 24; Rennie 2003, 16). Unsurprisingly this did little to persuade these 'old European' governments of the case for war.

The French and German governments showed unity of purpose in opposing the conflict including a joint public statement after a bilateral heads of state meeting in January 2003 (Usborne 2003, 1; Connolly 2003, 15; Black 2003, 5). For Germany there remains a large Second World War legacy that acts like a self-denying ordinance on deploying armed forces outside of German borders (Lander 2003). Schroeder's election announcement that Germany would not take part in US-led military actions merely served to reinforce this. Schroeder's position also acted as a strong marker for German foreign policy preferences – an adherence to minimum force and optimized coalitions with legitimate international backing, again a reaction to legacy of the mid twentieth century. The French government's position was different; the EU should have a foreign policy independent of the United States and that acts as a counter-weight to American hegemonic power. The French position did not exclude the use of military force, but to place it very firmly within the auspices of UN Security Council consent. By contrast those governments, considered by inference as being in 'new Europe' by Defense Secretary Rumsfeld, declared themselves to be supportive of the American Administration's position in an open letter published on 30 January 2003. The British, Czech, Danish, Hungarian, Italian, Polish and Portuguese governments' stated that they believed Iraq to be a threat to global peace and that they believed the US and EU shared common values that required protecting (Evans-Pritchard 2003, 14; Walker 2003, 10). A further ten NATO accession states issued a similar open letter supporting the American Administration.[1]

In early February 2003 the US and the British governments pressed for a new UN resolution to provide legitimacy for an armed conflict against Iraq. As a counter measure the German, and French governments argued that a new Resolution was precipitous and that the weapons inspectors should be given more time to complete the job given to them by Resolution 1441 (Stevenson and Preston 2003). Their position was supported by the Head of the UN inspectors, Hans Blix and by former

---

1 The governments include Romania, Slovakia, Albania, Bulgaria, Croatia, Estonia, Latvia, Lithuania, Macedonia and Slovenia.

leading inspectors like the American, Scott Ritter (Bone 2003; Bone 2003a). Having been given support from leading figures in the weapons inspectorate, the French and Russian governments threatened to veto a newly tabled resolution from the British and American governments in the Security Council (10 March). A further week of intense diplomacy followed and on 17 March the British and American administrations withdrew their draft resolution and finalized their plans for war. In Britain the decision to go to war had immediate and serious political consequences for Tony Blair's government because of the resignations of former Foreign Secretary and then Leader of the House of Commons, Robin Cook and the Secretary of State for Development, Claire Short and the million strong public march through London opposing the war (Cook 2003; Freedland 2003).

Despite heavy criticism of its position from the public, the media, and its own MPs the British government stuck to its original assessment that the Iraqi government was in breach of Resolution 1441, which legitimized a military response. It also argued that Iraq was in breach of Resolution 678 which had been passed at the end of the first Gulf war in 1991 and that obliged Iraq to surrender all weapons of mass destruction (Yoo 2003; de Torrente 2004; Kagan 2004). Thus, by a slightly convoluted and tortuous rationale the American and British governments constructed legitimacy for the military assault on Iraq on 19 March 2003.

The EU's Response

The war on Iraq itself and the debate that preceded it was conducted by states. The EU's contribution to the debates and the road to war was marginalized and therefore provides an interesting perspective on how the Commission views its role in a Europeanized defence and security policy. As seen earlier in this book the Commission opted to remain aloof in the ESDP negotiations on the grounds that it saw them as being between states 'holding' competency on these issues. However, with a Commissioner for External Relations in place, the Commission, through its representative and former British Cabinet Minister, Chris Patten chose to publicly comment on Iraq. Furthermore, the Commissioner agreed with the British and American position, highlighting Saddam Hussein as a threat to world and Iraqi domestic peace armed with WMD (Patten 29 January 2003). Patten also positively suggested that an armed intervention might become necessary to avoid the UN being humiliated – an interesting rationale in the context of the British and American governments having proposed the contentious resolution in the UN requesting the option of military force.

Whilst the debate about the legitimacy of the war raged on there was international unity behind the belief that the Iraqi government was responsible for the escalation of the crisis. This extended to EU heads of state from both sides of the divide over the efficacy of conflict (Patten 29 January 2003; Blair 3 February 2003). Even those opposed to the conflict, like Vladimir Putin, suggested that the Iraqi government could remove some of the pressure on it by cooperating with the weapons inspectors (Stewart 2003, 5). The disagreements were, therefore, not about Iraq as a problem in the international system – but the tools with which the international community sought to deal with it.

The leading 'old' Europeans – the French and German governments – were key to demonstrating the 'European' consensual style of security policy. They viewed the British government's behaviour as destabilising the world and making it less secure. What is more, the French and German governments correctly predicted that the unilateral action by the American-led coalition would erode international unity on tackling terrorism (Helm 2003, 1; Harmden 2003, 11; Bone and Webster 2003, 14). They could have taken this point a step further to include the difficulty the American-led coalition would face in the post-conflict reconstruction phase of the war, with governments who normally support reconstruction or peace-keeping efforts, withholding assistance because they viewed the initial war as illegitimate and illegal. This has proved to be a significant problem for the US, UK, Australian and Polish coalition that has failed to make the transition – on the ground -from high-end war-fighting to peace-keeping. That the coalition appears to still be entrenched, in 2006, in a series of counter-insurgency campaigns can be attributed either to their continued presence in Iraq and the absence of an international peace-keeping force, or to the intractability of an enemy that has found an effective set of operational tactics (Haskini 2003; Hoffman 2006, 103-121). The absence of a wider number of European military actors assisting in the peace-keeping or peace-enforcement activities in Iraq has left the coalition members exposed to the political consequences from Iraq. A good example of one of the consequences is the Madrid train bombings, which has been attributed in policy circles to the Spanish government's support for the Iraq war and resulted in Aznar's pro-war government losing the subsequent election.

The German government questioned the wisdom of the war in the context of the war against terrorism, again something given credibility by the Madrid and London bombings, that were a key feature of 2004 and 2005. The German Foreign Minister, Joschka Fischer argued that seeking stability and solutions at source in regional conflicts would be a far more effective way of dealing with the problem of international terrorism (Beeston, Watson and Webster 2003, 1). Fischer paid particular attention to the on-going tensions between Israel-Palestine, which he argued was the key to all the troubles in the Middle East and by implication, for terrorism exported to the 'west' (Fischer 13 March 2003). He argued that a war against Iraq would have serious consequences for the Middle East and might even lead its 'Balkanization' – a reference clearly designed to resonate with the memories of the 1990s for European governments who had suffered strong criticisms following their collective and individual responses to the Yugoslavian civil war (Fischer 19 March 2005; Dover 2005).

In the European debate on Iraq one of the key schisms that opened up was between the British government, on one side, who viewed Iraqi possession of WMD as the key threat to regional and global security and the French and German governments, on the other, who argued that Iraqi WMD was an issue to be tackled alongside other more pressing Middle Eastern issues, such as Israel-Palestine. As a result the French and German governments saw the UN process and Resolution 1441 as a means to identify what materials and weapons programmes Iraq were developing and to then respond to those findings. The French government were keen to disarm Iraq if it was shown to possess WMD, whilst the British government had concluded that Iraq was in breach of UN Resolutions and therefore could be subject to forcible regime change (Fischer 19 March 2003; Fischer 20 March 2003; Webster 2003, 1; Delves-Broughton 2003, 14). Both the British Prime Minister and Secretary of State for Foreign Affairs, Jack Straw, drew wider implications for the international community if action was not taken against Iraq – that taking action would deter other 'rogue' states from trying to acquire and use weapons of mass destruction (Blair 28 February 2003; Blair 18 March 2003; Straw 9 January 2003; Straw 11 February 2003). Even with the benefit of only three years hindsight this seems to have been a bad judgement call as Iran and North Korea appear to have accelerated their nuclear weapons programmes, because they view acquisition of WMD as a means to ensure they are not attacked by an American-led military coalition.

As the coalition moved towards war against Iraq Joschka Fischer complained that the British government kept subtly changing the grounds for war and that in doing so was making the diplomatic efforts to prevent war impossible (Fischer 13 March 2003). This is a charge that the British government would publicly reject but which diplomats speaking on the condition of anonymity privately felt had showed them to have done a 'good job'. Fischer's assertion highlights some of the problems inherent in trying to create a common foreign, security and defence policy. The British government's shifting rationale for attacking Iraq highlights the problems inherent in an intergovernmental system that broadly defines European external relations policy. In transforming the rationale for war from it being a consequence of Saddam Hussein's complicity in the attacks on the World Trade Centre in 2001, to the need to prevent his attempts to develop or acquire WMD, and finally onto the need to remove Saddam as a potential proliferator of these technologies, and as a threat to regional security, the British government brought to the fore a tension within the EU. This tension exists between the EU as a closely co-operating club of nations, or as a fledgling super-state. One thing that is clear from the Iraq example is that the stronger the disagreements between at the intergovernmental level the more problematic future formal integration becomes. But paradoxically, these tensions also provide more latitude for the European Commission to deepen integration on pre-agreed areas.

A major line of disagreement at the intergovernmental level between the British, French and German governments was the nature of the intervention. This disparity went to the heart of very different conceptions of a Europeanized security, defence and foreign policy. Notably, the French and German governments' approach to Iraq fitted more closely into patterns established by other EU foreign and defence initiatives – strong normative foundations but with consensus at its core. The French government argued strongly that it was unhelpful for single states to believe that they could resolve international disagreements unilaterally, whilst the German government said it wanted to encourage consensus politics and the rule of international law, both positions carrying a clear critique of British and American diplomatic conduct. The British government's approach was far closer to the American position – an ideological underpinning prioritising the liberation of the Iraqi people and a promotion of world stability, but attached to a divisive policy framework where consensus was optional

(Blair 7 January 2003; Blair 31 January 2003). The imposition of a particular model of political and economic governance by the American and British invading force echoed of imperialism, the sort of practice that had been rejected by the German, Spanish, Italian, Belgian, and Portuguese governments because of their individual historical legacies, mostly in Africa. The British government's position therefore went outside of established EU foreign policy practice and means that any further defence and foreign policy integration and common positions are likely to continue proceeding on a lowest common denominator basis.

Unsurprisingly, perhaps, the EU pursued a series of positions that emphasized consensual decision making in the international community and as a result, the creation of a truly multilateral international system. The European Commission was therefore keen to talk up the UN as the most appropriate forum for resolving international disputes and also to suggest the strengthening the CFSP and ESDP frameworks to make them more effective. European Commissioner Chris Patten talked in strong terms about the Iraq conflict producing a return to a 19th century 'balances of power' international system which he argued threatened the institutions created after the Second World War, including both the UN and EU (Patten 20 March 2003). Speeches like this highlight the extent to which a Europeanized foreign and defence policy has been created. Patten and French and German officials clearly asserted a European way of doing foreign policy and were willing to argue strongly for it. Far from this being formal Europeanization, it is the Europeanization of foreign and defence policy practice.

Whilst Iraq was not directly an EU defence or foreign policy issue it has become, by association, a European issue. The disunity between EU governments put the CFSP under pressure and raised questions over the Europeanization of other issues (Patten 20 March 2003). European Commissioner Chris Patten argued that this disunity was particularly damaging between those governments who had taken 'firm national policy positions as if they spoke for the European Union as a whole', which applied to the British, French and German governments equally (Patten 12 March 2003). Out of adversity though, EU officials viewed this crisis of European identity as an opportunity to build upon areas of common agreement and good practice like for example, in the Balkans (Patten 13 March 2003; Patten 20 March 2003).

Further diplomatic declarations by, for example, Javier Solana suggested that the Iraq war would be a turning point in EU relations whilst Romano Prodi described this diplomatic impasse as a 'moment of truth' for the EU, presumably in terms of whether a foreign and defence policy capable of progressing beyond the lowest common denominator is possible (Solana 24 March 2003; Prodi 26 March 2003). The Greek Presidency, through Foreign Minister George Papendreo, suggested that the only way for the EU to get past lowest common denominator policy making would be to develop pan-European approaches to Middle Eastern issues (Papendreo 6 May 2003). Solana and Papendreo also argued that the EU should produce a European equivalent to the American National Security Strategy to guide European action and to produce a greater sense of cohesion on foreign and defence policy formulation, something that was done in December 2003 (Papendreo 6 May 2003). From this evidence we can suggest that a Europeanized security policy is limited to those issues that the 'big' European states are not involved with. Moreover, whilst 'the European approach' is typified by consensus and humanitarian norms, these can be over-ridden by European governments taking unilateral action. The problems of intergovernmentalism – as discussed at length in the earlier chapters of this book – are as pronounced in the Iraq example and in practice seem to undermine the attempts to create a Europeanized polity.

The French government argued that a Europeanized security and defence policy was essential to stability within the international system (de Villepin 11 December 2002). As a reflection of their political desires the French sought to advance the idea of the EU being one pole in a multi-polar world. By this rationale the military strength of the EU has to be enhanced to provide credibility to its position as an alternative locus of world power (Chirac 22 January 2003). Thus, the French government's view is not too dissimilar to the EU's institutional view. Patten, Prodi, Solana and Papendreo all argued that the EU should focus on how it could be used to assist the UN's central, but damaged role in world affairs (Patten 12 March 2003; Papendreo 6 May 2003). As two correctives to the British and American coalition on Iraq, the Greek Presidency argued that the EU was an obvious counter-weight to US hegemonic power and, furthermore, a union of shared values, ideal for tackling global issues like WMD proliferation (Simitis 26 March 2003).

The political motivations for the EU counterbalance to the UK and US is interesting insofar as it highlights the deeper problems of common policy making in the Union, and that some influential EU member governments have a very distinct notion of what it means to be a member of the EU and in the Europeanization project. The lack of common-cause between European governments on these issues suggests that the Europeanization of security and defence policy will remain typified by lowest common denominator policy making, unless there is a substantial development on the part of EU member governments to put aside narrow national self interests.

Support for the concept of global multi-polarity also came from the French government who believed that the US-UK war against Iraq would result in global instability through blow-back from Islamic terrorists and the artificial creation of a 'clash of civilisations' (Chirac February 2003).[2] The French government also believed, on a point of principle, that removing a head of state was an error, establishing a dangerous precedent that could result in the international system reverting to a 19th century system of 'survival of the fittest' (de Villepin 2 March 2003). In a more immediate sense the removal of Saddam Hussein had the predictable knock-on effect on other proliferating countries like North Korea and Iran who now face potential military interventions to prevent the further development of their WMD programmes. To avoid such outcomes, the German government focussed on improving UN institutions, particularly those involved in weapons inspections, as a means to uphold the UN's position as global policeman and leading institution in rolling back proliferation and thus obviating the need for unilateral military action.

The British government's repost to the French and German government's position was to focus on the effectiveness of the UN in solving difficult problems. Thus the

---

2   For example, Chirac said 'It would create a large number of little bin Ladens. Muslims and Christians have a lot to say to one another, but war isn't going to facilitate that dialogue. I'm against the clash of civilisations, that plays into the hands of extremists'.

British government's implicit argument was that US-UK led action therefore provided credibility for the UN in helping to deal with the threat to international stability (Blair 31 January 2003). This is a curious understanding of the Iraq campaign and their view of the EU and the UN is, as a result, that making a claim about the effectiveness of these institutions is more important than finding international consensus. Tony Blair's publicly stated position in 2003 was that the Iraqi crisis should be resolved through the UN, but that the UN would have to become more pro-active in seeking a resolution. What this amounts to is a clear indication that the US-led coalition would adhere to UN rules so long as they moved in a direction that was both agreeable to the coalition, and one that they were heading in regardless of extraneous diplomacy (Blair 3 February 2003; Blair 12 February 2003). This position is deeply problematic for the EU because of the inbuilt assumptions regarding consensus and a norms based foundation.

Despite the obvious schisms all the EU's leading governments expressed their desire to retain strong diplomatic relationships with the United States. The British government retained the strongest desire to be close to the US – seeing it as important to the cohesion of the 'free world'. The German government kept stressing that its opposition to the war did not constitute a recalibration of its strategic position in the world and even the French government sought to stress that the crisis over Iraq should not be construed as being hostile to the US and that they envisaged continuing strong relations. How much of this is diplomatic posturing and the niceties of international relations is difficult to tell. As a statement of intent it is clear that all three leading EU governments did not wish to destabilize trans-Atlantic relations, even though there were pronounced policy differences.

A Failure of Common Purpose

The Iraq case study is a strong example of why it is, and will continue to be, inherently difficult for the EU to formulate a coherent foreign, security and defence policy. The majority of European governments were in favour of a common approach to Iraq that emphasized the importance of multilateral and consensus approach to the agreed problem of an Iraq with a serious WMD capability. Disunity between governments was caused by the unconditional support given to the US' course of action in seeking to topple Saddam Hussein without the mandate and authority of the UN. The British government's side of this disagreement was informed by their efforts during the 1990s to police Iraqi compliance with UN Resolutions made before, during and after the first gulf war. Conveniently, perhaps, the British government decided there was little point continuing the containment policy of the 1990s, particularly in the light of repeated Iraqi breaches of UN resolutions. Thus, the British government thought that military action against Iraq would ensure that these repeated infractions would end permanently and if the action was supported it would unify the world behind an American conception of global security.

In pursuing this singular course of action the British government provides strength to the argument that narrow self-interest is the largest stumbling block to a fully fledged common EU security policy; and without a see-change in the politics of the EU this will remain a significant challenge to the Union and one likely to cause it to remain typified by lowest common denominator outputs.

The EU's central institutions – the Council and the Presidency – emphasized the role of the UN as a forum for conciliation and appropriate for disarming Iraq. The European Council tried to provide a summary of a unified position in its statement on the 17 February 2003 that emphasized Iraq's responsibility to comply with UN resolutions and to argue that armed conflict should be a last resort (Greek Presidency 17 February 2003). It was quite clear however that the member governments were engaged in open disagreement on many of these points.

The French and German government positions were couched in legal terms (French), and that the proposed UK-US military action was unacceptable (German). As previously mentioned Chancellor Schroeder opposed military action during the August/September 2002 election campaign, a position that some believe enhanced the chances of his coalition's eventual victory on 22 September (Chandler 2003; Lambert 2003). The pledges Schroeder made during the election campaign put the German government at one end of anti-war sentiment. He argued that the UN Resolutions had their remit restricted to disarmament and this was not to be achieved by armed force. Schroeder's overall position was that war should be a last resort and indeed should only be triggered when a strategic ally was being attacked – which he accepted for Afghanistan and 9/11 – but even then only when the UN had issued a mandate for such action. This, the Chancellor said, was a result of German historical legacies – particularly the Second World War – which particularly qualified the German people to advocate military reticence.

The Consequences for the EU's Institutions

The example of the Iraq war highlights the difficulties faced by the European Commission and Parliament. Commission officials were effectively hamstrung by the actions of the major European governments in their diplomacy over the Iraq crisis. Once the British, French and German governments had adopted strong positions any comment by Commission officials would be open to interpretation as either supportive of or detracting from that position. The Commission could be accused of becoming openly politicized. This accusation was levelled at Chris Patten who made a public statement arguing that armed action might be justified to uphold the sanctity of the UN, which was a clear replication of the official British government position. The Commission's difficult position on Iraq is partly exacerbated by individual Commissioners reverting to national positions, but more importantly that the Commission lacked an independent legal personality to make security policy pronouncements on behalf of the EU. Patten sums this tension up neatly when he said:

> The Commission is not a member state. We of course contribute to the development of the Union's Common Foreign Policy and we are deploying the instruments within our competence to make it more effective. But many of the issues we are discussing go to the heart of national sovereignty' (Patten 29 January 2003).

In the face of stark levels of disunity over Iraq the EU turned in on itself and focussed on bolstering the narrow security roles the EU already plays. As mentioned in Chapters Two and Four the success of the ESDP was dependent on the so-called 'Berlin Plus' arrangements being codified. This was achieved, somewhat surprisingly given the circumstances, on 17 March 2003 (Robertson 17 March 2003). Further extensions to existing EU security activities occurred at a Council meeting (18 March 2003) with the decision for the EU to discharge NATO operations in Macedonia through Operation Concordia which became the first EU badged military operation. This was followed up with Operation Artermis, which was an EU-badged but French led peacekeeping operation in the Democratic Republic of Congo to suppress inter-ethnic tensions and violence. Both these operations were conducted with agreement from the member governments. In these cases agreements were relatively simple to achieve because the activities were covered by readily agreeable humanitarian norms. By contrast, Iraq was so divisive because it was a war of aggression and of choice, containing very few humanitarian characteristics. These divisions did lead, arguably, the creation of a European Security Strategy in December 2003, which aimed to find common agreement on security norms and practices across the Union, a paradox of deepening integration at a time of disunity.

The Lasting Legacy – A Fractured Identity and the British Presidency of the EU (2005)

The lasting legacy of the divisions over Iraq were felt further than on the Europeanization of security, defence and foreign policy. As seen above, there were strong improvements made to the existing range of EU security areas in the months following the onset of the Iraq war. This section explores, through the example of the British Presidency of the EU – in the final six months of 2005 – whether the disunity caused by the Iraq conflict spread across the full range of EU policy competencies.

The UK Presidency began on 1 July 2005 in the context of the effective rejection of the EU's Constitutional Treaty by French and Dutch publics, and a Luxembourg Presidency that had failed to reach an agreement on the EU budget. Across the policy board the EU was rightly seen by many commentators to be a 'club in crisis' (Henley 2005; Financial Times Leader 2005, 12). The UK government set out its own expectations for its Presidency in two White Papers: *Priorities for the UK Presidency of the Council* (23 June 2005) and *'Prospects for the EU in 2005: The UK Presidency of the European Union'* (30 June 2005). These papers separated out the UK's aspirations into three sections: economic reform and social justice, security and stability, and Europe's role in the world with a final paragraph pledging to 'take forward the discussions on future financing'. Both papers provided strong signalling that the government appreciated that it would have to pick up unfinished business from the Luxembourg Presidency, but with the British rebate as a contested area the position of the British government as Chair of the EU, this was inopportune.

In keeping with the focus of this book this section ought to centre on defence and security policy. However, in the context of the 2005 British Presidency this chapter explores the disunity in the EU created by the Iraq conflict, as a defence and security issue, that has spread to other sectors of European public policy making and informal Europeanization. These non-defence areas can therefore be included in the wider analysis of defence related Europeanization. That a large disagreement on one policy area should heavily impact on negotiations across the full spectrum of European policies directly contradicts the work of liberal intergovernmentalists who suggest the each policy area is negotiated on a rational basis and separate from other issue areas. The example of the 2005 British Presidency would suggest that this is not the case and further, that the UK's support for the US led war on Iraq has put back the further formal Europeanization of defence by some years, if not indefinitely.

The British Presidency set out to achieve agreements on the budget reforms (2007-13), accession talks with Turkey, progress on stabilizing financial services and chemical processing (known as REACH) as well to make significant ground on environmental and climate change policy. The mood music prior to the UK's Presidency augured well for an engaged and positive British government. Prime Minister Blair's speech to the European Parliament (23 June 2005) raised expectations that the UK would lead radical debates on the future of European integration (Jones and Rennie 2005, 11; Financial Times Observer 2005, 14). The speech was received warmly by most EU governments, although the failure to follow through with some of the bolder statements during the Presidency has been the cause of some discontent (Stephens 2005, 19). The British Presidency, achieved the substantive elements of its programme, including the budgetary legacy from the Luxembourg Presidency, but did very little to improve pan-European relations arguably as a hangover from the disunity surrounding military action on Iraq and its continued fallout. This is a paradoxical position as CFSP and ESDP are policies dominated by member governments and unanimity. It should follow, therefore, that disagreements are lost within an agreed political system that understands 'opt-ins' and 'opt-outs' of member governments. However the evidence suggests that governments clearly act outside of the constraints of individual policy areas and take a broad view of diplomacy that leads to implicit or explicit linkages, again something that liberal intergovernmentalism rejects.

As with all EU Presidencies, the British government had very limited scope to influence the six monthly agenda. It could use its restricted privileges as Chair of the Union to push the EU's business forward. Institutionally, it could facilitate this through acting as Chair for Heads of State and Government, Ministerial and other committee and working group meetings, in representing the Council of Ministers at the European Parliament and the European Commission and to act as EU representative to third countries and international organizations. As a result, the British government acted as the chief facilitator for an established agenda, brokering deals on different issues. That the UK has been central to the disagreements on the EU budget is unfortunate, and holding the position of Chair made its antagonistic position even starker.

The 'programme of action' for the British Presidency was part of the Multi-annual Strategic Programme for the period 2004–6, designed by the Irish, Dutch, Luxembourg, UK, Austrian and Finnish Presidencies (Multi-Annual Programme 2006). The Luxembourg and British Presidencies submitted their annual Operational Programme of the Council for 2005 and were also tasked, as are all Presidencies, with managing the EU's responses to large international events. For Britain this was particularly onerous due to the terrorist attacks on the London transport system in July 2005 that highlighted the shifting nature of European security away from territorial defence and onto homeland security, as well as managing the European programme in the absence of a fully functioning German effort, due to the attempts to formulate a functioning coalition government (September 2005). By happy chance the British government also held the Presidency of the G-8 Presidency alongside the Presidency of the EU. The two Presidencies remained separate and distinct – the G8 Presidency focused on broad global issues like world poverty and climate change, whilst the EU Presidency worked its way through negotiations on institutions and budgets.

Benchmarking Success

Any number of state, sub- and supra- state actors are able to legitimately pass judgement on the success or otherwise of a European Presidency and these judgements are invariably highly contested. From a European Union perspective, the British Presidency was judged well because it secured an agreement on the budget, but poorly because of the political consequences of those negotiations. As previously mentioned, similar damage was done to the British government's reputation as a result of the rapid loss of momentum between the Prime Minister's speech to the European Parliament in June 2005 and the mid-point of the Presidency. The failure to implement radical policies and instil a sense of direction to the European project was seen as constituting a missed opportunity. The British government's concept of a successful Presidency, on the other hand, included success in these areas but also the protection of key national interest areas such as retaining as much of the budget rebate, secured by Prime Minister Thatcher in 1984, as possible (Daily Telegraph Editor 2005, 17).

In procedural terms the British Presidency was judged to be a success. As Chair of the large number of committees and working groups the FCO and Cabinet Office were once again effective in co-ordinating positions and institutions (see Chapters 2 and 3). The one exception to this was the informal foreign ministers meeting in September which suffered from rare poor organization (Browne 2005, 41). Complaints about the British government's diplomatic and negotiating style were more widespread however – a good example of this came in October with the informal Heads of State summit at Hampton Court, London. The Slovakian Prime Minister, for example, complained that he and other Heads of State had not been given agendas or briefings for the meeting (Editor: The Observer 2005, 32). Most of the new EU member states saw the meeting at Hampton Court as an opportunity for the British government to use up some the time of its Presidency and thus avoid difficult issues like budgetary reform. However, Prime Minister Blair's call for an energy security policy was greeted with enthusiasm and has become a much larger issue since the British Presidency through the Austrian Presidency, and through the global exposure given to the issue as a result of the disagreements between Russia and the Ukraine over the supply of natural gas and concerns about global warming (Herbstein 2006, 32).

On foreign and security policy the British Presidency managed to retain some European unity in the face of some considerable challenges, such as Iran and US 'renditions'. This cohesion is somewhat surprising given the schism over Iraq and more generally on the direction of the ESDP. The tension hanging over from Iraq were not eased by revelations about the American policy of 'extraordinary renditions' (the removal of suspects from or through continental Europe for interrogation all over the globe) and further that the CIA had established interrogation bases in Europe without the permission of host governments (Watt 2006, 27). The universal outrage this caused in the EU prompted a unified response and a collective request for clarification on US policy and practice in this area.

The latest challenges have included the diplomatic standoff with Iran over their nuclear technology programmes, whilst the strategically and economically sensitive relationship with China was rocked by negotiations over voluntary export restraints to limit the impact of Chinese textiles and shoe imports – the so called 'bra-wars'. Bringing these tensions under control and delivering cohesion across the Union was an important challenge for British diplomats and one in which they achieved some notable and surprising successes.

Domestic Security Policy

The developments at Saint Malo and Nice were premised on territorial defence and humanitarian intervention, whilst the post 9/11 security environment has been dominated by 'homeland security' issues in the UK and across the rest of the EU. As a key security player the British government divided its work on these issues into: counter-terrorism, people-trafficking and enlargement. The British government viewed opening accession negotiations with Turkey as strategically important and achieved this in early October. The rationale for this desire rests on Turkish accession providing greater levels of regional and global stability in the future, even with the strong Austrian, French and German government and public resistance to this further enlargement.

Counter-terrorism policy came to the fore because of the attacks on London in July 2005 – but had been preceded by the adoption of the Hague Programme in June 2005. The Presidency also made significant strides in reaching agreement to harmonize, for law enforcement purposes, the retention of telecommunications, email and internet data in all member states for up to two years. The German, Greek, Italian, Portuguese and Slovakian governments as well as many civil society groups all raised concerns about civil liberties implications and costs of the measures (Laitner 2005, 8). The Presidency managed to get a qualified majority vote for a Directive on the retention of data, but this may be subject to a future legal challenge in the European Court of Justice.

The focus on homeland security since 2001 poses the larger question of whether defence and security policy should be refocused on to these domestic concerns. Insofar as they provide a case study for Europeanization, the measures taken to support government counter-terrorism efforts have been successful and have included pan-European policing agreements, common arrest warrants, limited intelligence sharing and increased powers of data acquisition and retention, bringing common working practices and importantly a sense of a truly pan-European attempt to counter the terrorist threats posed to mainland Europe.

The opening of accession negotiations with Turkey was seen as a large diplomatic success by the British and American administrations. This success is even more stark when viewed in the context of a veto threat from the Austrian and German governments who wanted to continue the debate about the nature of the EU's relationship with Turkey (Browne 2005, 42). However, British negotiators managed to publicly identify the Austrian government as an awkward and vulnerable negotiating party, but as a result these tactics left central and eastern EU members feeling isolated because of the number of bilateral negotiations conducted by the British government.

The German general election and helpful declarations by the UN War Crimes Tribunal greatly assisted British efforts. The inconclusive German general election prevented a Christian Democrat, and therefore anti-Turkish, representation at the General Affairs Council while the UN reported that Croatia had fully cooperated with efforts to detain the suspected war criminal General Gotovina, which allowed British negotiators to persuade their Austrian counterparts that in exchange for Turkish accession talks, talks with Croatia should also begin (Wagstyl 2005, 8; Moravcsik 2006, 2). At this most intergovernmental level the British government were able to play a very conventional diplomatic role, moving between the various member governments finding compromize on these difficult issues; showing the benefit of standard international relations explanations for European negotiations and diplomacy.

External Relations and External Security

The British government managed to retain a measure of EU foreign policy cohesion throughout the Presidency, whilst not actually deepening formal integration, even on sensitive issues like Iran's development of nuclear technologies. Cohesion on Iran was made considerably easier by President Mahmoud Ahmadinejad's call on 26 October for Israel to be 'wiped off the face of the planet', which was badly received by Tony Blair as President of the European Union, and by other EU leaders (Webster 2005, 4; La Guardia, Helm and Rennie 2005, 8). The EU3 (Britain, France and Germany) persisted with attempts to negotiate with Iran over its nuclear energy programme, which is widely seen as a cover for a nuclear weapons programme, that is unacceptable to most EU governments and particularly to the US who labelled Iran as a member of the 'axis of evil' – countries who support terrorism and seek to undermine the 'west'. In January 2006 the EU3 declared that they were no longer able to negotiate with Iran without the Iranian government making some concessions (Sherwell 2006, 24). This has left the international community with limited choices about whether and how to escalate the crisis in a way that puts pressure on the Iranian government. The EU-3's approach has been resolutely through collective responses, rather than unitary action.

EU cohesion on the Iranian issue, and therefore the semblance of a Europeanized foreign policy has been made possible by the overwhelming presence of a unifying norm against the proliferation of nuclear materials. This position is particularly held, in Europe, by the French and British governments who are already nuclear powers and outside Europe by the American Administration who view the theocratic regime in Tehran as a threat to American national security interests. The presence of this non-proliferation norm raises the bar on the lowest common denominator agreements possible in intergovernmental negotiations – hence the quality and rigour of the European position.

On less sensitive defence and security issues the EU further developed its international presence during the six month Presidency. In September 2005, the European Union launched the first ESDP operation outside Europe and Africa, the monitoring mission in Aceh (Indonesia), with support from the Norwegian, Swiss, and a number of ASEAN governments. The success of these missions is more symbolic than an impressive show of military capabilities. Furthermore, on 15 November the Council adopted a joint action that officially launched the EU Police Mission in the Palestinian territories (EUPOL–COPPS) as of 1 January 2006, further evidence of the EU engaging in humanitarian operations although the Israel-Palestinian-Lebanese clashes in 2006 have disrupted these efforts. The missions have, however, served to reinforce the view that the EU has found a niche foreign policy identity that serves to support post-conflict reconstruction and other soft-security roles.

The other Middle Eastern issues dominating European politics were more problematic. The British government had wanted the EU to become more involved in Iraq, but this has still not occurred because of fractures in domestic support for the war and post-conflict reconstruction efforts in countries like Spain, Italy and France. From the British government's perspective, the more countries it can involve in the reconstruction effort, the greater its legitimacy will be and prospectively the less danger it will face as an occupying force. Negotiations to increase political and trade cooperation with Iraq have yet to start and nor has a Commission Delegation Office opened in Iraq. Nonetheless, the EU Political Directors did initiate a dialogue with Baghdad on 24 October 2005 and a decision was taken to extend EUJUST LEX (the Rule of Law Mission for Baghdad), which is positive step for European involvement in Iraq.

Economic Reform and the 2007-2013 Budget

The Europeanization of defence and security policy has impacted on the wider Europeanization programme. As a civilian and economic superpower the principal focus of any EU Presidency should be the stabilization and promotion of the EU's trading status. The British Presidency, as with the foreign policy emphasis of Prime Minister Blair domestically, was more engaged in security policy than economics. This was partly due to the prevailing security situation in Britain, partly because of the government's wider security interests in the Middle East, and also because the Prime Minister had developed his Premiership to bolster his reputation as an international statesman, whilst leaving his Chancellor to drive a domestic policy agenda. However, it was a joint priority of the Barroso Commission and the UK Presidency to reinvigorate the Lisbon agenda. They placed particular emphasis on streamlining business regulation which included reform of chemical regulation (REACH) – finally agreed in December 2006, and development of the Financial Services Action Plan and the Services Directive. The Commission caused a number of headlines when it published a communication (25 October) calling for a three year programme of reform and consolidation of 222 pieces of basic legislation and 1,400 Acts (Parker 2005, 8). The Commission's proposals included scrapping 68 pieces of new legislation which met with criticism from the French government in particular. The persistent legitimacy questions faced by the Commission following the Santer commission have placed a renewed emphasis on the Council and achieving unity amongst Member governments. Indeed, the current situation has put a renewed emphasis on governments as the lead players in the EU, which means there is greater scope for disagreements in one policy area to spill over into unrelated areas.

The UK Presidency was also at the forefront of moves to further integrate the EU's financial services market. The Commission's Green Paper on Financial Services Policy 2005–10, provided details of the proposed reforms, which were then duly adopted without controversy, even though the UK and French governments had previously disagreed on these issues. The European Parliament's Internal Market Committee ended its internal disagreements and voted for the Services Directive on 22 November which allows it to come forward for a first reading in the European Parliament in 2006. The Services Directive is broadly in line with British government thinking, highlighting an under-published truth that, just as with ESDP, despite its 'awkward partner' stance the British government manages to shepherd through initiatives that are in its interests, regardless of the dominant political and media discourse that the EU imposes disadvantageous measures on the UK (Forster 2002).

The final few months of the British Presidency was blighted by arguments over the budget and future financing of the EU. By tying this debate to a discussion about agricultural subsidy and the CAP the British government highlighted the damage that can be inflicted on formal and informal Europeanization by narrow national interests and two major UK-centric issues in particular. First, the UK budget rebate and second, the promotion of certain types of economic reform. These issues were very clearly foregrounded in the diplomatic wrangling over the 2007-13 budget in late 2005. The British government would have preferred to postpone discussion of this issue until after its Presidency, as it had done with the European Constitution, but EU states and the Commission did not allow the issue to slip off the British Presidency's agenda. The British strategy had two divisive elements: First, the UK Presidency linked reform of the UK rebate to reform of the CAP, which it said was no longer compatible with European economics. In doing so the British government laid itself open to the charge of opportunism (Sunday Times Editor 2005, 16; Rennie and Helms 2005, 1). Second, it used the same delaying tactics that had been successful on the Turkish accession issue to try and force the debate on CAP.

The British government presented its detailed budget proposal to its fellow EU members on 5 December. The proposals aimed to reduce the burden on the current net contributors to the budget through cutting the regional aid planned for the Central and East European member states 'by no more than 10 per cent'. British officials tried to justify this reduction on the basis that the East European member states have failed to spend a large amount of aid within the two-year time limit. The reduction would be linked to an extension of the time limit in which the East European states would be allowed to spend their aid, as well as a 2009 review of spending, to include the CAP. A key point of the British proposals was that they tried to disentangle the reform of CAP reform from the UK's budget rebate – which had been done presentationally – through the reduction in the rebate being part of a British desire to support the accession states. These proposals were received badly amongst EU governments but a negotiated position did emerge through reducing the British budget rebate by one billion pounds a year – although in cash terms it would continue to grow (White 2005, 11).

The large EU governments' cash contributions will increase because of this budget in a large redistribution of wealth to the former Soviet bloc countries part of the enlarged EU area. Furthermore, the UK managed to get agreement from the French government that a review in 2008/9 would examine the workings of the CAP, although this is a relatively minor concession, given the history of delays aimed at avoiding reform of this policy area. It is difficult to judge whether the diplomatic schism over Iraq was an important contributory factor to the similarly divisive developments on CAP and the British budget rebate. However, the CAP is seen by the French government as an area of core national interest and they treat it as such in negotiations. The perception of the British government flaunting it's 'special relationship' with the United States and constructing itself as being above the EU's day-to-day politics gives the British government's status as an 'awkward partner' a different dynamic, including a great deal of resentment.

There are few objective reasons for the UK to occupy a 'special' role within the EU – the legacy of Empire is a dim, distant historical relic, as is victory in World War Two. The nuclear deterrent is struggling to find a role in a new security environment framed by asymmetric threats and the power of UN has been dented by inertia and inaction on important events like Rwanda (1994) and Darfur (2005/6) both of which seemed to unify world opinion but have produced little action. As a club of unitary states the EU has historically struggled to channel the needs of huge state egos into useful action – the diplomacy at the end of 2005 over the Budget rebate and CAP demonstrates this point clearly.

Summary

This chapter has explored the effects of the Iraq war – the diplomacy leading up to it and the fallout from it – on what might be termed the informal Europeanization of security policy and wider EU policy areas. This research suggests that Europeanization is a relatively fragile political phenomenon. Whilst strong and significant advances have been made to produce unified positions and common understandings across the Union on security policy the behaviour of individual member states in following narrow national interests has been shown to derail the EU's unity of purpose. The UK's unilateral decision to join the US-led coalition and play a leading role in the military action stood at great odds with the EU's consensual and law-based security and foreign policy preferences. In turn, the Commission was unable to forge a strong position on the Iraq crisis for fear of being seen to favour one particular side of the debate, and moreover, did not feel empowered to do so. The example given of Chris Patten making a public statement that appeared to reinforce the British government's position did nothing to help this sense of paralysis in the Commission.

Crucially, the diplomacy concerning the Iraq crisis is part of a wider European contest to frame the nature of EU defence, security and foreign policy. The first side of this contest typified by the French and German government positions on Iraq which sees the EU as part of an international system of collective security apparatus' that explicitly reject the notion of unilateral military action – which was favoured by the British and American administrations in relation to the problem of Iraq. The collectivist position also emphasizes the rule of international law, the responsibility of major states to uphold this law and to protect smaller states from the affects of globalization whilst pointing towards the unity of the EU as an institution of shared experiences and political outlooks.

The British counter-position is that the EU is a political system rather than collecting house for common culture, values and experiences. The British government's instrumentalist position is the EU will remain operation and useful for all the time in which the separate institutions and governments remain committed to trying to find common solutions to policy issues, where those issues suit pan-European policies. Indeed, the British version of this model can be summed up as intergovernmental insider-advocacy – that is one which is happy to retain the unanimous elements of the EU, but with an aspiration to convince other governments of the wisdom of the British position. That such contests are taking place over the future direction of European security should not be a surprise – but that the protagonists have such different ideas is perhaps surprising and indeed worrying for the future of the Europeanization of security, defence and foreign policy. This points towards a conclusion, that is supported by the evidence in this chapter, that the EU will continue to deepen integration on issues underpinned by readily acceptable international norms, such as humanitarian intervention, but that cohesion on issues that fall outside of this bracket will be problematic because of behaviour of national governments pursuing narrow national interests.

This chapter also explored the effect of the Iraq crisis on the Europeanization of issues outside of the security sphere. It did this through the prism of the British government's Presidency of the EU in the last six months of 2005. Within these examples the Europeanization can be seen as a disparate political phenomenon. Despite the widespread disagreements over the Iraq crisis the normal business of the EU continued unabashed. The British Presidency achieved a budget agreement, accession talks with Turkey and movement on REACH and the Services Directive. However, in achieving the successes on Turkey and the budget the British government incurred huge political costs and goodwill in the Union, because of its diplomatic strategies and approaches.

The budget deal was a necessary evil for the UK, costing the government 7.2bn GBP over 7 years and some bad press coverage in the UK. On issues such as the rebate and CAP the negative effect of the Iraq crisis on EU diplomacy was overshadowed by more pressing narrow national preferences; in the case of the budget from the British government and in the case of CAP by the French government. However, all the negotiations occurred within the diplomatic context of the British government being poorly regarded by its fellow European governments because of its publicly negative attitude towards the EU and because of its self-constructed and self-important role as a bridge across the Atlantic to the Bush Administration in America.

One of the positive elements of the British Presidency was that the structural constraints of the Chairman role placed the British government under a political obligation to engage positively in negotiations and to try and advance a Europeanizing agenda. Free from the constraints of the Presidency in 2006 the British government will of course be free to return to an 'awkward' partner strategy particularly as this plays well with the 'Euro-sceptic' British media and a instinctively Euro-sceptic public (Forster 2002). Ultimately, the British Presidency achieved much of what it wanted to do substantively, whilst failing to achieve the level of reform stated by Prime Minister Blair in his June 2005 speech to the European Parliament. The British government returned, once again, to its position of 'awkward partner' in Europe, leaving the impression that it is happy for the EU not to reform. The British government's style of diplomacy was roundly criticized during the Presidency; the habit of tabling last minute amendments and proposals was seen as a form of brinkmanship; aimed at hijacking the diplomatic process, whilst in normal diplomatic terms this is seen as part of the essential statecraft involved with these processes.

The day-to-day Europeanization of defence and security policy under the British Presidency continued at a good pace. The EU was still able to run and lead peace support and advanced policing roles in Bosnia, the Congo and greater levels of support to Afghanistan and the Palestinian territories, although the EU's involvement in the Palestinian areas has been very recently thrown into doubt with Hamas' victory in the general election (La Guardia and Rennie 2006, 2). This has been exacerbated by the conflict between Israel, the Palestinian authority and Lebanon over the kidnapping of three Israeli soldiers that saw Israel take military action against Palestine and Lebanon to try and recover their men (Guardian – Agencies 2006; MacIntyre 2006). The long term future of the EU as a foreign, security and military actor looks to be in providing niche support to the failing and failed states and post-conflict reconstruction areas; whilst individual EU states use their high-end military capabilities in taking part in international coalitions of the willing. The corrosive effects of pan-European disagreements on the war on Iraq are likely to reignite if the US / UK coalition proposes taking military action against Iran which is seen as having a more demonstrably 'western' population than Iraq – 2006 and 2007 could therefore see the beginning of the end for the common foreign and security policy making in the EU, if the debate over Iran drives the US/ UK coalition down a military route. The Europeanization of security policy proceeds smoothly whilst there is a unifying international norm underpinning the policy, but outside of this narrow situation the logic of an anarchical international system – where the EU and Europeanization projects are still at the whim of individual nation states asserting their national strength on narrow self interests – prevails, providing a validation of the liberal intergovernmentalist framework of analysis. However, the next chapter throws these conclusions into sharp relief by highlighting the influence and control exerted by supra- and trans-national actors over Europeanization.

Chapter 7

The Europeanization of the Arms Trade

This chapter explores the Europeanization of the legal arms trade at the national and supranational level. It focuses on the how the British arms trade operates and then situates it at the European level. In doing so the chapter argues that the arms trade is both the 'fast and slow track' of Europeanization. Whilst the European Commission and arms manufacturers are at the forefront of an increasingly Europeanized arms trade, national governments are concerned with protecting national economic interests that are now anything but national because of the internationalization of defence industries through mergers, acquisitions and joint projects. Furthermore, this research suggests that the Commission and manufacturers are using the 'homeland security' agenda to force a Europeanization agenda, distorting the preferences of national governments away from the stated security goals of the ESDP by steering the securitization of national policy to meet economic objectives through state-private networks of officials and manufacturers. The juxtaposition of the deeply insular national trade against an emerging and vibrant pan-European trade will be explored through a typical procurement and sales cycle. This structure will help bring to the fore the elements of the cycle particularly affected by national and supranational pressures, and the particular officials and institutions involved. The chapter will show that the intergovernmental foundations of defence are being eroded by a trade driven cross-pillar approach; a supranationalist attack on core national sovereignty.

The Arms Trade as Power Politics

The legal arms trade in Britain is viewed by government officials as being a core function of the state and an indispensable part of the British economy (Dover 2007). Moreover, the legal arms trade has foreign policy implications – the British government's view is that they can garner favour from third parties and exert insider advocacy over other countries foreign or domestic policy (DESO 2006). The two leading examples of this belief concern arms exports to Saudi Arabia since the 1980s and India and Pakistan in 2002-3 in which officials described the British government's decision to maintain export levels to potentially warring countries as insider advocacy (MoD Interview March 2005). Sales to Saudi Arabia were justified on the grounds of being able to influence a strategically important government in the Middle East (Stavrianakis 2007). It should come as little surprise, therefore, that the British government lends this trade its full institutional support.

On the European stage the EDA provides the EU with an ability to influence the development of technology and, by inference, the procurement and sale of these materials. By extension the arms trade should now be considered as a tool of diplomacy at the disposal of the EU as well. However, with this new diplomatic tool comes the tension inherent in national arms programmes. The EU's established role as a humanitarian foreign policy actor provides part of this tension within its arms trade activities. The EU has been at the forefront of efforts to control the proliferation of weapons and military technologies. Its efforts in policing the Ottawa Treaty concerning landmines have met with scholarly acclaim (Long 2002; Dover 2006). The EU has enjoyed similar sentiments on its work to ensure a Code of Conduct for the arms trade is codified – a set of provisions aimed at making the trade more transparent and less open to claims of corruption (Bauer 2003; Davis, Hirst and Mariani 2001; Council of the EU 2005).

In practical terms the EU has thus far tried to demonstrate its arms related diplomatic strength through the medium of non-proliferation policies and actions. In the ongoing case of Iran, the EU – through the EU-3 – has adopted increasingly tough positions (through 2005/6) to try to stop and then roll back the Iranian government's programme to develop nuclear energy, with the commonly held assumption that this programme will naturally result in a weaponized nuclear programme (Bowen and Kidd 2004; Bahgat 2006). In the case of China the exact opposite approach has been taken. Member states, concerned with improving trade relations with China, have lobbied extensively for the EU's arms embargo on China to be lifted. This has been an ongoing issue since 2004 and has received a great deal of media attention (Minder 2004; Agence France Presse 2005; Buckley 2005). The human rights abuses perpetrated by the Chinese government on political dissidents, their problematic position on Taiwan (from an American perspective) and the Chinese economy's emergence as a potential hegemonic power, have all made the issue of trading military equipment with China more politically difficult.

However, within a framework of trying to achieve preferential trading terms with China, the sale of arms has become a bargaining chip that many within the European political elite are willing to trade. From a national perspective, the UK and BAE Systems have publicly declared that they will not sell military equipment to China regardless of the EU's position because they wish to remain closer to the US government's position on the issue. This demonstrates the influence of arms manufacturers on the direction of national policy and the commensurate affect this has on the European stage – with the ban on exports to China remaining.

The European Commission sees the arms trade as a useful way of improving the EU's position on the world's economic stage. The Commission believes both that defence manufacturing will contribute to meeting the Lisbon Agenda targets and that military technology will spin out to improve civilian technology industries. The EU has therefore moved from a position of being a non-military, foreign policy actor, at the forefront of arms control and non-proliferation initiatives, to a state-like actor with policy tensions between a desire to promote a thriving arms trade and the competing desire to control the proliferation of these technologies. What is clear, however, is that the trade dimension (including the Lisbon agenda) has facilitated the growth of a Europeanized and internationalized arms trade; one in which the EU has replicated state-like institutions like the UK's DESO into the EDA – evidence of the UK government uploading its policy and institutional preferences into the supranational level.

Whilst the EDA and the EU's defence and foreign policy identity remains an intergovernmental policy area there is considerable merit in the argument that the Europeanization of the arms trade has taken on its own dynamic and internal pace. The influence of lobbying on the EDA and member governments in tandem is driving the European defence procurement agenda to a position where it is considering network enabled capabilities to remain on a par with the United States (Hayes 2006, 27). The EDA's and Commission's desire to increase arms sales might also be part of a post-Cold War version of an arms race, the dash for market share, as firms from America, Russia and Europe vie for contracts around the world. The competition for market share is partly a raw economic equation of boosting balances of trade, but it also serves a foreign policy purpose of buying, or more precisely selling, influence into those client countries – particularly as the contracts often contain maintenance clauses that extend the commercial relationship into the medium term.

As an interesting footnote to these economic and trade developments, it is significant to note that the EU's Code of Conduct on arms sales has not had a significant effect in reducing the number of exports made by EU countries. Uncharitably this might indicate that the Code may have been a rather public attempt by the EU to retain its humanitarian actor tag, rather than a serious attempt to reduce proliferation (Larsen 2002; Bretherton and Vogler 2006).

The EDA's desire for technological parity with the US is partly driven by economics, but also driven by the consideration of power politics, both nationally and supranationally. For the British government, in particular, the political dimension is covered by the desire to act as a useful military ally of the US. The EDA's programme of action for 2005-6 demonstrates this point neatly: the priorities are stated as Strategic Lift (normally used for deploying military assets into high intensity military theatres), Air-to-Air Refuelling and C4ISTAR (Command, Control, Communication, Computing, Intelligence, Surveillance, Target Acquisition and Reconnaissance); a concept that has gained a higher profile since 2003 and the Iraq war (Potts 2002; Fulton 2003; EDA 2006). The EDA's flagship programmes for 2005/6 centre around projects that the United States military has been at the forefront of developing. For example, Unmanned Aerial Vehicles (UAVs) are technologies that the American and Israeli military forces have used in preparing reconnaissance for tactical bombing or infantry movements – a recent example being the 2006 Israeli action against the Lebanon (O'Sullivan 2004; Massy-Beresford 2006). The EDA's stated desire is that European built versions of this technology should remain 'interoperable' with American built technology, reinforcing the thesis that the European Commission's vision of defence technology is one that supports US-led military actions – a direct echo of the British government's position.

Given the post-conflict reconstruction work that European member states are involved with currently, and presumably will remain involved with, a new generation of Armoured Fighting Vehicles (AFVs) and inter-operable C3 technologies (Command, Control and Communications) are required. These technologies are being designed and dealt with by both the EDA and manufacturers, a move designed to improve the ability of the European militaries to participate in wars of choice. The US has voiced dissatisfaction, however, with the development of a European owned and controlled satellite system (known as Galileo), which the US views as an unnecessary addition to European capabilities, seeing as America offers good access to their surveillance and spy satellites (Parker and Thornhill 2005; Agence Europe 2004). The development of the 'Galileo' project is seen from the EU's perspective as an attempt to gain a foothold in the global satellite market, opening up European civilian and military applications. Whilst space cannot officially be militarized these satellite systems do offer militaries the ability to assess enemy capabilities and view enemy ground movements; a significant capability and a statement of intent on the EU's part.

Nationally, the transfer of military and dual-use materials are facilitated and strongly supported by the Defence Export Services Organisation (DESO) and Defence Attachés (DAs) who use privileged access to officials in government procurement agencies to unlock foreign trade opportunities. Furthermore, DESO and the arms manufacturers use their respective position within and access to the UK Ministry of Defence (MoD) to shape the ministry's domestic procurement practices for the benefit of the manufacturers. The vast majority of the British government's and EU's efforts on the arms trade are focussed on the presumption to sell arms, rather than to control or monitor their end use. There is only slight evidence to suggest that there has been a curtailment of trading, despite the weight of evidence from NGOs of inappropriate end-use or re-sale of UK or EU built and sold arms. Importantly both the promotion and monitoring of arms sales occurs mostly at the nation-state level with only little of it occurring at the supranational level.

'Too Close for Comfort': Government, Manufacturers and the Pre-licensing of Exports[1]

The arms trade is an emotive issue, arousing strong views amongst campaigners who argue the moral and economic cases against the arms trade while industry insiders advocate the political, strategic and counter-economic case for continued export activities. The trade has attracted criticism on wider fronts, such as on corruption and the impact of the arms trade in fostering violence in the recipient countries (Barkawi and Laffey 2001).

The industry commentator Joe Roeber, whose book on corruption in the arms trade was too contentious to go into print following threats of litigation from arms manufacturers to his publisher, suggests that the trade is the 'most corrupt legal sector of the economy' (Roeber 2005). Roeber also contends that in the late 1990s the CIA estimated that the arms trade accounted for 40-45% of the total corruption in world trade despite only amounting to less than half of one percent of the total trade. However, British arms exports have continued to prove to be highly lucrative for the UK Treasury as well as, as previously mentioned, an area in which officials believe asserting considerable influence over recipient countries; whilst industry figures emphasize the economic advantages of the arms trade to the UK.

In 2004 UK arms exports reached a five-year trading high, according to figures released by DESO, exports totalling US$8.2 billion, up $400 million from 2003. In

---

1   This subtitle echoes Stavrianakis' PhD (Stavrianakis 2007).

terms of market share this translates to a 20% share of the world market in 2004, putting the UK second behind the United States (DESO 2006; Isenberg 2005). For the British government, therefore, the arms trade is a national, rather than European issue, although there is interview evidence that the British government made significant efforts to ensure that a British official was appointed as the first head of the European Defence Agency (EDA) (Dover 2007, 30). The arms manufacturers see the trade as internationalized – the increasing overlap of shareholdings, projects and procurement strategies mean that 'flag-carrying' companies are no longer entirely tied to individual nations, but this disjuncture has not resulted in friction between the manufacturers and the British government. Arguably the manufacturers have benefited from good relations with both the British government and European Commission; the decision of the Commission to fund some research and development work introduces an interesting dynamic into the arms trade – the supranational funding of materials to be sold through state-private networks to the British procurement agencies. This means that, by a complicated process, the British government is influenced by both national and European producer group pressure.

The British government's approach to the arms trade can by typified by a strong pro-trade preference that forms an essential part of the British government's wider external relations policy. This agenda manifests itself most strongly through DESO whose raison d'etre is to support the transfer of military and dual-use equipment (Norton-Taylor et al 1996, 15). One interviewee characterized this preference as being a free-market philosophy under which the default is to sell as much material as possible but within a framework that exerts control over exports within given criteria (Interview 23IS). As previously suggested, the case of Saudi Arabia provides strong evidence for this claim through the long established and important links to British arms manufacturers. Evidence of the strength of this trade link is shown by the answer to the Freedom of Information Act query placed by The Guardian newspaper that revealed 161 of the 600 employees at DESO were assigned to the 'Saudi Armed Forces Project', which specifically facilitates arms sales to Saudi Arabia (Leigh and Evans 2005). The government's effort in promoting and supporting the arms trade, and particularly in exporting equipment to Saudi Arabia, coupled with an overlap between public and industry officials highlights the extent to which public and private interests have elided.

Uploading British Preferences to the Supranational Level

One way in which the UK has uploaded its defence preferences to the supranational level is through the establishment and remit of the EDA. The EDA's role is to advance collaboration between companies and countries on the development of defence equipment. Nick Witney, the current British Chief Executive of the EDA (and former UK MoD and FCO official) and also Head of the group tasked to design its institutional elements, has been keen to extend the role of the EDA and critics argue, generate further manufacturing contracts for British industry (Tigner 2004; Interview 14IS). Arms manufacturers had a large role in the working groups that designed the EDA: high ranking European Commission officials sat with representatives of BAE Systems and EADS as well as the President of the European Defence Industries Group to advise on how the new institution should operate, providing a key voice opportunity to manufacturers and providing greater evidence of a fundamental elision of public and private interests. As a result of these working groups the EDA has been greeted by anti-arms trade campaigners as a strong signal that the EU has taken on a military identity. More notably perhaps are the comments of two interviewees that the installation of Witney as the head of the EDA was a key UK government position in the intergovernmental negotiations that secured the establishment of the agency (Interview 13IS; Interview 14IS). Having a 'Brit' as the head of the agency would ensure that British interests were secured.

British officials anticipate that Witney will help steer the EDA towards a British conception of what the Agency should seek to achieve. In trying to balance a quasi think-tank role of identifying and plugging gaps in European military capabilities, whilst also being an institutional guarantor of EU defence manufacturing interests pushes the EU into a potentially contradictory position. Evidence of this tension was seen within days of the Agency being established with the largest EU arms manufacturers taking out a full page advert in some British newspapers to emphasize their vision for the EDA (The Times; The Telegraph 15 June 2004).

The danger for the EDA is that it will lose its strategic overview of how to plug the capabilities gaps that exist within the European military portfolio – based on the sort of operations the EU and its member governments' wish to conduct – as a result of becoming a conduit for the lobbying attentions of the major arms manufacturers. Moreover, its strong links with a European Commission which is determined to promote a high-technology, research-led industrial base, an enhanced internal market and an increasingly neo-liberal industrial policy pushes the EDA down certain avenues of activity. At the time of writing none of these avenues appear to disadvantage British manufacturers, or go against the British view of the European arms trade.

The EDA – Institutional Structure, Legal Basis, Membership and Budget

The European Defence Agency was originally agreed within the Convention on the Future of Europe, a pre-cursor to the European Constitution in October 2003 (European Convention Secretariat 2003). The EDA should have been established as part of the Constitution in 2008 – however, subsequent referendums in France and the Netherlands in 2005 have effectively killed it off (Scolioni 2005; Lichfield 2005). Member States have begun, however, to resurrect the elements of the Constitution that they thought were meritorious, and included in this tranche of measures are the EDA provisions. The role of the Agency was debated extensively between Member Governments and by the Defence Working Group – which was composed of national government representatives, those with Ministerial experience at the national and supranational level, and manufacturers – which again reflects the extent to which a state-private network exists, to determine government policy and procurement practices, in the European arms trade.[2]

During the Thessaloniki Council negotiations the French government pushed for the agency to reflect their political desire for a fully-fledged common defence policy by having the EDA as a pan-European procurement and development agency – incorporating equivalent roles to the UK government's DESO and Qinetiq into a supranational agency. The British government, having argued all the way through the Saint Malo process that capabilities should be at the heart of the Europeanization project, simultaneously tried to protect and advance British arms manufacturer interests. The British position, reflecting British pragmatism and this dual approach, pushed for an EDA that would coordinate mutually convenient and advantageous projects as they occurred, without being too prescriptive (Interview MoD Official 2005). The German and Italian governments, argued however, for a light-touch agency to ensure common procurement trends across Europe, reflecting their concerns about the EDA undermining NATO and providing inflationary pressures on national defence budgets. The outcome, as expressed in the Conclusions of the June 2003 European Council meeting at Thessaloniki provided a pathway for the EDA to be formally established with a mix of British and French preferences – as with Saint Malo – as the underlying operational understandings:

> The EDA is an intergovernmental agency in the field of defence capabilities development, research, acquisition and armaments. This agency, which shall be subject to the Council's authority and open to participation by all Member States, will aim at developing defence capabilities in the field of crisis management, promoting and enhancing European armaments cooperation, strengthening the European defence industrial and technological base and creating a competitive European defence equipment market, as well as promoting, in liaison with the Community's research activities where appropriate, research aimed at leadership in strategic technologies for future defence and security capabilities, thereby strengthening Europe's industrial potential in this domain (EU Council Greece 2003).

A Joint Action brought the EDA into existence on 12 July 2004 as an agency in which member states can voluntarily opt in or out of its remit thus allowing the 'neutral' countries to have internal debates about whether they wished to become members of a supranational defence organization (EU Council Joint Action 2004). The British and French governments engaged in a lengthy debate about whether the EDA should be governed by unanimity or by majority vote – the decision that emerged was that states retain a right of veto over the involvement of non-EU countries in

---

2 Javier Solana (High Representative for the CFSP), Gen. Rainer Schuwirth (Head of EU Military Staff), Corrado Antonini (President of the European Defence Industries Group), Jean-Louis Gergorin (EADS), Laurent Giovacchini (DGA, French Ministry of Defence), Peter Lundberg (Assistant DG, Defence Equipment Agency, Sweden), Mr Anthony Parry (BAE Systems), Gen. Carlo Cabigiosu (former KFOR Commander General), Alain le Roy (Special Envoy of the European Union in the FYROM), Gen. Gustav Hagglund (Chairman of the EU Military Committee), Lord Robertson (Secretary-General of NATO and former UK Secretary of State for Defence), Alain Richard (former French Minister of Defence), and Christopher Patten (Commissioner for External Affairs) (EU Council doc. CONV 461/02, 2002.

the EDA. In turn, the French government won the debate over the EDA's autonomy, allowing the EDA to request and fund new projects whilst the British government secured a provision that means the EDA's budget is decided by unanimity. The intergovernmental nature of the EDA is underlined by the Agency's steering board, which is composed of 24 EU defence ministers, meeting biannually at Ministerial level (or by proxy through their designated officials), who effectively control the EDA. In theory, therefore, the EDA should be a tool of national governments, but a central argument of this chapter is that the EDA has managed to go beyond the narrow confines of state control and develop its own distinct and Europeanized agenda.

The Agency has a staff of around 80 officials who ultimately report to the High Representative, Javier Solana. The EDA has official links to the 24 member governments who are associated with the Agency. The Agency is staffed by those seconded from national bureaucracies and also by direct recruitment into the agency (EDA Open Recruitment 2006). Nick Witney was appointed as the 'Head of the Establishment Team', which broadly equates to Chief Executive. Under him is the German, Hilmar Linnenkamp.

Whilst the effect of a pro-sale operating principle is marked on the behaviours of the EDA it is similarly pronounced on the UK's Embassy officials and for DAs attached to those embassies (Phythian 2001). Defence Attachés are not expected to get involved in any covert intelligence activities but are expected in the course of their duties, to collect openly available military information (Steele 2004, 282). They spend a great deal of time liaising with the host armed forces and arms companies and are therefore an invaluable source of military information to those wishing to access their knowledge (Clarke 2000, 730).

Similarly, the success of an Ambassador's period of tenure is partly judged upon whether he or she has assisted in securing a significant quantity of export trade, including arms sales, for UK companies (Interview 24IS). For the purposes of supporting the efforts of manufacturers, a British company, is one which brings in or maintains employment in the UK (Interview 03IS; Interview 23IS). Former British Ambassador to the US, Christopher Meyer, illustrates the reciprocity of such relationships having been invited to join the Board of UK arms manufacturer GKN, whilst simultaneously holding the Chairmanship of the Press Complaints Commission (Barnett 2005; Meyer 2005).

For British diplomats seeking to secure rapid entry to the higher echelons of the diplomatic community a successful spell in a trade division of a UK embassy is essential, demonstrating the importance of trade to the overall British foreign policy effort (Interview 24IS; Interview 28IS). This can be viewed as an extension of the age-old function of government to promote trade as a symbolic and material encapsulation of its international status. The institutionalization of trade targets and the expectation on embassy staff to assist arms manufacturers in selling their products demonstrates a virtuous or vicious circle (depending on one's perspective) whereby state-sponsorship of private interests skews national foreign policy. The repeated reviews of the structure and costs of the diplomatic service have also led to an increasing emphasis on export assistance to UK companies, and have effectively made these state institutions, better agents of manufacturer's interests.

A key function of UK embassies abroad is to support and facilitate arms sales. Embassies act as an essential marketing tool for the arms companies and assist in resolving contractual glitches. DAs are the arms companies' principal point of contact in the country they hope to sell to; the DA reports directly to the Ambassador in weekly (and daily – depending on the progress of the sale) review meetings (Interview 24IS). Between 25-40% of a DAs time is spent on facilitating arms sales – including being directly tasked by DESO (something which is unique to the UK system) – this suggests arms sales are a significant part of the DA's role. Direct tasking from DESO is unique to the UK, however the use of Attachés in this role is quite commonly found in competitor European, Russian and American governments (Dover 2007). The proximity of the manufacturer, MoD, DESO, and DAs is partially illuminated through the MoD Defence Attaché committee that decides on which countries should receive UK DAs. This committee has DESO representation and one of the explicit criteria for a DA being sent to a country is the possibility of creating or further opening up a market for UK arms exports (Interview 24IS; Interview 36IS). DESO's intervention on this committee suggests the extent to which this small part of the MoD guides state power – in this instance guiding state power onto very localized issues concerning defence contracts.

The European Commission's involvement in defence industries has manifested itself in promoting research and development in defence industrial sectors – although mostly through dual use technology (de Vestel 1995; EU Commission 1997; EU Commission 1996). There have been several lines of resistance to the Commission's involvement in funding defence research – the first has been Treaty provisions expressly forbidding it (particularly Article 223 Treaty of Rome and Article 296 Treaty of Amsterdam) and partly because of the political-cultural point that the EU is a civilian rather than military superpower (Treaty of European Union 1992; Treaty of Amsterdam 1998; Morth 2000).

However, through a series of Communiqués the Commission provided a gradual justification for its involvement in funding defence research. Through these self-empowering ordinances the Commission can now help fund aerospace, general defence and security research, and because a clause in one of the communiqués removed the distinction between military and civilian funding the Commission has a potentially large role in defence industrial policy (European Commission 2003; European Commission 2003a). The Group of Personalities (a group of Commissioners, research institute representatives, MEPs and arms manufacturers who meet in near secrecy) 2004 report argued that, in addition to the EDA managed projects and dual-use research projects, a further one billion euros should be invested in security research, demonstrating the Commission's commitment to investments in security equipment (European Commission 2003a). Furthermore, the Commission has provided support to ailing defence firms and supported employees made redundant by arms manufacturers who have closed, a role normally played – on a case by case basis – by national governments (Bishop and Griapos 1995).

The European Commission has proved itself to be a cheerleader for manufacturers through the establishment of pro-trade advisory committees at the supranational level. These committees are weighted heavily with arms industry insiders and Commissioners, which is only notable because they do not appear to have devoted such efforts to other industries. The Committees have each focussed on an aspect of the defence trade – MEP Elmar Brok has chaired the 'Group of Personalities' whose remit has been to focus on research and development in the security sector, especially to expand work on homeland security technologies. As the Group of Personalities report states:

> Technology itself cannot guarantee security, but security without the support of technology is impossible. It provides us with information about threats, helps us to build effective protection against them and, if necessary, enables us to neutralize them. In other words: technology is a key 'force enabler' for a more secure Europe. At the same time, the security dimension of technology itself is changing, because technology is very often multi-purpose. Civil and defence applications increasingly draw from the same technological base and there is a growing cross-fertilisation between the two areas (Group of Personalities 2004).

Such words could have been written by the marketing division of an arms manufacturer, which poses a series of questions about how much critical distance officials can have when the representatives of manufacturers are on the committees and, moreover, the extent to which a state-private network exists between the European Commission – effectively the government of the EU – and private business interests. This is a relationship that exactly mirrors the situation at government and regional level in the UK. Quite why public officials work so hard to ensure that private industry continues to profit from defence sales is difficult to comprehend – but that this network exists, as Seymour Melman, and Marc Pilisuk and Thomas Hayden suggest, is clear (Melman 1970, 19; Pilisuk and Hayden 1965, 69). The Commission's behaviour on defence trade fits within Giandomenico Majone's description of it being both a regulator and policy entrepreneur, and perhaps even within Laura Cram's description of the Commission as an opportunist (Majone 1996; Cram 1997).

The Commission's 2003 communiqué on military equipment, and particularly its economic advantages, demonstrates eliding the interests of the Commission and the arms companies (European Commission 2003). The Commission claims to be able to show pre-eminence, as in other areas of Community law, over member governments on the issue of arms control – which, according to it, should now be considered in the light of the EU defence industrial bases' competitiveness. This places at the supranational level the operating assumptions within the UK's arms licensing and control processes; that economic considerations have priority over moral and non-proliferation concerns. This also reflects the success of the British and French governments in uploading their preferences into the supranational level. Both governments operate their arms trades on this basis and have steered the EU down the same path, perhaps unsurprising given that Britain, France, Germany and Spain account for 80% of the defence spending in the EU (European Commission 2005).

The arms trade has been a permissive area for Europeanization because it has become framed as a predominantly trade, rather than security issue (Morth 2000). One of the interesting trends within the arms trade is that the EU's defence industrial base is increasingly international. It is misleading to talk of BAE Systems, for example, as a British firm – 40% of its shareholders live in the United States and it has business ties across the whole EU area. So, whilst national governments have adopted protectionist policies regarding their arms manufacturers both the Commission and the manufacturers themselves have both Europeanized and internationalized. The Commission's support for the manufacturers is in part a recognition of the manufacturers' lobbying efforts, and in part a realization of the Commission's desire to engage in defence policy and to shape defence and security policy through influencing on industrial policy (Treaty of Amsterdam 1998).

Arms manufacturers spend a great deal of time and money lobbying national governments (both politicians and officials) and now, at the European level, the Commission and the Parliament. Across all the EU's policy competencies some 15,000 professional lobbyists operate within Brussels to steer EU decision-making (European Commission 2006). For the arms industry the umbrella grouping 'Aerospace and Defence industries Association of Europe' (known as the ASD), was formed in 2004 from the European Defence Industries Group, the European Association of Aerospace Industries and Eurospace, and the Association of European Space Industry (ASD Website 2006). Replicating the revolving door between the arms trade and government departments, the first three Chairmen of the ASD were Mike Turner, BAE System's CEO, Pier Francesco Guarguaglini, Chairman and CEO of Finmeccanica and Thomas Enders, CEO of EADS, thus representing the most significant arms manufacturers in Europe and showing the institutional strength behind the lobbying effort. The ASD represents a 'who's who' of the multi-billion Euro European arms trade and within the European Commission, which sees itself as an ambassador of European trade and the European Parliament, with constituency employment concerns, the ASD represents a very serious player on the EU lobbying stage.

The so-called post-Cold War peace dividend, represented by cuts in national defence programmes, saw European arms manufacturers being squeezed in a global defence market increasingly dominated by American firms. Much of the EU manufacturers' lobbying on the Commission has focused on policy responses that react to the dominance of American manufacturers, a desire to improve EU market share and to increase the number of orders in their order books, something that was not assisted by the negotiation of the ESDP. The Commission's trade-driven response was to suggest that there needed to be further consolidation of EU defence firms either through acquisition and merger and/or through greater levels of harmony within the defence procurement practices, resulting in pan-European research, development and economies of scale. To meet this end some €570million was dedicated to 'space and security' in the EU's 2005 budget (European Commission 2005a). On the face of it the Commission's approach to the arms trade looks like a repeat of its conduct with other industries – driven by a conviction that consolidation and mergers will produce greater efficiencies in the defence industrial base (Sandler and Hartley 1995; cf Dunne and Perlo-Freeman 2003).

One weakness in the EU's approach – a product of the desire to legitimize its influence over the arms trade – has been the uncritical approach and belief that improvements to the European defence industrial base will result in advances in high end civilian technologies. This phenomenon, known as the 'trickle-down effect', is a claim made by defence manufacturers to ground their technologies in the civilian sphere, but is one countered by the campaigning organizations and NGOs (Gusterson 2004, 27-33). The European Commission, as the work of James March attests, has internalized both sets of the manufacturers' lobbying output. In the first instance the need to spend more on 'traditional' defence equipment, skewing procurement away from fulfilling the Petersberg tasks and into high end (and therefore expensive) technologies, but latterly in adopting the 'homeland security' agenda that allows manufacturers to develop high-end niche products (March 1994, 221-272). The internalization of these messages has been deepened by the formation of groups such as the European Advisory Group on Aerospace, which was established by the Commission in 2001 and whose membership includes representatives from the European Union's supranational institutions and arms manufacturers (European Commission 2006a).[3]

The composition of the Aerospace Advisory committee is worthy of note because of the 'Star 21' report recommending large increases in funding to aerospace companies, tax concessions, and favourable business conditions alongside the foundation of the 'Galileo' satellite system (European Commission 2002). More recently, in April 2005, the European Security Research Advisory Board (ESRAP) has been established by the Commission. Fourteen of the Board's 50 seats have been taken by industry representatives, a further 14 by academics and researchers, eighteen have gone to representatives of national security and defence ministries, whilst 4 seats have been occupied by EU officials (Hayes 2006, 25).

The lack of transparency of the Board is worrying given that it has been established and staffed in secret, holds meetings away from public or Parliamentary scrutiny, without public outputs, and whose remit is to advise the Commission on 'strategic missions' and priority areas for security research, including FP7. The Board also advises on implementation issues such as the exchange of classified information and intellectual property rights and on the use of publicly owned research/evaluation infrastructures. Whilst the absence of transparency should be of concern to those who hold democracy dear, this network is also acting to dominate the formulation of preferences, at the European level, to an entirely trade driven agenda that then serves to download these preferences to the national level and reinforce the effects of this network. For the purposes of analyzing Europeanization the main point is that domestic producer groups almost exclusively provide the interests that are adopted at the national and supranational level. At the core of European defence the governments issued their strategic preferences through the ESDP, which have now

---

3 Membership included Philippe Busquin (European Commissioner for Research), Pascal Lamy (European Commissioner for Trade), Erkki Liikanen (European Commissioner for Enterprise and the Information Society), Loyola de Palacio (Vice-President of the European Commission, responsible for Relations with the European Parliament, Transport & Energy) and Chris Patten, Member of the European Commission, Responsible for External Relations, Carlos Westendorp y Cabeza MEP (Chairman Industry, Foreign Trade, Research and Energy Committee) and Karl von Wogau MEP. Whilst from the arms manufacturers members included Jean-Paul Béchat, Chairman and CEO SNECMA, Manfred Bischoff, Co-chairman EADS, Sir Richard Evans, Chairman BAE Systems, Jean-Luc Lagardère, Co-chairman EADS, Alberto Lina, President and CEO Finmeccanica, Denis Ranque, Chairman and CEO THALES and Sir Ralph Robins, the Chairman of Rolls-Royce.

been steered by the effects of terrorist attacks on EU soil but also by the influential agenda of these industry interests.

The 2001, 2004 and 2005 attacks on New York, Madrid and London respectively are encouraging the acceleration of the Europeanization of the arms trade. Homeland security is a cross-pillar issue, situated in the Justice and Home Affairs pillar but increasingly pushed towards the security and economic spheres with the Commission showing an enthusiasm for promoting its role, and the utility of technology solutions to the threat posed by terrorists. These supranational policy entrepreneurs have succeeded, in this limited area, in taking defence research, development and procurement beyond the intergovernmental level. Therefore, whilst it is still technically possible to fall back on liberal intergovernmentalist theory that 'states are still in control', the Commission, the EDA and the manufacturers have made this suggestion all but redundant in the case of homeland security, and the technologies springing out of this agenda. This research suggests that the supranational level has gained a large influence over domestic research, development and procurement policy making intergovernmental negotiations less relevant in this sphere.

Product Design and Development

The first stage in any arms transfer is the design and development of marketable defence products, but it might also be the sale of old stock. Finding suitable products for domestic and international markets open to UK arms manufacturers is a key challenge in maintaining healthy order books. Accordingly, the British government's privileged knowledge of the requirements of external militaries is invaluable information to arms companies and is available from government sources, including DAs. While there is little evidence that suggests that UK government agencies, including the intelligence services, routinely play a commercial marketing role for arms companies, evidence exists of assistance being given to manufacturers when the government is uncertain of its investment in a project. At that point there is evidence that the intelligence services, in particular, are tasked to conduct intelligence-led assessments of a project's commercial viability. A notable example of this happening is in the case of the Merlin HM K1 helicopter produced by GKN Westland in the late 1980s (Dover 2007).[4] The majority of evidence points towards the process being geared towards arms companies creating equipment and systems and then making a great effort through lobbying and back channels to influence government policy into requiring these products (Tigner 2001). Because of competition between national industries – which is problematic for the reasons stated before – there seems to be very little information sharing between European governments on where opportunities lie, although with the increasing internationalization of the arms trade, companies are no longer tied to a single country affiliation.

A significant material advantage given to the UK's arms manufacturers comes in the form of research and development space on UK Ministry of Defence land. At

---

4 Commercial viability does not always equate to technical excellence however, and this project has received some inglorious reviews (Page 2006, Chapter 5).

sites near Bristol and in Wiltshire, for example, BAE Systems and their subsidiary companies, Thales, MBDA, and Raytheon have significant research and development units. The commercial basis on which these sites exist is not publicly available, but it is a note for future research that the extent to which the Ministry of Defence subsidises the arms trade through indirect subsidies like these is an important area for investigation. What the positioning of these research and development units do is to provide a day-to-day revolving door between UK military personnel, Ministry of Defence officials and the arms manufacturers. This relationship makes a great deal of sense given the sensitivity of the technologies being developed, and the control over the development of technology that the government wishes to exert.

However, this proximity does reduce the space between government officials and the arms manufacturers – the number of secondments from the Ministry of Defence and the armed forces to arms manufacturers and vice versa is an indication of a relationship that arguably constitutes a state-private network in its own right and is the key influence over national and supranational government policy on this issue.

An interesting paradox within British domestic policy formulation is that the manufacturers and European Commission are engaged in a rapid Europeanization of the arms trade whilst governments, and particularly the British government, are intent on an isolationist policy, so the assistance given to the manufacturers by the EU is actually aiding and abetting a policy outcome that the government does not favour.

The development of new technologies has traditionally occurred at the state level on the basis of national procurement requirements. The terrorist attacks on New York, Madrid and London since 2001, for example, have opened up new commercial possibilities for arms companies in the $100bn 'homeland security' market (Hayes 2006, 3; Taverner 2003). There is very little evidence that governments have been placing requirements on arms manufacturers to create products suitable for homeland security, aside from biometric identity cards in the UK. Rather, the manufacturers have been operating in a highly permissive environment in which technical innovations are openly welcomed by the government and in turn influencing government homeland security policy, demonstrating the important influence of informal networks in guiding these developments (Interview 14IS; Interview 25IS). The political salience of 'homeland security' has allowed companies to push cutting edge technologies enthusiastically to national governments and through European Commission committees, which has opened up the possibility for a fully Europeanized arms trade.

Given the EDA's research and development functions, and the potential it has to accelerate the Europeanization of the arms trade, the Agency's budget only covers the costs it incurs – so, for example, staff and building costs which runs to €1.9mil (on 2004 figures) (EDA 2006a). The Agency's influential research and development costs are funded by individuals or groups of member governments establishing and running projects through the EDA framework which appears to be a truly intergovernmental endeavour. The EDA acts as a facilitator for multinational projects and as a research organization able to identify gaps in the capabilities-catalogue and in national and supranational procurement projects. It also acts as a conduit for the complementary interests of arms manufacturers, their lobbyists and the European Commission, which has thus far steered the Agency's policy outputs.

The EDA is creating a culture change within the European arms trade. The Europeanization and internationalization of the arms trade has been underway for some time through acquisitions, mergers and joint working arrangements. What the EDA and the input of the Commission has provided is an institutional push – at the supranational level – for common procurement and increased defence equipment budgets; in its own words 'a coherent approach to EU procurement'. Officially, the EDA's tasks are set out in the core documents associated with the 2004 Joint Action. As a result the Agency has been asked to co-ordinate: "defence capabilities development; armaments co-operation; the European defence, technological and industrial base and defence equipment market; research and technology" (European Defence Agency 2006b). And:

> ..to work for a more comprehensive and systematic approach to defining and meeting the capability needs of ESDP (supporting, for example, the "Headline Goal 2010" initiative – which is clustered around the idea of forming up 'battlegroups'); to promote equipment collaborations, both to contribute to defence capabilities and as catalysts for further restructuring of the European defence industry; to promote European defence-relevant R&T, as vital both to a healthy defence technological and industrial base and to defining and satisfying future capability requirements. This will involve pursuing collaborative use of national defence R&T funds, in the context of a European policy which identifies priorities; to work, in close cooperation with the Commission, on steps towards an internationally competitive market for defence equipment in Europe (European Defence Agency 2006b).

The EDA is, therefore, an institution dedicated to reshaping European defence procurement and with it carries the political and economic aspirations of both the manufacturers and the Commission – and tangentially the economic aspirations of the British government.

Old Wars versus New Wars – Plotting a Strategic Direction

The Saint Malo process and the ESDP have not turned out to be particularly profitable for arms manufacturers in Europe. The 'capabilities catalogue', far from providing a flood of new orders, has refocused European governments on being able to deploy a minimum force level, based on prior capabilities. The manufacturers, their lobbyists and the Commission had hoped that the EU would attempt to close the capability gap between the EU members and the United States (Yost 2000; Kagan 2003). Unfortunately for the manufacturers the Petersburg Tasks, which frame the ESDP, demands that the money available is spent on filling low-technology capability gaps rather than developing high end technology to keep up with the technological advances made year on year by the American defence industrial base. The manufacturers, for obvious reasons, would like the EU to positively address this EU-US capabilities gap, and therefore seek to influence government policy in this regard.

The Global War on Terror (GWOT) and the homeland security agenda offers the Commission and manufacturers an opportunity to push through the advances in technology and increases to the budget that they clearly desire. The European Commission's enthusiasm for an active role in the EU's arms trade has existed since the mid-1980s. Successive Commission Presidents have provided economic justifications for their interest in the arms trade – arguments that resonate with the spurious economic arguments deployed in the national context (Oxford Research Group 2004). The Prodi Commission (1999-2004) typifies this approach having spent a great deal of time highlighting and working on promoting European defence industries as part of a broad portfolio of economic concerns (Morth 2000). Moreover, the codification of the ESDP in 2000 – despite the Commissioners' reluctance to become involved in the Saint Malo process – encouraged the Commission to become involved in defence industries as part of its wider interest in foreign and security policy. The Commission has belatedly realized that economic advantage and technological progress will not come from the ESDP. In a demonstration of the intergovernmental nature of defence and the arms trade, as a sub-set of defence policy, member governments have rejected the Commission's attempts to engage with traditional defence procurement areas.

However, in the post-9/11 world the Commission has been able to support and push for so-called 'dual-use' technologies with security applications. Ben Hayes lists these as including: 'Myriad local and global surveillance systems; the introduction of biometric identifiers; electronic tagging and satellite monitoring; "less-lethal weapons"; paramilitary equipment for public order and crisis management; and the militarization of border controls' (Hayes 2006, 3).

The arms manufacturers and the Commission have managed to take advantage of the homeland security agenda because of a series of fortuitous circumstances. First, national governments have responded to the threat posed by so-called Islamic terrorists in a securitized manner – the national emphasis has been on security-technology solutions to this threat (mostly surveillance and monitoring equipment). Second, government agencies involved in local and national security have been buying more equipment for their officers. In Britain there has been a large growth in the market supplying police with 'security technologies' as well as seeing an increase in the number of private security companies (Krahmann 2005; Kinsey 2005). Lastly, arms manufacturers and computer firms have found ways to collaborate on security projects – mostly in the fields of surveillance and counter-surveillance. In short, the political and economic agendas of the arms manufacturers, national governments and the European Commission have merged to create additional opportunities in this field. The interests that are aggregated by national and supranational governments are exclusively those of business interests, to the exclusion even of the armed forces.

The Licensing of Arms Sales

Before British military or dual-use equipment can be transferred to third countries (aside from government gifts) a DTI licence has to be obtained by the manufacturer. Eight criteria are used, and have to be considered by the DTI in deciding whether to grant a full licence to export military or dual use equipment. The information for the assessment is provided by manufacturers and triangulated against open and secret information provided by government departments. These politically but not legally binding criteria are: Respect for the UK's international commitments and obligations (UN and EU sanctions); respect of human rights and fundamental freedoms in the country of final destination; not exacerbating tensions in the country of final destination; preservation of regional peace, security and stability; the national security of the UK, of territories whose external relations are the UK's responsibility, and of allies, EU Member States and other friendly countries; the behaviour of the buyer country with regard to the international community, as regards in particular to its attitude to terrorism, the nature of its alliances and respect for international law; the existence of a risk that the equipment will be diverted within the buyer country or re-exported under undesirable conditions; the compatibility of the arms exports with the technical and economic capacity of the recipient country (FCO Document 2000).

The 'Smart Front End Committee' which considers all license applications, and sifts the contentious ones for further consideration, is composed of representatives from the MoD, FCO, DFID and DTI are taken on the basis of unanimity. Where consensus cannot be reached, discussions go to successively higher levels of officials (outside of a formal committee structure) until it reaches the political sphere with Junior Ministers, Secretaries of State and eventually the Prime Minister who, like officials, are politically but not legally bound to make their judgments with reference to the eight criteria. Ultimately, therefore, it is the decision of national politicians whether exports licenses are granted; the influence of lobbying money, party donations and the large number of ex-ministers with arms manufacturers directorships can only be speculated upon.[5] Whilst there is a European 'Code of Conduct' for arms sales, its recommendations are for national implementation rather than to police a 'European arms trade' at the supranational level. Control of licenses for military equipment are vested (in the British context) in the Department for Trade and Industry – because licensing is primarily a trade, rather than military or foreign policy issue area.

Arms sales and Defence equipment manufacturers almost invariably approach the government before commencing research or manufacturing work on a particular product to ensure that the start-up costs for either of these activities are not wasted through a straightforward license refusal. There are two formal processes whereby manufacturers make pre-license enquiries. One is known as the 'Ratings' process and the other as F680 process, and the assessments of a range of government departments, including the Defence Intelligence Staff (DIS) play a role in the replies companies receive (Interview 18IS; Interview 36IS; Scott 1996, C2.8-11, C2.29-31 and K7.2)

The F680 process is run by the Ministry of Defence, more precisely, the Directorate of Export Services Policy (DESP) within DESO (Scott 1996, C2.29-

---

5 For example, John Major is the European Director of the Carlyle Group, Malcolm Rifkind is the Chairman of Armor Group, and Michael Portillo was until May 2006 a Non-Executive Director of BAE Systems.

31). The process obliges 'List X' companies like BAE Systems, GKN and MBDA – who handle material with a classification of 'confidential' or above – to apply for a license before they promote their products. Materials requiring listing are provided in the 'Manual of Protective Security', which is issued by the Cabinet Office and often contains sensitive information about commercial agents in the country, political figures and general assessments about the stability or political situation within a particular region (Interview 04IS; Interview 23IS). There is reciprocity of information between the government and the arms manufacturers with commercially sensitive information being passed to UK government officials under a duty of confidentiality, but outside of a formal intelligence sharing arrangement (Interview 23IS; Scott 1996, E10.30-3). That this arrangement exists supports a central argument of this chapter that the British arms trade constitutes a state-private network of key government and industry officials. There is very little need for arms manufacturers to hold the types of information that they receive from the British government – the proximity between the government and the manufacturers suggests a tension between the Europeanization in the industry and the isolationism of the British government. However, the strength of the British arms trade and the closeness of the relationship between government and industry might be cause to think that the government is subtly uploading British preferences onto the European stage or that the manufacturers have managed to get their interests adopted at the national and supranational levels.

Non-List X companies (who can handle 'unclassified' or 'restricted' material) are not obliged to seek F680 clearance for promotions, but may need to have an F680 clearance to pursue full Licenses from the DTI (DESO 2005). The process helps prevent unauthorized disclosure of protective market (classified) assets; it gives companies an indication of what markets may provide viable export opportunities for their products, whilst also potentially speeding up the assessment of any eventual export license application made through the DTI (DESO 2005). The process can, however, be used to license an arms transfer that occurs outside the UK, and therefore represents a straightforward way of gaining authority for brokering arms. The F680 process involves the submission of a written application to the MoD using the F680 form. On receipt of the form, officials within DESP circulate the contents to 'MoD Advisors' – which includes a wide range of views from country and technical experts. (Interview 36IS; Interview 26IS. Interview 18IS).

Since 1999 F680 forms have also been circulated to the FCO and DFID for their assessments. The FCO circulate these forms to their Counter Proliferation, Country Officers and Human Rights Departments as well as MI6 (Interview 36IS). These assessments are based mostly on pre-existing information, but with some new intelligence information often forming part of the assessment, showing a reactive approach to creating assessments at the pre-licensing stage and places an emphasis on the quality of inter-agency information sharing and ad-hoc networks of officials.

The departments involved in the F-680 licensing process have lists of destinations they believe are problematic. The countries on their lists reflect the differing priorities and worries within the departments; and often replicate the stereotypes of particular departments (Interview 36IS; Interview 10IS). For example, the Treasury has concerns about whether a client government will pay, the DFID is concerned about the impact of a sale on development issues and future regional or national stability, the MoD on the implications for UK interests at home and abroad and the FCO on the implications for the stability of regions (Interview 36IS; Interview 13IS). The informality at this stage highlights the pro-trade preferences of the British government, that the process is resolutely state-based, and a willingness to deny pre-licenses only when overwhelming evidence is presented. At the full licensing stage the collection of information is far more pro-active with a greater emphasis on freshly collected sources.

The DTI run an independent process to F680 known as 'Ratings'. This process decides whether a license is required to export particular goods through the Export Control Organisation. Enquiries are made through the Export Control Organisation's Technical Assessment Unit which comprises a team of engineers and scientists all of whom have worked for arms manufacturers to advise exporters on technical issues; a structural position that belies the proximity of the government to arms manufacturers (DTI 2005; Interview 23IS). This is a change from the situation outlined by Sir Richard Scott, in his report on arms to Iraq, which highlighted the lack of expertise within the technical units at the DTI (Scott 1996, C2.8-11). The post-Scott arrangement is a powerful commercial tool and provides a partial explanation of why UK arms manufacturers are such successful exporters of materials around the world.

Contract Negotiation, and Sales

Once the manufacturers have received F-680 clearance they are free to engage in marketing activities to sell their products. Arms manufacturers are able to call upon the full machinery of the British state to support these efforts – depending on conditions that will be outlined – and this section demonstrates the extent to which the government views the arms trade as an extension of the national interest – contrary to a Europeanized policy.

DESO's role is to provide support for defence sales which includes research and providing negotiating assistance for manufacturers (Interview 24IS; Interview 36IS, Scott 1996, C2.22-3). DESO provides this support through its officials in London and in Embassies globally as well as through the Defence Attaché system (Scott 1996, C2.26). The EU has no comparative capability like DESO. It focuses, through the EDA, on capability assessment and research and development.

In September 2006 DESO was accused of helping manufacturers immorally profiteer from the Iraq war and the rapprochement with Libya – a document obtained under the Freedom of Information Act shows the efforts being made by DESO to ensure that British manufacturers secure entry into Iraqi and Libyan markets and demonstrates the single mindedness of DESO in achieving its goals (Barnett 2006). DAs are very well placed to provide 'privileged' information to arms manufacturers, in an ad hoc manner, as they are routinely invited to briefings by their host governments; as well as in the course of their duties networking with senior officials in their host nation's military. DESO regularly task DAs with providing various kinds of logistical, political or knowledge based assistance to manufacturers – which is in marked contrast to other governments. The DA's assistance feeds into every stage of the marketing, and sales process – making the DA the British government's person on the ground in these sales. Again, the EU has no comparative capability to this – because the EU has not entered into a direct selling arrangement with the arms trade, like national governments have done and because defence attachés are part of national militaries.

Unlike competitor nations, British arms manufacturers are able to contact DAs directly, establishing a discreet link between the provider and consumer of privileged information. DESO will provide, through its 'Partners Network', contact details of the relevant DA and Embassy staff that can assist throughout the life of the negotiation (DESO 2005a). The British government makes no charge for the DA's assistance in trying to secure contracts – this is in contrast to the charges made by Embassies for their assistance to other industries). The relationship between DESO, Attachés and manufacturers highlights the state-based foundations of the arms trade. The transformation of the trade to reflect commercial Europeanization (mergers and acquisitions) and political Europeanization (the Commission's efforts in R&D and strategic direction) is occurring outside of the state-based frameworks but with the British government keen to steer the Europeanization process.

British government assistance to manufacturers extends out to having the Defence Attaché and occasionally embassy officials present at the sales presentation to foreign government procurers (Dover 2007; Scott 1996, C2.26). Anecdotally, this is often a persuasive factor in any sales pitch – there is a badge of credibility carried by British officers because of the perceived quality of UK forces on active service and demonstrates the conflation of interests between the British government and arms manufacturers. Moreover, it provides a direct link through which British government support for a manufacturer can be made explicit to a foreign procurement official (Interview 24IS; Interview 18IS). The Embassy and the Attaché are also able to use their links with the foreign government to smooth over any problems that emerge during the negotiations and in extreme circumstances Ambassadors will be willing to write to the foreign Defence Ministers to press the case for procuring British arms (Interview 24IS; Interview 19IS). These roles step outside what the Embassy is officially tasked to do for an arms manufacturer but falls within the government's 'can-do' attitude towards arms transfers.

A high-profile measure of assistance from the British government is the official visit to potential customers from a high-ranking official from DESO or a Junior Defence Minister. In publicly important cases such as the negotiations with the Saudi government, the Secretary of State for Defence and even the Prime Minister will be involved in official visits, emphasising the political support given to the arms trade. DESO's close day-to-day relationship with the large UK-based arms manufacturers such as BAE Systems, means they are able to provide high-level support and advice to both the manufacturers and the Embassy staff that accompany official visitors. Circumstantial evidence of this close relationship can be seen with the current head of DESO, Alan Garwood, having previously been the head of sales at BAE Systems and his predecessor, Charles Masefield, worked for Vickers before running DESO to then go on to become vice-Chair of BAE Systems after leaving DESO in 1998. This interchange of government and commercial posts brings commercial experience to Whitehall and skews the government's policies and preferences towards certain outcomes. This is not so much the aggregation of domestic producer group pressure, than the import of institutional memory.

The Scott Report demonstrated the lengths to which the British government is prepared to go in support of a strategically sensitive and important transfer of arms (Scott 1996, K7.1-3). The examples, as previously mentioned, of high-level political support being afforded to BAE Systems' successful attempts to sell the Saudi Arabian government Eurofighter aircraft in a deal worth about £40bn, and the parallel attempts to sell military aircraft and small arms to India and Pakistan respectively during their nuclear stand-off in 2002, provides evidence of the full machinery of government supporting these transfers (Norton-Taylor and MacAskill 2002). Because the Saudi Arabian example is ongoing the evidence is largely circumstantial, however through official and secondary source reports it is clear that BAE Systems' marketing effort to the Saudi Arabian government has been supported at the very highest level by the Prime Minister and the Secretary of State for Defence, both of whom have made personal trips to Saudi in pursuit of this contract (Guardian 2005). Previous British Prime Ministers including Ted Heath, James Callaghan, Margaret Thatcher and John Major, as well as members of the British royal family have all intervened in large Saudi arms deals, the latter option is unavailable to French competitors due to their Republican constitution. This can be seen clearly in the example of the 'Al-Yamamah' deal in which the Saudis bought a fleet of Tornado aircraft (Financial Times 1988; Interview 03IS). Michael Turner, BAE Systems' Chief Executive, stated his recent aims clearly: 'The objective is to get the Typhoon into Saudi Arabia. We've had 43 billion pounds from Al Yamamah over the last 20 years and there could be another 40 billion pounds' (Flight International 2005). This deal has been complicated partly by reports that the Saudi Arabian government had agreed to buy 90 Rafale aircraft from French-based Dassault Aviation in April 2005, but also that the Saudis had demanded that the UK Serious Fraud Office (SFO) investigation into BAE Systems be dropped as part of the deal – a deal with a private British company, not the British government. The SFO investigation has looked at the legality of $2bn of commissions allegedly made to five agents in Saudi Arabia, and is a bone of contention between the two governments (Isenberg 2005).

The Saudi case study has all the prima facie elements to make it a good example of where centralized state support applies to the arms trade. It is a good example of where the British government has a clear interest in supporting a financially lucrative and strategically important transfer of arms and dual use technologies. What is more, the Saudi market represents a key area in which the British government has historically worked to suppress the competition presented by French defence companies partly because of the economic loss this would present, but also because of the number of human intelligence sources that can be placed in Saudi Arabia as a result (Interview 03IS). Within the British government's understanding of the arms industry it would be perverse and surprising therefore if the full machinery of the state, were not to be utilized in support of transfers that give the UK a balance of payments surplus and political leverage over events in the Middle East. The Saudi case study represents a strong example of national protectionism in the context of an arms industry that is clearly internationalising; a paradox within this issue area.

End-Use Monitoring

The end-user monitoring of arms and dual-use materials is also done on a state-level basis; with the exception of studies like the 'Small Arms Survey', which is compiled in Switzerland with the help of international non-governmental organizations (Small Arms Survey 2006). One of the curiosities within the British arms trade is that the UK Parliament is entirely excluded from licensing until after the transfer of materials is complete. There is no prior role for the House of Commons Quadripartite Committee, which scrutinizes strategic exports licenses and is constituted of the Select Committees of the MoD, FCO, DTI and DFID and came into existence in 1999.

The main function of the committee is to provide judgments about the licensing process in the previous parliamentary year and to do so largely on policy grounds rather than in respect of the detail of particular transfers (Interview 24IS; Interview 36IS). The Government has argued 'that prior scrutiny of export licence applications raises unacceptable constitutional, legal and practical difficulties' (Quadripartite Committee 2005). Moving scrutiny from post-hoc to prior would remove the delegated responsibility that the DTI holds within the arms transfer process, and also put pressure on the relevant government departments to respond transparently to questions that are posed to them about process, something the government has been unwilling to do even after the publication of the Scott Report.

The Quadripartite Committee argued in the 2001-2004 Parliament that there should be a limited trial of prior Parliamentary scrutiny, for example on government gifts of military equipment, which do not require a license. This would remove some of the latitude the government has to make arms transfers to governments that government-insider NGOs, like Saferworld, suggest have established track records in transferring arms to problematic destinations or are problematic recipients in their own right (Saferworld 2005). Moreover, there is little in the way of end-use monitoring of arms transfers by the government. The rationale for this is that once the manufacturer has cleared the F680 and full license process the potential for misuse or misappropriation of the materials transferred has been reduced beyond a point where it is 'economically feasible' for the government to investigate (Interview 24IS; Interview 26IS). Campaigners have argued that the British government should have taken action in high profile cases where end-use restrictions have been broken by recipient governments. These include the prohibition on the Indonesian government using Hawk jets in offensive operations over East Timor, the use of British made tanks in the occupied Palestinian areas, and armoured cars for internal repression in Uzbekistan (Norton Taylor 2005; Joffe-Walt 2006; Nevins 2002, 643). In these circumstances DAs are tasked, by the Government, to monitor the end use of these technologies, which is structurally problematic in the context of one of key functions being to facilitate arms sales. NGOs concerned with the arms trade have campaigned strongly for a formal system of end use monitoring, but this looks unlikely to be achieved in the short-term. The EU has been a strong supporter of humanitarian foreign policies including the restrictions on landmines and other 'problem' munitions, but as it becomes an advocate of expanding the EU's defence industrial base it also becomes subject to the tensions between a pro-sale and ethical concerns.

The final state-based government institution engaged in end-user monitoring is HM Customs and Excise. Customs Officials serve the function of monitoring and examining air, sea and land passengers and their baggage, freight and mail to ensure there is no smuggling of goods or goods in excess of established regulations (Scott 1996, C3.1-10; Butler 2004, 37). They process customs documentation and therefore have a role to play in the export of weapons and dual-use material. Customs officials played a significant role in the events leading to the Scott Inquiry, succeeding ultimately in interrupting an attempt to breach official government policy towards Iraq (Scott 1996, C3.1-71). Outside of this very high profile example of where two government departments worked against each other, Customs Officers play an important role in preventing the transfer of arms through the illegitimate trade, which is their main focus (Department of Trade and Industry 2005a; Butler 2004, 37-8). In the post-September 11 world there is a great deal more institutional co-operation between national 'policing' institutions – such as Customs and Excise, intelligence, and counter-proliferation units.

However, there remains a disparity between government support for the arms sales and efforts to monitor their end use. This can be explained through the disparity between the political motivation to sell military equipment and the less compelling desire to discover reasons for halting transfers and also for the state-based foundations on which the arms trade seems to rest; the competition between states drives the political motivation to export 'at all costs', while the EU seeks to increase the levels of trade through competition and cooperation between EU states and in competition with the other big arms exporting blocs – America, Russia and China.

Conclusion

The Europeanization of the arms trade is a multi-paced and multi-levelled political and economic phenomenon. European arms manufacturers have been subject to mergers and acquisitions that have effectively Europeanized the defence industrial base. Europeanization has become – to a lesser degree – internationalization with the enhanced presence of European firms in the American arms market and increased American ownership of European firms. The European Commission has manoeuvred to increase its influence over the European defence industrial base; including funding research and development projects. The British government appears to be on the slow-track of arms trade Europeanization as its day-to-day conduct is highly protectionist. However, even here the analysis is not clear cut – the British government lobbied very heavily to have Nick Witney installed as the Head of the EDA; a situation not dissimilar to the uploading tactics seen in the Saint Malo Accords (see Chapters 2 and 4). The British government's tactics seem to be to try to create the greatest possible value for 'UK Plc' from the inevitable Europeanization of defence industrial base commercially, whilst trying to shape the preferences and policies of the Commission. All these behaviours fit neatly within the liberal intergovernmentalist traditions of government action but with the large footnote that in this instance the EU's institutions and arms manufacturers are the most persuasive actors in the process.

From a national perspective, a key theme that emerged during this research was that UK government officials have elided the government's identity and interests with those of the commercial manufacturers. There was a notable use of collective terms by government officials such as 'we go and sell', 'we negotiate', and 'our kit' whilst maintaining a notable caution in providing information on the processes that lay behind transfers. However, the proximity and overlap of government and private officials, interests and movement of money suggests the governmental and private spheres have merged, raising large questions about the extent to which a state-private network operates within the British government.

The conflation of interests raises two points for further research, firstly about the efficacy of public money being spent in the promotion and facilitation of arms sales and secondly, whether the protection of sensitive markets for private businesses is a realization of an age old function of state – the further development of economic diplomacy. The privileged position of the defence industry in the decision-making processes of the government is a contested area. Explanations range from the extent to which defence manufacturers provide funding for political parties, to the level of integration and inter-changeability between employees of manufacturers and civil servants, right up to international political-economy critiques such as those made by Seymour Melman, for example, which argues that government officials are top-level managers of defence capitalism (Melman 1970, 13). There are also foreign policy-led explanations for the pre-eminence of defence industries, namely that high-end defence technologies produce additional political credibility for the British government on the international stage, through enhanced capabilities and trade links. What remains out of these many competing explanations, some of which require further empirical testing, is that defence manufacturers hold a special position within the British government's policy formulation processes and now hold an equally advantageous position within the European Commission and European Parliament's decision making apparatus.

The Europeanization of the arms trade at the supranational level has adopted the same inherent tensions that are present in national defence industry policies. The EU was, until the codification of the ESDP provisions within the Nice Treaty, a civilian superpower which had eschewed a military identity. The ESDP rapidly developed into a policy defined by the projection of humanitarian norms in peace-keeping and peace-support roles while 'high-end' security remained vested at the national level. However, the Europeanization of the arms trade has marched on apace – the Commission, in particular, has brought together the EU's economic superpower role with its involvement in defence industrial policy. More particularly, the Commission's thinking on defence industrial policy has been coloured by its view that the high-technology of the defence industries will spin-out to support advances in the civilian technology sectors.

The EU's work as an active supporter of non-proliferation looks set to continue. The Union has been at the forefront of initiatives to control the proliferation of small and light weapons and high-end military technologies (Manners 2002; Dover 2005). However, the EU has fallen into the same pattern of behaviour as the big EU defence exporting countries (Britain, France and Germany) who have used defence exports as a means by which to secure foreign policy leverage over client states. An example of this is the recent French and German government efforts to lift the arms embargo on the Chinese government – a move that deeply resonates with a trade agenda.

The Europeanization of the arms trade will continue apace so long as it is tied to European industrial policy and homeland security agendas. The involvement of the European Commission in defence research and the transnationalization of defence manufacturers will only serve to deepen and widen Europeanization. The corollary to this is the behaviour of European member states who have continued to adopt protectionist policies towards their defence manufacturers. In this respect the manufacturers and Commission appear to be more progressive than member governments who have yet to realize that the arms trade has internationalized. A point for further research is the extent to which lobbyists at the supranational level can generate European policies that are imposed on member governments, and furthermore, impose policies on member governments than run contrary to the interests of member governments. This represents a potential paradox of Europeanization.

Conclusion

Europeanization is a multileveled and multi-paced political phenomenon. The contrast between the negotiation of the ESDP, which was conducted exclusively between governments, and the Europeanization of the arms trade, which is talking place almost exclusively outside the control of governments, is marked. Similarly, the pace of Europeanization has varied greatly. For nearly fifty years, after the Second World War, the Europeanization of defence outside of NATO structures, proceeded at a snail's pace and with a great deal of reluctance from large parts of the European defence community. Yet between October and December 1998 an agreement was formulated and signed that uprooted previous European thinking on the subject. Furthermore, the attacks on Madrid and London in 2004 and 2005 have presented the European Commission and arms manufacturers with the opportunity to Europeanize the arms industry (albeit through a vanguard of homeland security equipment) that will, in all likelihood, result in a pan-European defence procurement, and research and development base. Europeanization can perhaps be typified as an opportunistic phenomenon; requiring the fortunate placement of key political and bureaucratic figures and historical contingency to succeed.

The institutional actors involved in Europeanization are national governments and their departments, the central institutions of the European Union, and sectional interest groups such as manufacturers, universities, think-tanks, the armed forces and lobbyists. The case study of defence integration highlights that Europeanization of one policy is often dependent on the progress or status of other issues. For example, whilst the ESDP was negotiated as a discreet item at the Nice IGC, its origins lay in the British government's unwillingness to participate in the single currency project. Further integration –from 2003 onwards – has been hindered by the European wide schism brought about by the British government's decision to join America's war of choice against Iraq.

Whither the State? Europeanization to Trans-Nationalization

The structures of state – governments, government departments, their officials and the politicians that control them, are vital to the formal Europeanization of policies. The 'large' EU governments (Britain, France and Germany) have a particularly sizeable influence on the direction and speed of Europeanization in general, but specifically within defence integration. Put starkly, ESDP could not have happened without the convergence of member state preferences. The creeping influence of the European Commission in defence policy has been undermined by the preeminent role of governments. Whilst the Commission had limited involvement in the negotiation of the ESDP – a self-denying ordinance based on a belief that the convergence of national interests across Europe was only possible if it was seen to be outside of the process – the first few years of the ESDP in operation has seen the

Commission take a renewed interest in external relations and the military facets of that policy. The Commission has, therefore, allowed itself to become involved in Europeanization – deepening security integration and pressing for a more prominent role in EU external relations policy.

Moreover, in the case of the arms trade, the Commission has played a very prominent role in advancing the direction and level of arms sales; including directing research and development money. Balancing its role as a funder of defence research and development and yet a constraint on the proliferation of these technologies, the Commission is gaining state-like attributes. It is interesting to note that it has tacitly adopted the tensions inherent the state activity on the arms trade – the problem of promoting trade versus promoting arms control; a tension that resolves itself at the state level at promoting the sale of equipment unless there are compelling reasons not to.

The final institutional set of actors within Europeanization are sectional and producer group interests. This research has argued that think-tanks and institutional interests – apart from large business interests – have very little influence over the Europeanization of defence, aside from to offer vocal support for the policies being pursued. The exception of business is made because of the influence of the major European arms manufacturers in directing the Europeanization of the arms trade, procurement and the continued securitization of homeland security. Arms manufacturers have made use of state-private networks at the domestic and European levels to ensure the policies at both these levels advance their interests. The British government, the European Commission and parts of the European Parliament have all elided their interests with the interests of the major arms manufacturers. The success of the manufacturer's strategy has been to tie their interests domestically to the relative success of the economy, and to Britain's influence around the world; and supranationally to a cross-pillar agenda that makes arms sales a part of routine European trade. This study has further argued that the manufacturers are at the forefront of expanding their international horizons having successfully entered American defence markets (and vice-versa), which means they now effectively engage in a global trade that transcends the European.

What all of these examples highlight is the extent to which sovereignty has been transferred, gifted or eroded from the control of national governments; and therefore this transfer is a key element of Europeanization. The EU is, at its core, a tool by which governments can express and secure their national interests; but as we have seen the influence of supra- and trans-national actors and interests can advance distinct European agendas over and above the core interests of national governments. When governments purposefully seek to transfer elements of their sovereignty to the EU they do so on the basis that this locks in governments, preventing defections from intergovernmental agreements and thus binding one legislature to another.

The concept of sovereignty has played an important role in the European integration literature and in popular discourse about the UK's role in the EU. In broad terms, sovereignty can be defined as what ties the international to the domestic through linking independence from outside interference (autonomy) with the government's authority over its internal jurisdiction (Hinsley 1986, 158). This is also known as the 'Westphalian System' and as Francis Hinsley argues, '…these two assertions are complementary. They are the inward and outward expressions, the obverse and reverse sides of the same idea.' James Caporaso argues that the importance of Westphalian concepts of sovereignty are to demonstrate that domestic and international political systems are distinct and to also show how the domestic and international political systems interact with each other (Caporaso, 1996, 26-52). This system is premised on the role of national boundaries and third party governments respecting the internal authority of their partner governments. This approach is limited when applied to the EU because of the multiple levels of governance in the Union as a product of the transfer of national sovereignty to supranational institutions.

The creation and operation of the EU is premised on the delegation and pooling of sovereignty. Indeed, many analysts like Tanja Börzel, James Caporaso, and Liesbet Hooghe have argued that an important consequence of European integration (and sovereignty transfer) is that the autonomy and authority of EU governments is weakened (Börzel and Risse 2000, 45-59; Caporaso 1996, 29-52; Hooghe and Marks 2001; Risse-Kappen 1996, 53-80; Sweet and Sandholtz 1997, 297-317). Approaches to sovereignty within the EU have focused on the multi-levelled nature of actors and authority within the Union. The constructivist approach has argued that sovereignty and statehood are inter-subjective rather than a description of facts (Jachtenfuchs 1997, 43). Liesbet Hooghe and Gary Marks argue that, '..one does not have to argue that states are on the verge of political extinction to believe that their control of those living in their territories has significantly weakened' (Hooghe and Marks 2001, 27). Hooghe and Marks also argue that 'authority' rather than the competencies a government holds, is the crucial determinant of sovereignty (Hooghe and Marks 2001, 5-6). Moreover, they argue that economic and political control by the EU affects the ability of member governments to act and that governments cannot be said to be sovereign if the only competency they retain is the defence of their territory (Marks, Hooghe and Blank 1996, 431-378). Other multilevel governance theories, like that advanced by Ben Rosamond, describe the EU in broad terms encapsulating power relationships at different moments during policy formulation and negotiation. Analysis of these interchanges leads to Rosamond's description of the EU as a 'polycentric polity' – a political system with multiple sites of substantial political control (Rosamond 1999).

Alexander Wendt's approach to the question of sovereignty is informed by practical considerations. He advances the argument that if governments deal with each other in a way that indicates they believe they are sovereign, they are (Wendt 1992, 410). Furthermore, Wouter Werner and Jaap de Wilde argue that '…the reality of sovereignty consists in its use and acceptance' (Werner and de Wilde 2001, 304). There is, therefore, no settled position concerning the EU and national sovereignty but there is a growing and diverse literature on the subject. This research fits within the literature on Westphalian sovereignty because it argues that sovereignty transfer was a critical element in the British government's negotiating positions concerning ESDP. It further suggests that in the post Nice IGC era, and with the developments in the homeland security agenda, 'Westphalian' concepts of sovereignty within the EU suffer from varying degrees of false consciousness. The ability of any European state to act autonomously in the defence sector – be it projecting military power, in procurement, or in homeland security – has been replaced by a complex set of transnational interactions between governments, state agencies and industrial interests. Governments formally establish the arrangements through which most of these interactions take place; however the development of the Europeanized arms trade has highlighted how the European Commission and manufacturers can do this outside of state-created institutions.

The transfer of sovereignty from the British government to the EU as a result of the ESDP negotiations was very limited. The key areas in which the transfer of defence and security sovereignty has occurred is in line with a liberal intergovernmentalist critique that EU negotiated outcomes reflect and codify informal arrangements between member governments. Peacekeeping in the Balkans, for example, established good levels of cooperation between British and French armed forces in the field. The ESDP negotiations focused on issues where common interests lay. Examples of this lie in agreements which have already been reached on research, development and procurement projects through the single market provisions, resulting in projects like Eurofighter Typhoon.

The significance of the Europeanization of defence lies in the potential it has to take European defence and security policy into areas where eventually larger transfers of sovereignty will occur.

Formulating a Europeanized Defence Policy

Domestic policy formulation has proved to be a rich area of inquiry for this research. The formulation of preferences and policies, to use Moravcsik's taxonomy, is a crucial part of the formal Europeanization of domestic policy. It was particularly crucial in the negotiation of the ESDP 1998-2000; in which a convergence of British and French government preferences were required for negotiations to succeed. In the context of minor changes in British defence policy that have often taken years to finalize, the Saint Malo accords were completed with unusual haste. This speed was the product of the PM's desire to announce publicly, a pro-European policy initiative that would be seen as credible to Britain's European partners and his involvement in the policy – including resolving the debate between the FCO and MoD – lends weight to the notion that Saint Malo was a cornerstone of Labour's first term European policy.

The preferences at the heart of Labour's European defence policy have remained consistent across all the examples presented in this book. Their core desire – to be a 'force for good' in the world – is strained by the war in Iraq and by the supply of weapons to fragile regions, but on the government's understanding of its own actions these policies remain consistent with this core goal. Similarly, the preference for collaborative rather than unilateral defence ventures to build credible coalitions of the willing, constitutes another facet of the preferences behind ESDP, Britain's international security commitments and the practice, but not necessarily the theory behind British arms trade policy.

Stable, historical 'preferences' are an effective way to examine the formulation of British defence policy. The transatlantic security preference has driven the British government's efforts to create an ESDP that supports, rather than undermines NATO;

motivates the government's internal EU diplomacy, its decisions over Iraq and its procurement strategies. In the case of Saint Malo, the Cabinet Office, MoD and FCO officials invested a great deal of time in meetings with other EU government and US State Department officials to secure the continued pre-eminence of NATO to European security. If the Saint Malo initiative was a fundamental shift of preferences – as some claim – it is unlikely that UK officials would have invested so much time ensuring that the trans-atlantic security guarantee was a prefix to every public announcement on this policy.

Liberal intergovernmentalist approaches to Europeanization argue that that domestic policy is created through the rational aggregation, by government, of domestic interest group preferences. In the case of Saint Malo and the ESDP these domestic interest groups were difficult to find, particularly given the evidence that the policies had been formulated by the core executive and then they had gone out to seek support for this new policy from key interest groups. The influence of interest groups on the Saint Malo initiative domestically varied greatly, but the positioning of key policy officials was a crucial determinate in the progression of the policy. For example, Richard Hatfield, as the Policy Director of the MoD, is said to be the originating author of the Saint Malo initiative. The positioning of other officials involved in interdepartmental relations and advising the PM about policy, such as Emyr Jones-Parry as Policy Director of the FCO and Stephen Wall as the head of the European Secretariat of the Cabinet Office, were also important but less crucial. Although driven initially by the MoD the agreement of the Cabinet Office and FCO gave the initiative credibility and momentum within Whitehall, which facilitated its development for negotiation at the European Council at Nice. These developments were of course also assisted by the fortuitous positioning of key political allies like Peter Mandelson, Minister without Portfolio and George Robertson, Secretary of State for Defence (1997-1999) who offered cabinet level support for the initiative and on his personal staff, Roger Liddle, his personal political advisor (now of the European Commission), and within the Cabinet Office Stephen Wall who, as former UK ambassador to the EU, was able to offer keen insights into how the British negotiators would be able to deliver their package of measures.

The analysis of domestic policy formulation within this study touches upon a growing body of literature on epistemic communities – '…agents working on a commonly acknowledged subset of knowledge issues and who at the very least accept a commonly understood procedural authority as essential to the success of their knowledge activities' (Cowan and Foray 2000, 212-253). The outcome from the Saint Malo initiatives were driven by a small group of influential actors within the MoD, FCO, Downing Street and European Secretariat of the Cabinet Office support the notion that the core executive was an epistemic community. The decision to go to war in Iraq was similarly decided a small clique of the political, intelligence and civil service core executive, whilst the arms trade is run – at the Board Room and political level – by a state-private network of interlocking and exchangeable arms manufacturers, Cabinet and Junior Ministers, and Ministry of Defence and Department of Trade and Industry Officials. Policy formulation at this micro-level brings out the politics of personalities and the role of well placed policy activists.

However, without the structural context these micro-level analyses only tell part of the story.

Research on epistemic communities can be located within a broader literature concerning public administration that has focused on theories of networking, governance, institution building and cooperation. The work of James March and Johan Olsen has explored the impact of the infrastructure of political institutions and how this impacts on policy formulation (March and Olsen 1984, 738; Weaver and Rockman 1993). Institutional explanations of policy-making argue that officials mould institutional policy preferences and that the importance of leadership provided by politicians and officials cannot be underplayed. Moreover, Peter Haas has expanded the notion of community within these groups defining them as '...[A] network of professionals with recognized expertise and competence in a particular domain and an authoritative claim to policy relevant knowledge within that domain or issue-area' (Haas 1992, p.3). All the accounts of domestic policy formulation presented within this book can be analysed in these terms and locating these processes within this extant literature provides an avenue for future research.

Sectional interest groups like the armed forces only had a limited role in the decision to adopt Europeanized defence policies. The armed forces were ostensibly ambivalent about the war in Iraq, seeking legal clarification before carrying out the invasion. The forces are a key element, in political and human resource terms in the arms trade's state-private network and European military industrial complex. There is a growing body of evidence that despite their close involvement in research, development and procurement the British armed forces do not hold a great deal of influence over arms manufacturers or the procurement process (Page, 2006). Furthermore, Saint Malo would have been politically difficult for the PM to sign if the Chief of Defence Staff, Lord Guthrie, had been opposed to it, just as the Iraq campaign was made more problematic for the Prime Minister by the request from Admiral Sir Michael Boyce about its legality.

The preferences of commercial and manufacturing interest groups played a less significant role in the ESDP process than one might have reasonably expected – the evidence from the first few years of the ESDP reflects this; since defence manufacturers have benefited very little from it in terms of new orders. However, in the development of a Europeanized defence policy, and particularly in homeland security and counter-terrorism, the arms manufacturers, along with the European Commission are playing a very large role in generating additional research and development projects and in providing procurement requirements. The overly 'securitized' response from European governments to the perceived threat from terror has opened up these opportunities but the manufacturers have been very effective in using their insider position with the British government and the European Commission to steer favourable outcomes on these issues.

Sectional interest groups and analysts, like the Centre for Defence Studies, King's College London, Bradford University's Department of Peace Studies, the Heritage Foundation in the United States, the International Security Information Service, Demos, RUSI and the Centre for European Reform, continue to exert pressure and influence on UK government policy through publications, policy forums and informal meetings with politicians and officials engaged in UK defence policy formulation. However, there is very little evidence that this pressure affects the British government's approach to defence policy. Sympathetic hearings for government policy, such as that given by the Centre for European Reform's Charles Grant to the Saint Malo proposal and, for example, by two Demos reports to the commercial securitization of homeland security, merely provide favourable mood-music to current initiatives (Demos 2005; Demos 2006).

Intergovernmental Negotiations

Intergovernmental bargaining is the second element of the formal Europeanization of British defence policy. The liberal intergovernmentalist perspective from which this book has been written highlights the rationality of governments when negotiating at the European level. Following Robert Putnam this rationality occurs at the supranational and domestic levels, as he puts it 'the two-level game' (Putnam 1992, 436). The essence of his work is that governments negotiate to maximize their national interests in an issue specific area or across a broad range of issues but that any agreement struck between governments must also satisfy interests within domestic constituencies. In short, no national government can negotiate and agree to measures that jeopardize the electoral survival of the government.

A practical example of this comes through the series of informal negotiations between the UK and French governments, particularly the respective British and French Ministries of Defence, which were based on a series of lowest common denominator agreements (Walter 2003).[1] However, this is not the case for the multiple bi-lateral negotiations between UK officials bargaining with officials from other EU governments. This type of negotiation developed along higher than lower common denominator lines, because vetoes were likely to be used in security and defence policy if the proposed agreement went beyond a perceived domestic win-set.

Similarly, issue linkage, log-rolling and side-payment negotiating tools were not present in the ESDP negotiations at Nice, although the negotiated outcome was greater than lowest common denominator because less influential governments were able to incorporate these in the final policy without disrupting the core tenets of the agreement. However, a fundamental reality of this type of government behaviour is the political judgment of what is and is not electorally significant. The decision to go to war with Iraq prompted a large public response – over a million people marched through London on February 16 2003 – and received a similarly severe response from European Heads of State. Nevertheless, the Prime Minister and his government judged correctly that the war with Iraq would not cost them the 2005 General Election.

When it comes to the formal Europeanization of defence, governments are the principal units in the international system but not all governments have the same influence over the direction of European negotiations. Their influence is determined by their respective interest in security and defence policy, their ability to project their

---

1 This conclusion feeds into an emerging niche political literature in German political science known as 'Durchwelsten' which argues that policy formulation is an iterative product of successive lowest common denominator agreements.

preferences and create coalitions of governments around a policy area. Evidence of this is provided by the agreed texts at Saint Malo and the Presidency Conclusions of the European Council at Nice that outline the ESDP – the final negotiated output remained very faithful to the spirit of the original text – a point that was highlighted by key members of the British negotiating team in interview evidence. In the case of the ESDP the European Commission and Parliament had particular views which they asserted in the General Affairs Council at Nice but which were excluded by the member governments from the informal bi- and multi-lateral negotiations between the government on ESDP. However, once the ESDP framework was established the European Commission and Parliament have been able to exert some useful pressure in shaping the direction of ESDP, through the extension of peacekeeping and peace support operations in Africa (through Operation Artemis) and in the Balkans.

The self-created perception of defence as an area of core sovereignty meant that the negotiating parameters established by the British and French MoD and Foreign Office negotiating teams were extremely difficult to break. The absence of persuasive interest groups opposing the policy and a very large Parliamentary majority gave UK negotiators considerable leeway. The red-lines established by the UK core executive were difficult to breach partly because of a self-imposed discipline and partly because of the public expression of these red-lines by the FCO. The outcome of Saint Malo, which was exceptional within post-second world war and EU history, was a lowest common denominator agreement between France and the UK. The common interests between the French and UK governments were, for some interviewees, surprisingly considerable and enough to create a substantive policy initiative. To achieve convergence between the other EU governments at the Nice European Council, the original Saint Malo outcome was extended through allowing policy tools to be added to the final agreement by post-neutral countries like Ireland and Sweden such as humanitarian and peace support roles.

The negotiated ESDP therefore provides a lowest common denominator agreement between all the European governments, as the Presidency Conclusions did not breach any of their fundamental preferences. Importantly, then, the Saint Malo negotiations were the crucial moment in the development of the ESDP, rather than the IGC at Nice, which would be a more natural site of substantive progress. Whilst governments were still the principal players in these negotiations it reduces the importance of the IGC in the formal Europeanization of defence and means that researchers should focus more sharply on the meetings that lead up to IGC negotiations.

Governments act as gatekeepers between the domestic and international bargaining tables. The evidence from the case studies presented in this book strongly supports this view. This gatekeeper role serves to keep domestic political actors from the international bargaining table. The negotiations at the Nice European Council were conducted by a small cadre of negotiators from the Cabinet Office, COREPER, FCO and MoD. These negotiators were few in number and acted on behalf of their departments with delegated authority around the red-lines established by the PM and core executive. These negotiators would only refer back to their department when they felt an issue was close to the agreed red-lines or was an area without an established departmental position. Aside from these narrow circumstances the officials and ministers acting as negotiators operated in a vacuum with control over the flow of information back to their home departments.

Neither parliamentarians, nor Labour party officials were kept informed of how the negotiations were proceeding. The co-ordination between the UK MoD, FCO, Downing Street, European Secretariat of the Cabinet Office and UKREP before the Nice negotiations (February-December 2000) clearly established British negotiating positions. The UK negotiating team placed great emphasis on the coordination of the negotiating strands, through COREPER, and in briefing the political negotiators about the issue area and how British interests might be maximized. This research strongly suggested that the UK negotiating team acted in a closely coordinated way facilitating their role as a gatekeeper between the domestic and international bargaining table.

ESDP was negotiated separately from the institutional and procedural reforms that were a significant part of the business at the Nice European Council and there was therefore, very little issue linkage. Evidence from the British negotiating team at Nice suggested that the negotiations concerning ESDP were all but concluded before the final four days of the IGC at Nice (7-11 December 2000). The gatekeeper role was also present when the British government held the Presidency of the EU in 2005, although the development of the ESDP and the processes behind the European arm trade highlight how supra- and trans-national actors are able to circumvent the gatekeeper role of government by deepening integration without going back to governments' for successive permissions.

In the formal Europeanization of defence policy – through Treaty amendment – not only are governments the principal actors in the international system, but the EU is merely a forum through which the co-ordination of national policies can be regulated by a third party without needing to continually create new agreements. An important function of ESDP is that it serves as a way of avoiding having to create new agreements between governments for each new piece of defence policy collaboration. In ESDP this should be limited because of the scope of operations that can be conducted in the policy's name; however where defence policy takes on cross-pillar dimensions (notably with the arms trade and homeland security) a greater degree of control over policies is vested within the supranational institutions of the EU.

A Liberal Intergovernmentalist Revival?

This book has been written from a liberal intergovernmentalist slant, because this approach offers the largest number of analytical assumptions and hypotheses about Europeanization. This approach has been subject to a number of theoretical critiques (Budden 2002; Young 1999, 805-10; Diez 1999; Wincott 1995; Forster 1998; Caporaso, Scharpf and Wallace 1999). Some of the criticisms in the extant literature have argued that international negotiations are not a process in which governments try to maximize national interests in each issue area. Furthermore, they argue that negotiators are willing to accept disadvantageous negotiations on some issues providing that the entire negotiated package has more potential benefits than costs (Peterson and Bomberg 1999; Richardson 1996, 14-24). These criticisms have not been validated by the example of the ESDP negotiations.

Philip Budden, Anthony Forster and Helen Wallace have argued that LI fails to take full account of the role of the EU's supranational institutions and does not adequately explain the process by which governments formulate policy (Budden 2002; Forster 1999). The evidence presented in this book reinforces and extends these views. In the case of the ESDP, British domestic policy formulation was not a process by which governments aggregate the preferences of domestic interest groups.

Rather, it was a process in which the core executive, in the context of positive externalities and an ideological platform, created a distinctive policy goal and then sought support from domestic producer groups. This research has highlighted that the formulation of British defence policy was not motivated by the preferences of domestic producer groups but was driven by a core executive of officials and politicians in Downing Street, the MoD and FCO. Furthermore, the European Commission and European Parliament (through key actors) have been able to advance Europeanized defence initiatives outside of the control of national governments – which suggests that greater attention needs to be paid to the Commission as an actor in Europeanization. This conclusion adds to the analysis of Budden and Forster who argue that LI's account of domestic policy formulation is inadequate and requires theoretical correctives.

The question of whether this book provides a revival of liberal intergovernmentalist theory overstates the case somewhat. Liberal intergovernmentalist approaches provide a useful way to analyse Europeanization – it is important to explore the domestic and European dimensions within Europeanization, which actors and institutions are involved and the behaviours they adopt. Where the approach falls short is in underestimating the influence of the EU's central institutions, and the linkages between very different aspects of EU policy on governments and negotiators. However, in suggesting patterns of behaviour amongst government officials and politicians this approach is highly informative, and importantly highly testable, opening up possibilities to conduct interesting empirical research on important Europeanization issues.

Europeanized Defence?

When British and French negotiators began their dialogue in 1997 – that resulted in the ESDP – all options were possible. For the French government, the utopia in 1997 of a European army and a common European defence separate from NATO was a theoretical possibility. For the British this dystopia was to be avoided at all costs. The British preference was for a European force that could support the Americans in wars of choice and show the EU to be capable of resolving issues on its own backdoor. Several years on and the path of ESDP now seems set; NATO is the pre-eminent security institution within Europe and the EU, acting in its own name, performs peace-keeping, peace-support and advanced policing roles. As part of a broader security identity it has been at the forefront of arms control and actions against landmines, as well as to provide force multiplication assistance to areas under post-conflict reconstruction. In these areas integration and operational experience has deepened, but not widened in the intervening time. This is not the case in procurement and homeland security where Europeanization has both widened and deepened at the behest of the European Commission, the European Defence Agency and the manufacturers, assisted by states that have radically securitized their policing and counter-terror agendas.

The great fear of eurosceptics, certainly in Britain, is that even the relatively small step that ESDP represents will result in a fully fledged European army and collective European defence. This simply has not been borne out by the first four years of the ESDP in operation. The US-UK war against Iraq has made collective EU military action – outside of NATO structures – problematic and looks likely to have consigned the ESDP into its peace-support activities for the medium term, at least. However, in the field of counter-terrorism and homeland security there are strong signs of Europeanization – through the proliferation of common practices and procurement.

A Europeanizing Future?

The example of the Europeanization of British defence policy has illuminated wider trends in the transformation of the British state and the European Union. Away from the excitable rhetoric of eurosceptic newspapers and politicians, the European Commission and European Parliament are gaining a foothold in the provision of defence and security in the EU area. It is clear that governments remain the final arbiters of all that goes on in the EU – all states retain the right to repeal their accession to the European Union and mostly have the right to veto provisions or to not sign treaty amendments that extend European powers. However, Europeanization is only partly about big treaty-based advances; it is mostly about small amendments, institutional tweaks and subtle developments. Certainly in the defence sphere European governments have absolute control over the large treaty-based developments. The codification of the ESDP at Nice was a triumph of Anglo-French diplomacy that saw a meaningful convergence of national interests. Once Treaty amendments are enacted, however, there are opportunities through entrepreneurial activism or through bureaucratic inertia for Europeanization to be deepened.

The specifics of the ESDP and the arms trade demonstrate the extent to which the EU institutions and big business can shape Europeanization. In this specific example the 'securitization' of domestic policing and counter-terrorism policies has allowed manufacturers and the European Commission to advance a Europeanized industry in advanced policing and surveillance technologies.

Finally, the real question that comes out of studies into Europeanization and the public's perception of these developments is the extent to which we are less British now, that the British government has less control of its or our collective destiny because of advances in the European project. The answer to this, rather large question, is that whilst a 'golden age' of state autonomy has in all probability never existed, and the British people and its government are subject to the influence, and pressure of supranational and transnational political and economic concerns, both in its domestic and European policies. The business of government has undoubtedly changed since the UK's entry to the EEC in 1972. Greater consideration has to be given to the decisions of an external body, and implemented into national law, even if this against the national interest.

In a softer way, the British way of doing politics has been forced to recognize a European way of working. The extent to which these realities affect 'British' or 'European' identities is less clear – the man on the street in Bristol still feels British and still has his British customs; even though he might eat food inspired by the Indian sub-continent and drink coffee inspired by the Turks. The transformation of the British state, certainly in defence, but perhaps on other issues as well, lies in the realization that independent state action is no longer as important as collective state action. How effectively the UK formulates partnerships within the EU, and uploads it preferences into the supranational level is now more important than its actions as a unitary state. This is the real lesson of Europeanization.

Bibliography

Acquantine, E (3 October 2002), *France pushes for EU defence industry* (Pravda: Moscow).

Aerospace and Defence Industries Association Website - http://www.asd-europe.org/ , accessed 4 August 2006.

Agence Europe (26 October 2004), *United States may destroy some Galileo satellites if used by hostile power* (Agence Europe: Paris).

Agence France Presse (25 April 1999), *Balkan states around Yugoslavia are to be offered a multi-million dollar political and economic aid package to bolster wavering support for NATO action over Kosovo, British newspapers reported on Sunday* (Agence France Presse: Paris).

Agence France Presse (21 March 2005), *Britain in bid to postpone EU lift on China arms ban* (Agence France Presse: Paris).

Agencies (30 June 2006), *Israel Pounds Gaza Targets* (The Guardian: Manchester).

Ahmed, K and Hinscliff, G (4 June 2000), *Blair appoints Euro 'enforcer' to crack whip* (The Observer: London) 4.

Albright, M (7 December 1998), *The Right Balance will secure NATO's future* (Financial Times: London).

Alexander, M and Garden, T (2001), *The Arithmetic of Defence Policy* International Affairs, 77(3) 509-529.

Allan, J (1998), *The British Labour Party in Opposition 1979-1997, Structure, Agency and Party Change, Unpublished Thesis* (University of Connecticut: Connecticut).

Allen, D (1996), *Conclusions: The European Rescue of National Foreign Policy* in Hill, C (ed.) *The Actors in Europe's Foreign Policy* (Routledge: London) 288-304.

Allen, R (1 May 2002), *Labour spins every 4 minutes* (Evening Standard: London) 6.

Andreani, G, Bertram, C and Grant, C (2001), *Europe's Military Revolution* (Centre for European Reform: London).

Arnold, C (2002), *How Two-Level Entrepreneurship Works: The Influence of the Commission on the Europe Wide Employment Strategy – Conference Paper* (American Political Science Association: Washington).

Asmus, R et al (1996), *Can NATO Survive?*, The Washington Quarterly 19(2) 79-101.

Assembly of the WEU (3 June 2003), *Document A/1817 Parliamentary scrutiny of the ESDP in national Parliaments –debates and replies to Parliamentary questions tabled in WEU countries* (Assembly of the Western European Union: Brussels).

Austrian Presidency of the European Union (25 October 1998), *Austrian Presidency Informal Summit Press Conference*, Reproduced in Maartje Rutten (2001) *From Saint Malo to Nice* (Western European Institute for Security Studies: Paris) 1-3.

Axelrod, R and Keohane, R (1996) *Achieving Cooperation under Anarchy. Strategies and Institutions*, in Oye, K (ed.) *Cooperation under Anarchy* (Princeton University Press: New Jersey) 226-254.

Bahgat, G (2006), *Nuclear proliferation: The Islamic Republic of Iran*, Iranian Studies 39(3) 307-327.

Bailes, A (1996), *European defence and security: The Role of NATO, WEU, and EU*, Security Dialogue 27(1) 55-64.

Bailes, A (2000) *Under a European Flag* (Foreign and Commonwealth Office: London).

Balz, D (2 October 1997), *Britain's Prime Minister assumes Presidential air, Blair uses strong personality to consolidate power* (The Washington Post: Washington DC) A20.

Barkawi, T and Laffey, M (2001), *Democracy, Liberalism, and War: Rethinking the Democratic Peace Debate* (Lynne Reiner: London).

Barnett, A (20 November 2005), *Prescott blasts 'fop' envoy over book earnings* (The Observer: London).

Barnett, A (24 September 2006), *MoD targets Libya and Iraq as 'priority' arms sales targets* (The Observer: Manchester).

Bartley, W (1964), *Rationality versus the Theory of Rationality* in Mario Bunge (ed.) *The Critical Approach to Science and Philosophy* (The Free Press of Glencoe: London) 3-31.

Bartley, W (1984), *The Retreat to Commitment (second edition)* (Open Court: New York).

Bauer, S (2003) *The EU Code of Conduct on Arms Exports – Enhancing the Accountability of Arms Export Policies?*, European Security 12(3-4) 129-147.

Baylis, J (1975) *Defence Decision-making in Britain and the Determinants of Defence Policy*, Journal of the Royal United Services Institute for Defence Studies, 42-48.

Beaumont, P and Islam, F (3 November 2002) *Attack on Iraq: Carve up of oil riches begins: US plans to ditch industry rivals and force end of OPEC* (The Observer: London) 16.

Beeston, R, Watson, R and Webster, P (14 February 2003) *Battle lines drawn on day of decision* (The Times: London) 1.

Bennett, J (2002) *An Anglosphere Primer* (Foreign Policy Research Institute: New York).

Bennett, J (24 August 2003), *Anglosphere: Melting Pots and Harmonies* (Washington Times: Washington DC).

Bennett, R (14 May 1999), *Blair vows to put UK at the heart of Europe: PM stresses need for EU reforms but wants Britain to be a leading player* (Financial Times: London) 1.

Berger, S (27 October 1999), *Why isolation is not an option for American in the years to come* (International Herald Tribune: Neuilly Sur Seine) 8.

Berman, M and Carter, G (1993), *The Independent European Force: Costs of Independence* (RAND Corporation: New York).

Bettis, P and Gregson, J (2001), *The Why of Quantative and Qualitative Research: Paradigmatic and Pragmatic Considerations* in Farmer, E and Rojewski, J (eds.) *Research Pathways: Writing Professional Papers, Theses and Dissertations in Workforce Education* (University Press of America: New York) 8-33.

Bishop, P and Gripaios, R (1995,) *UK and European policy responses to defence restructuring: the case of Devon and Cornwall*, European Business Review 95(4) 25-33.

Black, I (23 January 2003), *Threat of War: Schroeder and Chirac want more time for inspectors* (The Guardian: Manchester) 5.

Black, I (16 December 2003), Interview.

Blair, T (1995), *1945 Anniversary Lecture to the Fabian Society*.

Blair, T (14 December 1998), *Oral Questions concerning European Council, Vienna*, House of Commons, Cols. 605-608.

Blair, T (7 January 2003), *Prime Minister's speech to the Foreign Office conference* (Foreign and Commonwealth Office: London).

Blair, T (31 January 2003), *Press Conference: Prime Minister Tony Blair and President Bush at the Whitehouse* (Downing Street: London).

Blair, T (3 February 2003), *House of Commons* (Hansard: London) Col. 21.

Blair, T (3 February 2003), *Prime Minister's statement to Parliament following his meeting with President Bush* (Downing Street: London).

Blair, T (12 February 2003), *House of Commons* (Hansard: London) Col. 858.

Blair, T (28 February 2003), *Joint Press conference with Spanish Prime Minsiter Jose Maria Aznar*.

Blair, T (18 March 2003), *House of Commons* (Hansard: London) Col.760-764.

Blunkett, D (2006), *The Blunkett Tapes* (Bloomsbury: London).

Bone, J (17 March 2003), *UN prepares to quit Baghdad as insurer backs out* (The Times: London) 12.

Bone, J (18 March 2003), *End of the Road for Diplomacy* (The Times: London) 6.

Bone, J and Webster, P (21 January 2003) *European allies move to thwart Blair war strategies* (The Times: London) 14.

Boon, P (2003), *COREPER* (European Documentation Centre: Tilburg University Library).

Borger, J (30 January 2002), *Anti-terror war is only starting Bush tells US: State of Union speech names states which pose big threat* (The Guardian: London).

Borger, J (29 January 2003), *US to rally support by releasing secret files* (The Guardian: London) 1.

Börzel, T and Risse, T (2000), *Who is Afraid of a European Federation? How to Constitutionalize a Multi-Level Governance System?* in Joerges, C, Mény, Y and Weiler, J (eds.) *What Kind of Constitution for What Kind of Polity? Responses to Joschka Fischer* (European University Institute:Florence) 45-59.

Boswold, D and Oppermann, K (2006), *Talking Win-Sets: Combining Two-Level Games and Discourse Analysis* (PSA Conference 2006: Reading).

Bourn, J (1994), *Securing value for money in defence procurement - Whitehall Paper Number 25* (Royal United Services Institute: London).

Bowen, W and Kidd, J (2004), *The Iranian Nuclear Challenge* International Affairs 80(2) 257-276.

Boyes, R (15 January 2003), *Berlin joins Paris in insisting on a new UN resolution before battle* (The Times: London).

Branch, A and Øhrgaard, J (1999), *Trapped in the Supranational-Intergovernmental Dichotomy: A Response to Stone Sweet and Sandholtz*, Journal of European Public Policy 6(1) 123-143.

Bremner, C (28 April 2003), *Paris and Berlin prepare alliance to rival NATO* (The Times: London).

Bretherton, C and Vogler, J (2006), *The European Union as a Global Actor* (Routledge: London).

British-French Summit Saint Malo (3-4 December 1998).

British Sociological Association (2002), *Statement of Ethical Practice for the British Sociological Association* (The British Sociological Association: London).

Brittan, Lord Leon (9 January 2003), Interview.

Brogan, B (23 November 2000), *Sniper fire over army that dare not speak its name* (The Daily Telegraph: London) 14.

Browne, A (22 September 2005), *Blair is a bad President, say critics* (The Times: London) 41.

Browne, A (10 November 2005), *Two years to sort out your human rights* (The Times: London) 42.

Bruckner, P (1990), *The European Community and the United Nations*, European Journal of International Law, 1(1/2) 174-195.

Brzezkinski, Z and Huntingdon, S (1982), *Political Power: USA / USSR* (Viking Press: New York).

Buckley, C (14 April 2005), *For U.S. and EU, a tricky 'strategic triangle' with China* (International Herald Tribune: Berlin).

Budden, P (1994), *The United Kingdom and the European Community, 1979-1986 - Unpublished DPhil thesis* (University of Oxford: Oxford).

Budden, P (2002), *Observations on the Single European Act and 'launch of Europe': A less 'intergovernmental' reading of the 1985 Intergovernmental Conference*, Journal of European Public Policy 9(1) 76-97.

Bulletin Quotidien (24 April 1999) *Italian Minister Climbs Down from Condemning TV bombing* (Bulletin Quotidien: Paris).

Bulletin Quotidien Europe Number 7854 (2 December 2000), *Tight Schedule for Ministers* (Bulletin Quotidien: Paris).

Bulletin Quotidien Europe Number 7854 (2 December 2000), *Chirac's Rounds* (Bulletin Quotidien: Paris).

Bulletin Quotidien Europe, Number 7855 (5 and 6 December 2000), *Last Ministerial Conclave did not broach issue of weighting of votes in Council – hardening of positions over ceiling for Commission* (Bulletin Quotidien: Paris).

Bulletin Quotidien Europe Number 7855 (5 and 6 December 2000), *Council approves report on ESDP for Summit* (Bulletin Quotidien: Paris).

Bulletin Quotidien Europe Number 7856 (6 December 2000) *Mr Fischer is optimistic but realistic over result of Nice Summit* (Bulletin Quotidien: Paris).

Bulletin Quotidien Number 7863 (14 December 2000) *Next March Parliament will give its detailed opinion on Nice Treaty. In meantime Constitutional Committee's analysis is very severe and very concerned* (Bulletin Quotidien: Paris).

Bulletin Quotidien Europe Number 7865 (16 December 2000), *Draft text to be subject of legal and linguistic review next week – Commission considers it was not able to fully play its role as mediator in Nice and that working of EU Council must be improved* (Bulletin Quotidien: Paris).

Bulmer, S (1994), *The Governance of the EU: A New Institutionalist Approach*, Journal of Public Policy 13(4) 351-380.

Bulmer, S (1997) *The Governance of the EU: A New Institutionalist Approach* in Nugent, N (ed.) *The European Union (Volume II)* (Dartmouth Press: Aldershot) 49-78.

Bulmer, S and Edwards, G (1992), *Foreign and Security Policy* in Bulmer, S, George, S and Scott, A (eds.) *The United Kingdom and EC Membership Evaluated* (Pinter Press: London) 145-160.

Bulmer, S, Jeffery, C and Paterson, W (1997), *United Germany in an Integrating Europe* in Peter Katzenstein (ed.) *Tamed Power. Germany in Europe* (Ithaca: New York) 1-48.

de Burca, G (2001), *The European Court of Justice* (Oxford University Press: Oxford).

Butler, N (2004), *UK White Papers on Defence and Foreign Policy*, Disarmament Diplomacy 75.

Butler, Lord R (2004) *Review of Intelligence on Weapons of Mass Destruction* (The Stationery Office: London).

The Cabinet Office (November 2002) *An Introduction to the Cabinet Office* (The Stationery Office: London).

Campbell, M (1998), *Oral Questions Concerning European Council, Vienna* (House of Commons: London) Col. 611-12.

Capabilities Commitment Conference (20-21 November 2000), Brussels.

Caporaso, J (1996), *The European Union and Forms of State: Westphalian, Regulatory or Post-Modern?*, Journal of Common Market Studies 34(1) 29-52.

Caporaso, J, Scharpf, F and Wallace, H (1999) Symposium on *The Choice for Europe Journal of European Public Policy* (March 1999).

Centre for Defence Studies (20 November 2001), *Making sense of the Helsinki Goal* (King's College London: London).

Chalmers, M (1995), *Military spending and the British economy* reprinted in Coates, D and Hillard, J (eds.) *UK Economic Decline* (Harvester Wheatsheaf: London) 287-91.

Chalmers, M (1997), *The Strategic Defence Review – British policy options*, Journal of the Royal United Services Institute, 142(4) p.37.

Chandler, W (2003), *Foreign and European Policy Issues in the 2002 Bundestag Elections*, German Politics and Society 21(1) 161-184.

Chirac, J (22 January 2003), *Declaration at the 40th Anniversary of the Treaty of Elysee* (Ministry of Foreign Affairs: Paris).

Chirac, J (February 2003), *Interview* (French Ministry of Foreign Affairs: Paris).

Chomsky, N (2002), *9/11* (Seven Stories Press: New York).

Christiansen, T (April 2000), *Reform of the European Commission: Whither informal networks?* (ECPR Joint Sessions of Workshops: Copenhagen).

Cini, M (1996), *The European Commission* (Manchester University Press: Manchester).

Clark, D (11 March 1997), *Labour's Defence and Security Policy* (UK Defence Forum: London).

Clarke, M (July 1998), *How strategic was the review?*, Disarmament Diplomacy, Issue Number 28.

Clarke, M (8 July 1998), *How the MoD came to rewrite our foreign policy* (The Independent: London)

Clarke, M (2000), *British and French Security: Mirror Images in a Globalized World*, International Affairs, 76(4) 725-739.

Clarke, M and Cornish, P (2002), *The European Defence Project and the Prague Summit*, International Affairs, 78(4) 777-88.

CNN Online (14 December 2000), *NATO battles EU over defence* (CNN: New York).

Cohendet, P and Meyer-Krahmer, F (2001), *The theoretical policy implications of knowledge codification*, Research Policy 30(9) 1563-1591.

Coker, C (1998), *Twilight of the West* (Boulder Press: Westview).

Cole, P (25 November 2000), *Britain and Europe: PM goes to war over Euro-army* (The Guardian: Manchester) 8.

Cologne Council (3-4 June 1999), *Declaration of the European Council on strengthening the Common European Policy on Security and Defence* (European Union: Cologne).

Commentary (31 October 1999), *A look at... America's role; new isolationists, old fallacies; the speech* (The Washington Post: Washington) b.03

Connolly, K (23 January 2003), *Schroeder's stand on Iraq risks bitter rift with US* (The Daily Telegraph: London) 15.

Cook, R (17 March 2003), *House of Commons* (Hansard: London) Col. 726.

Coughlin, C (2 December 2001), *Number 10 won't stop Bush going After Saddam whether or not Mr Blair has the Stomach for it* (Sunday Telegraph: London) 31.

Council of the European Union (2005), *Council Conclusions - 2678th GAC Meeting Press Release, Document 12514/1/05 REV* (European Council: Brussels) 14.

Cowley, P and Norton, P (1999), *Rebels and Rebellions: Conservative MPs in the 1992 Parliament*, British Journal of Politics and International Relations, 1(1) 84-105.

Cowley, P and Quayle, S (2002), *The Conservatives running on the spot* in Geddes, A and Tonge, J, *Labour's Second Landslide – The British General Election 2001* (Manchester University Press: Manchester).

Cowan, D and Foray, D (2000), *The explicit economics of knowledge codification and tacitness*, Industrial and Corporate Change 9(2) 212-253.

Coxall, W (2001), *Pressure Groups in British Politics* (Pearson: London).

Cram, L (1997), *Policy-making in the European Union* (Routledge: London).

Crawford, A (1 January 2006), *Mass Protest Planned for Iraq War 'Architect'* (The Sunday Herald: Glasgow) 13.

Croft, S, Dorman, A, Rees, W and Uttley, M (2001), *Britain and Defence 1945-2000, A Policy Re-evaluation* (Pearson /Longman: London).

Crotty, M (1998), *The Foundations of Social Research: Meaning and Perspective in the Research Process* (Sage: California).

Daadler, I and Lindsay, J (2003) *American Unbound: The Bush Revolution in Foreign Policy* (Brookings Institute: Washington).

Daddow, O (2000), *The Historiography of European Integration – PhD Thesis* (University of Nottingham: Nottingham).

Darby, P (1973), *British Defence Policy East of Suez 1947-68* (Oxford University Press: Oxford).

Davis, I, Hirst, C and Mariani, B (2001), *Organised crime, corruption and illicit arms trafficking in an enlarged EU* (Saferworld: London).

De Vestel, P (1995), *Defence Markets and Industries in Europe: Time for Political Decisions?* Chaillot Papers No.21 (Institute for Security Studies: Paris).

Defence Export Services Organisation,'F680 Process', www.deso.mod.uk/arms_control.htm, accessed 18 October 2005.

Defence Export Services Organisation, 'DESO Partners' http://www.deso.mod.uk/partners.htm, accessed 26 October 2005a.

Defence Export Services Organisation, 'About DESO' www.deso.mod.uk/origin.htm, accessed 10 May 2006.

Delves-Broughton, P (14 March 2003), *Paris tries to cool row with a softer tone* (The Daily Telegraph: London) 14.

Demos (2005), *From national security to networked security* (Demos: London).

Demos (2006), *The Business of Resilience* (Demos: London).

Denver, D (2003), *Elections and Voters in Britain* (Palgrave: Basingstoke).

Department of Defense (2000), *United States Security Strategy for Europe and NATO* (Department of Defense: Washington).

Department of Trade and Industry, 'Ratings Process' http://www.dti.gov.uk/export.control/applying/ratenq.htm, accessed 18 October 2005.

Department of Trade and Industry News Story 'Exporter who tried to send Military Components to Iran caught By Customs and fined £70,000' http://www2.dti.gov.uk/export.control/applying/multicorecustomsfine.htm; accessed 12 July 2005.

Description of REACH provisions, European Commission website, <http://europa.eu.int/comm/environment/chemicals/reach.htm>, accessed 16 November 2006.

Description of the European Scrutiny Committee, Houses of Parliament website, <http://www.parliament.uk/parliamentary_committees/european_scrutiny.cfm>, accessed 16 November 2006.

Diez, T (1999), *Riding the AM Track through Europe, or: The Pitfalls of a rationalist journey through European integration*, Millennium: Journal of International Studies 28(2) 355-369.

Dorman, A (1998), *An Examination of the Formulation and Implementation of British Defence Policy 1978-1989 – Unpublished PhD Thesis* (University of Birmingham: Birmingham).

Dorman, A (2001), *Reconciling Britain to Europe in the next Millennium: The Evolution of British Defense Policy in the Post-Cold War Era*, Defense Analysis 17(2) 187-202.

Dover, R (2005), *The EU and the Bosnian Civil War 1992–95: The Capabilities–Expectations Gap at the Heart of EU Foreign Policy*, European Security, 14(3) 297-318.

Dover, R (2005a), *The Prime Minister and the Core Executive: A Liberal Intergovernmentalist Reading of UK Defence Policy Formulation 1997–2000*, The British Journal of Politics & International Relations 7(4) 508-525.

Dover, R (2006), *The EU's Joint Actions on Anti-personnel Mines and Unexploded Ordnance: Finding a Security Policy Identity*, European Foreign Affairs Review, 11(3) 401-417.

Dover, R (2007), *For Queen and Company: The Role of Intelligence in the UK Arms Trade*, Political Studies, forthcoming Spring 2007.

Duncan-Smith, I (26 April 2001), *Minutes of Evidence Taken Before The Select Committee on the European Union (Sub-Committee C)* (The Stationery Office: London).

Dunne, P and Perlo-Freeman, S (2003), *The Demand for Military Spending in Developing Countries*, International Review of Applied Economics 17(1) 23-48.

Duff, A (1997), *The Treaty of Amsterdam: Text and Commentary* (Sweet & Maxwell: London).

Dunn, D (2001), *European Security and Defence Policy Debate: Counter-balancing America or Re-balancing NATO*, Defence Studies, 1(1) 146-55.

Earnshaw, D and Judge, D (1997), *The Life and Times of the European Union's Co-operation procedure*, Journal of Common Market Studies 35(4) 543-564.

Eastham, P (7 February 2000), *Cook flies into US storm over Euro army* (The Daily Telegraph: London) 2.

The Economist Global Agenda (26 March 2004), *The EU Constitution, Revived to Die Another Day?* (The Economist: London).

Eden, A (1960), *Full Circle* (Cassell: London).

Editor (28 December 2000), *The Voice of America* (The Daily Telegraph: London).

Editor (29 January 2000), *Euro-corps to command peacekeepers in Kosovo* (International Herald Tribune: New York).

Editor (20 March 2003), *War and After* (The Times: London) 21.

Editor (19 December 2005), *Blair will pay for his betrayal in Brussels* (The Daily Telegraph: London) 17.

Editor (27 October 2005), *So Much for Putting Britain at the Heart of Europe* (The Observer: London) 32.

Editor (18 December 2005), *A Costly Climbdown* (The Sunday Times: London) 16.

Egar, J (1993), *Hermeneutics as an Approach to Science*, Science and Education 2 1-29.

Elman, C (1996), *Horses for Courses: Why Not Neorealist Theories of Foreign Policy?*, Security Studies 6(1) 7-53.

European Convention Secretariat, The (18 July 2003), *The European Convention, CONV 850/03* (Brussels).

European Commission Communiqué (January 1996), *The Challenges Facing the European Defence Related Industry: A Contribution for Action at the European Level, COM(96) 10 Final* (European Commission: Brussels).

European Commission Communiqué (April 1997), *1998-2002, COM(97) 142 Final* (European Commission: Brussels).
European Commission, Star 21 Report, http://ec.europa.eu/enterprise/aerospace/report_star21_screen.pdf published online 2002, accessed 16 July 2006.
European Commission (11 March 2003), *European Defence - Industrial and Market Issues - Towards an EU Defence Equipment Policy. Document COM (2003) 113 final* (European Commission: Brussels).
European Commission (13 October 2003a), *A Coherent Framework for Aerospace: A Response to the STAR 21 Report, Document COM (2003) 600 final* (European Commission: Brussels).
European Commission "Research for a Secure Europe", Report of the Group of Personalities in the field of Security Research, European Commission, March 2004, http://europa.eu.int/comm/enterprise/security/doc/gop_en.pdf , accessed 1 October 2006.
European Commission "Frequently asked questions – New Commission initiatives on more open and efficient defence procurement", European Commission memo, 6 December 2005: http://europa.eu.int/rapid/pressReleasesAction.do?reference=MEMO/05/467&format=HTML&aged=0&language=EN&guiLanguage=en, accessed 1 October 2006.
European Commission FP7 proposal, COM (2005) 119, 6 April 2005, http://europa.eu.int/eur-lex/lex/LexUriServ/site/en/com/2005/com2005_0119en01.pdf, accessed 1 October 2006.
European Commission (May 2006), *European Transparency Initiative, (COM-0194)* (European Commission: Brussels).
European Commission Star 21 Advisory Group's website – http://ec.europa.eu/research/growth/gcc/projects/star21.html#01, accessed 12 October 2006a EU Council doc. CONV 461/02, 16 December 2002: http://register.consilium.eu.int/pdf/en/02/cv00/00461en2.pdf, accessed 25 September 2006.
EU Council Joint Action 2004/551/CFSP, http://ue.eu.int/uedocs/cmsUpload/l_24520040717en00170028.pdf, accessed 22 September 2006.
European Council (1998), *Resolution on the gradual establishment of a common defence policy for the European Union, Minutes of 14/05/1998, based on Document No. A4-0171/98 - Final Edition* (European Council: Brussels).
European Council (2000), *Regulation creating the Rapid Reaction Facility (COM(2000) 119 - C5-0272/2000 - 2000/0081(CNS)) to meet international crises* (European Council: Brussels).
Eurofighter GmBh (2 August 2003), *Eurofighter – Background Information* (Eurofighter GmBh: Berlin).
European Communities Amendment Act (18 July 2001) (Brussels).
Definition of IGC, EU Glossary of Terms, (http://europa.eu.int/scadplus/leg/en/cig/g4000.htm), accessed 16 November 2006.
EDA's open recruitment website http://www.eda.europa.eu/vacancies/vacancies.htm accessed 26 July 2006.
European Defence Agency Organisation Chart, http://www.eda.europa.eu/edaOrgChart.htm, accessed 20 August 2006.

European Defence Agency Financial Statements, European Defence Agency Website, http://www.eda.europa.eu/finance/EDA%202004%20Financial%20Statements. pdf accessed 26 July 2006a.

European Defence Agency website, background to the European Defence Agency, http://www.eda.europa.eu/background.htm, accessed 16 November 2006.

EU Greek Council–Thessaloniki; http://www.eu2003.gr/en/articles/2003/6/20/3121/, accessed 20 August 2006.

European Parliament (1998), *Resolution on the gradual establishment of a common defence policy for the European Union, Minutes of 14/05/1998, based on Document No. A4-0171/98 - Final Edition* (European Parliament: Brussels).

European Parliament (1999). *Recommendation on the establishment of a European Civil Peace Corps, Minutes of 10/02/1999, based on Document No. A4-0047/99 - Final Edition* (European Parliament: Brussels).

European Parliament (2000), *Legislative resolution on the proposal for a Council regulation creating the Rapid Reaction Facility (COM(2000) 119 - C5-0272/2000 - 2000/0081(CNS)) to meet international crises* (European Parliament: Brussels).

Evans-Pritchard, A (25 October 2001), *2003 target vote on Euro* (The Daily Telegraph: London).

Evans-Pritchard, A (31 January 2003), *New Europe' reads riot act to Paris and Berlin* (The Daily Telegraph: London) 14.

Evans-Pritchard, A and Jones, G (13 December 2000), *Blair Pledges to maintain Britain's veto* (The Daily Telegraph: London).

Factortame vs Regina (ex parte Secretary of State for Agriculture, Fisheries and Food) (1990-2001), All England Law Reviews (Sweet and Maxwell: London).

Financial Times (9 July 1998), *Al Yamamah II* (Financial Times: London).

Fioretos, K (1997), *The Anatomy of Autonomy: Interdependence, domestic balances of power and European integration*, Review of International Studies 23(2) 293-320.

Fischer, J (13 March 2003), *Speech held by Federal Foreign Minister Fischer in the German Bundestag as part of the European policy debate on 13 March 2003, on many other things the enlargement of the EU and the question of military intervention in Iraq* (Bundestag: Berlin).

Fischer, J (19 March 2003), *Speech by Federal Foreign Minister Fischer to the United Nations Security Council* (United Nations: New York).

Fischer, J (20 March 2003), *Speech by Federal Foreign Minister Fischer in the German Bundestag on 20 March 2003 on the war against Iraq* (Bundestag: Berlin).

Fisk, R (4 October 2002), *NATO used the same old trick* (The Independent: London).

Flaggard, S and Moravcsik, A (1993), *The Political Economy of Financial Assistance to Eastern Europe, 1989-1991* in Keohane, R, Nye, J and Hoffmann, S (eds.) *After The Cold War: International Institutions and State Strategies in Europe, 1989-91* (Harvard University Press: Cambridge) 282-285.

Flight International Magazine (June 21 2005).

Foreign and Commonwealth Office, UK (26 October 2000), *FCO Document HC 199-203W, Sanction Regimes, Arms Embargoes and Restrictions on the Export of Strategic Goods* (HMSO: London).

Forster, A (1998), *Britain and the Maastricht Treaty: A Critical Analysis of Liberal Intergovernmentalism*, Journal of Common Market Studies 36(4) 368-388.

Forster, A (1999), *Britain and the Maastricht Negotiations* (St. Antony's/Macmillan Press: Basingstoke).

Forster, A (1999a), *The State of the Art: Mapping the Theoretical Landscape of European Integration*, Journal of International Relations and Development 2(1) 1-19.

Forster, A (2001), *Prospects for an Independent Security Policy: Institutions and Capabilities* in Sjursen, H (ed.) *Redefining Security? The Role of the European Union in European Security Structures* (ARENA: Oslo) 15-33.

Forster, A (2002), *Euroscepticism in Contemporary British Politics: Opposition to Europe in the Conservative and Labour Parties Since 1945* (Routledge: London).

Forster, A and Blair, A (2002), *The Making of Britain's European Foreign Policy* (Longman Press: London).

Freedland, J (24 October 2001), *The latest control freakery may have damaged the New Labour brand, but the Blair brand remains pristine* (The Guardian: Manchester) 21.

Freedland, J (19 March 2003), *Dilemmas of War* (The Guardian: Manchester).

Freedman, L (1999), *The Politics of British Defence 1979-1998* (Palgrave: Basingstoke).

Freedman, L (2001), *Chapter 14 – Defence* in Seldon, A (ed,) *The Blair Effect* (Little, Brown and Company: London) 289-305.

Froehly, JP (2000), *The French Perspective: France's position towards ESDI and ESDP* (German Council on Foreign Relations: Berlin).

Fulton, R (2002), *11 September and Afghanistan: Implications for the SDR and UK C4ISTAR Requirements*, RUSI Journal 147(5) 66-71.

Garden, T (1989), *The Technology Trap* (Brasseys: London).

Garden, T (28 May 1999), *The Problem of European Co-ordination* (WEU Institute: Paris).

Garden, T (13 October 2003), *Whither ESDP: Trends and Challenges* (RAND Corporation: New York).

Garden, T (7 January 2003) *Interview.* Garrett, G (1992), *International Co-operation and Institutional Choice: The EC's internal market*, International Organization 46(2) 533-60.

Garden, T and Roper, J (11 November 1999), *Time for European Defence* (Centre for European Reform: London).

Garrett, G and Weingast, B (1993), *Ideas, interests and institutions: constructing the European Community's internal market*, in Goldstein, J and Keohane, R *Ideas and Foreign Policy* (Cornell University Press: Ithaca) 173-206.

George, B (7 January 2003) *Interview.*

George, B (June 1998), *Focus – The Higher Management of Defence: Parliament and National Security*, Journal of the Royal United Services Institute, 24-28.

German Presidency (24 February 1999), *Paper, Informal Reflection at WEU on Europe's Security and Defence* (German Presidency of the EU: Bonn).

German Presidency (13-14 March 1999), *Informal Meeting of EU Foreign Ministers Eltville* (German Presidency of the EU; Bonn).

Geyer, R (2003), *European Integration, Complexity and the Revision of Theory*, Journal of Common Market Studies 41(1) 15-35.

Gilpin, R (1981), *War and Change in World Politics* (Cambridge University Press: Cambridge).

Ginsberg, R (1989), *Foreign Policy Actions of the European Community: The Politics of Scale* (Lynne Rienner: Colorado).

Ginsberg, R (2003), *European Security and Defense Policy: The State of Play*, European Union Studies Association Review 16(1) 1-2.

Glarbo, K (1999), *Wide-awake Diplomacy: Reconstructing the Common Foreign and Security Policy of the European Union*, Journal of European Public Policy 6(4) 634-651.

Gnesotto, N (8 July 2001), *ESDP: A European View* (IISS/CEPS European Security Forum: Brussels).

Gnesotto, N (December 2002), *ESDP: The Way Forward*, Military Technology 17-20.

Gordon, P (1997), *Europe's Uncommon Foreign Policy*, International Security 22(3) 74-100.

Gourlay, C (2002), *The Spanish Presidency's agenda for conflict prevention and civilian crisis management* (International Security Information Service: Brussels).

Grabbe, H and Guerot, U (February 2004), *Could a hard core run the enlarged EU?*, (Centre for European Reform: London).

Graegar, N, Larsen, H and Ojanen, H (2002) *The ESDP and the Nordic Countries: Four Variations on a Theme* (The Finnish Institute of International Affairs: Helsinki).

Graham, R and Groom, B (12 December 2000), *A New Dynamic at Nice: The* Franco-German axis at the centre of Europe's post war development is giving *way to more fluid alliances based on industrial issues* (Financial Times: London) 27.

Grant, C (1998), *Can Britain Lead?* (Centre for European Reform: London).

Grant, C (May 2000), *European defence post-Kosovo* (Centre for European Reform: London).

Grant, C (21 January 2003), *Interview*.

Grant, W (2000), *Pressure Groups and British Politics* (MacMillan: London).

Greek Presidency of the EU (17 February 2003), *Conclusions: Extraordinary European Council, Brussels* (European Council: Brussels).

Grice, A (16 January 2003), *Blair warns future generations could be haunted by Iraq* (The Independent: London).

Grice, A and Brown, C (22 March 1999), *Blair faces backlash over 'control freakery'* (The Independent: London) 1.

Grieco, J (1996), *State Interests and Institutional Rule Trajectories: a Neorealist Interpretation of the Maastricht Treaty and European Economic and Monetary*

Union, in Frankel, B (ed.) *Realism: Restatements and Renewal* (Frank Cass Publishers: London) 261-306.

Groom, B (9 July 2001), *President Blair beefs up Downing Street: The Prime Minister is strengthening his office to ensure policy ideas are turned into action* (Financial Times: London) 2.

Groom, B and Norman, P (11 December 2000), *EU Leaders draw up outline deal on treaty revisions* (Financial Times: London) 1.

The Guardian (27 September 2005), *Saudi Arabia Links Huge Arms Deal to Expelling Dissidents* (The Guardian: Manchester).

Gunaratna, R (2002), *Inside Al-Qaeda: Global Network of Terror* (Colombia University Press: New York).

Gusterson, H (2004), *People of the Bomb: Portraits of America's Nuclear Complex* (Minnesota Press: Minnesota).

Haas, P (1992), *Introduction: Epistemic Communities and International Policy Coordination*, International Organization 46(1) 1-35.

Hague, W (1998) *Oral Questions Concerning European Council, Vienna* (House of Commons: London) Col.609-610.

Hague, W (26 April 2002), *What I learned about Tony – The Hard Way* (The Guardian: London & Manchester) G2 3.

Hamilton, D (15 December 2000), *US to Turkey, don't let EU-NATO deal collapse* (Reuters: Paris).

Harnden, T (17 February 2003), *Chirac playing into Saddam's hands says US* (The Daily Telegraph: London) 11.

Harnden, T (29 January 2003), *War is all but certain – Bush to reveal evidence linking Saddam to Al-Qaeda* (The Daily Telegraph: London) 1.

Harnden T and La Guardia, A (8 March 2003), *March 17: Deadline for War* (The Daily Telegraph: London) 1.

Harries, O (23 August 1999), *Three rules for a superpower to lie by* (New York Times: New York) A19.

Hartley, K (2000), *Evidence to the House of Lords Select Committee on the European Union', Sub-Committee C – The Common European Security and Defence Policy* (The Stationery Office: London) 38.

Hasenclever, A, Mayer, P, and Rittberger, V (1997), *Theories of International Regimes* (Cambridge University Press: Cambridge).

Haskini, A (2003), *The Insurgency in Iraq*, Small Wars and Insurgencies 14(3) 1-22.

Hatfield, R (2000), *The Consequences of Saint Malo* (Paris Institut Francais des Relations Internationales: Paris).

Hayes, B (April 2006), *Arming Big Brother – The EU's Security Research Programme* (Transnational Institute: Brussels).

Healey, D (1989), *The Time of My Life* (Michael Joseph: London).

Heath, D (3 December 1998), *Oral Questions* (House of Commons: London) Col.1108-1112.

Heisburg, F (September 2000), *European Defence: Making it work, Chaillot Papers 42* (Institute for Security Studies of the WEU: Paris).

Helm, T (17 February 2003), *Blair feels heat in war of words* (The Daily Telegraph: London) 1.

Helsinki Presidency (10-11 December 1999), *Presidency Conclusions, European Council, Helsinki, 10-11 December 1999* (Helsinki).

Henley, J (8 March 2003), *Threat of War; France issues threat to block resolution* (The Guardian: Manchester) 2.

Henley, J (15 June 2005), *EU crisis: Best of times, the worst of times at Elysee* (The Guardian: Manchester) 10.

Hennessy, P (1989), *Whitehall* (The Free Press: New York).

Hennessy, P (2000), *The Prime Minister: The Office and Its Holders since 1945*, Penguin Press: London).

Hennessy, P (4 April 2003), *Correspondence with Peter Hennessy, 'The Presidential Prime Minister'*.

Herbstein, D (9 January 2006), *Austria gains Europe's Mantle* (The Financial Times: London) 32.

Hill, C (1993), *The Capabilities-Expectations Gap or Conceptualizing Europe's International Role*, Journal of Common Market Studies 31(3) 305-328.

Hinsley, F (1986), *Sovereignty (2nd Edition)*, (Cambridge Unversity Press: Cambridge).

Hix, S (1994), *Approaches to the Study of the European Community and the challenge to comparative politics*, West European Politics 17(1) 1-30.

Hix, S (1999), *The Political System of the EU* (Macmillan: Basingstoke) 1-17.

Hoffman, B (2006), *Insurgency and counter-insurgency in Iraq*, Studies in Conflict and Terrorism, 29(2) 103-121.

Hogg, S and Hill, J (1995), *Too Close to Call* (Little, Brown and Company: London).

Hogwood B and Gunn, L (1984), *Policy Analysis for the Real World* (Oxford University Press: Oxford).

Holland, M (1995), *Bridging the Capabilities-Expectations Gap: A case study of the CFSP Joint Action on South Africa*, Journal of Common Market Studies, 33(4) 555-572.

Hooghe, L and Marks, G (2001), *Multi-Level Governance and European integration*, (Rowman & Littlefield: Boulder).

Hoogland, J (19 April 2001), *Stone by stone, NATO builds a new Kosovo*, (International Herald Tribune: Paris) 7.

Hopkinson, W (2000), *The Making of British Defence Policy* (The Stationery Office: London).

Hopkinson, W (17 January 2003) *Interview*.

House of Commons Select Committee on Defence (3 September 1998), *Examination of witnesses (Question 2960-2979) Thursday 23 July 1998* (The Stationery Office: London).

House of Commons Select Committee on Defence (3 March 1999), *The European Security and Defence Identity, Select Committee on Defence, 3rd Report* (The Stationery Office: London).

House of Commons Defence Select Committee (21 May 1999), *Third Special Report, The Future of NATO: The Washington Summit* (The Stationery Office: London).

House of Commons Select Committee on Defence (11 May 2000), *Eighth Report, European Security and Defence* (The Stationery Office: London).

House of Commons Select Committee on Defence (3 August 2000), *Tenth Special Report - European Security and Defence: Government Observations on the Eighth Report from the Defence Committee of Session 1999-2000* (The Stationery Office: London).

House of Commons Defence Select Committee (February 2001), Second Special Report, *Lessons of Kosovo: Government Observations on the Fourteenth Report from the Defence Committee of Session 1999-2000* (The Stationery Office: London).

House of Commons Select Committee on Defence (15 October 2003), *Uncorrected Evidence presented by Mr Simon Webb CBE, Policy Director of the Ministry of Defence, Dr Sarah Beaver, Director for the EU and UN, Ministry of Defence, and Mr Paul Johnston, Head of the Security Policy Department, Foreign and Commonwealth Office* (The Stationery Office: London).

House of Commons Select Committee on European Scrutiny (21 November 2000), *Twenty-Seventh Report of the Select Committee on European Scrutiny* (The Stationery Office: London).

House of Lords, Select Committee on the European Union (2000), *Session 1999-2000, 15th Report, The Common European Policy on Security and Defence* (The Stationery Office: London).

House of Lords Committee on the European Union (July 2001), *Select Committee C, The European Union's Policy on Security and Defence* (The Stationery Office: London).

Howard, M (1970), *The Central Organization of Defence* (Royal United Services Institute: London).

Howarth, J (1995), *France and European Security 1944-95, Re-Reading the Gaullist 'consensus'* in Jenkins, B and Chafer, T (eds.), *France from the Cold War to the New World Order* (MacMillan: London) 17-40.

Howarth, J (2000), *Britain, France and the European Defence Initiative*, Survival, 42(2) 33-55.

Howarth, J (2000), *European Integration and Defence: the ultimate challenge?*, *Chaillot Papers Number 43* (Institute for Security Studies: Paris).

Howarth, J (2002), *Why ESDP is Necessary and Beneficial for the Alliance*, International Relations and Security Network, 2002.

Howarth, J (2002), *The European Security Conundrum: Prospects for ESDP after September 11 2001, Policy Paper Number One* (Notre Europe: Paris).

Hubschmid, C and Moser, P (1997), *The Co-operation Procedure in the EU: Why was the European Parliament Influential in the Decision on Car Emission Standards*, Journal of Common Market Studies 35(2) 225-242.

Humphreys, M (2003), *Bargaining in the presence of strategic ratifiers* (Harvard Working Paper Series: Cambridge).

Hunter, R (2002), *After Helsinki: Getting the NATO-EU Relationship Right* (RAND: New York).

Hunter, R (2002a), *The European Security and Defense Policy: NATO's companion or competitor?* (RAND: New York).

Hura, M, McLeod, G, Larsen, E, et al (2000), *Interoperability: A Continuing Challenge in Coalition Air Operations* (RAND Corporation: New York).
Hutton, W (30 March 2003), *Comment Extra: The Tragedy of Unequal Partnerships*, (The Observer: London) 30.
Informal meeting of EU defence ministers (22 September 2000), (Ecouen: France).
Interview A (26 March 2002), Cabinet Office Official.
Interview B (6 March 2002), Foreign and Commonwealth Official.
Interview C (21 January 2003), Ministry of Defence Official.
Interview D (6 January 2003), Ministry of Defence Official.
Interview E (7 January 2003), Foreign and Commonwealth Office Official.
Interview F.
Interview G (20 December 2002), Foreign and Commonwealth Office Official.
Interview H.
Interview I (26 March 2002), Number 10 Downing Street Official.
Interview J.
Interview K.
Interview L.
Interview M (21 March 2002), Cabinet Office Official.
Interview 03IS.
Interview 04IS.
Interview 05IS.
Interview 10IS.
Interview 12IS.
Interview 13IS.
Interview 14IS.
Interview 18IS.
Interview 23IS.
Interview 24IS.
Interview 25IS.
Interview 26IS.
Interview 27IS.
Interview 28IS.
Interview 30IS.
Interview 36IS.
Interview 38IS.
Interview 39IS.
Interview with UK Ministry of Defence Official (December 2005).
Isenberg, D (5 October 2005), *Scandal Sours Saudi Arms Deal* (Asia Times: Hong Kong).
Jachtenfuchs, M (1997), *Conceptualizing European Governance* in Jorgensen, K (ed.) *Reflective Approaches to European Governance* (MacMillan: London) 39-50.
Joffe-Walt, B (29 July 2006), *Made in the UK, bringing devastation to Lebanon – the British parts in Israel's deadly attack helicopters* (The Guardian: Manchester).
Johnson, R (April 2001), *Missile Defence Debate Remains Intense as US Conducts Reviews*, Disarmament Diplomacy, 56.

Jones, G and Rennie, D (1 July 2005), *British Presidency to Seek EU Finance Deal* (The Daily Telegraph: London) 11.

Jonson, P (25 March 2003) *Interview.*

Jordan, A (1991), *The Commercial Lobbyists: Politics for Profit in Britain* (Aberdeen University Press: Aberdeen).

Jordan, G and Richardson, J (1987), *Government and Pressure Groups in Britain* (Oxford University Press: Oxford).

Jorgensen, K (1997), *PoCo: The Diplomatic Republic of Europe* in Jorgensen, K (ed.) *Reflective Approaches to European Governance* (Macmillan: Basingstoke) 167-180.

Jorgensen, K (1999), *Modern European Diplomacy: A Research Agenda,* Journal of International Relations and Development 2(1) 78-96.

Joshi, J (17 December 2002), *NATO, EU ink peacekeeping pact* (Agence France Presse: Paris).

Kagan, R (2003), *Of Paradise and Power America and Europe in the New World Order* (Vintage: Canada).

Kagan, R (2004), *America's crisis of legitimacy*, Foreign Affairs 83(2).

Kassim, H, Menon, A and Peters, G (2001), *The National Co-ordination of EU Policy: The European Level* (Oxford University Press: Oxford.

Kassim, H and Menon, A (11 February 2003), *European Integration since the 1990s: Member States and the European Commission (Paper)* (ARENA: Oslo).

Kellner, D (2003), *From 9/11 to Terror War: The Dangers of the Bush Legacy* (Rawson and Littlewood: London).

Kellstrup, M (1992), *European integration and political theory* in Kellstrup, M (ed.) *European Integration and Denmark's Participation* (Copenhagen Political Studies Press: Copenhagen) 13-58.

Keohane, R and Nye, J (1977) *Power and Interdependence. World Politics in Transition* (Little, Brown and Company: Boston).

Keohane, R and Hoffmann, S (1991), *Institutional Change in Europe in the 1980s* in Keohane, R and Hoffmann, S (eds.) *The New European Community. Decision making and Institutional Change* (Westview Press: Boulder) 1-40.

Key, R (10 January 2003), *Interview.*

King, G, Keohane, R and Verba, S (1994), *Designing Social Inquiry: Scientific Inference and Qualitative Research* (Princeton University Press: New Jersey).

King, T (July 1991), *Britain's Army for the 90s* (Ministry of Defence: London).

Kirkpatrick, D (1995), *The Rising Unit Cost of Defence Equipment – the Reasons and Results*, Defence and Peace Economics 6(4) 263-288.

Kirkpatrick, D and Pugh, P (1983) *Towards the Starship Enterprise – are the Current Trends in Defence Unit Cost Inexorable* (Aerospace: London).

Kinsey, C (2005), *Examining the Organisational Structure of UK Private Security Companies*, Defence Studies, 5(2) 188-212.

Kohler-Koch, B (1996), *Catching up with change: the transformation of governance in the EU*, Journal of European Public Policy 3(3) 359-380.

Krahmann, E (2005), *Regulating Private Military Companies: What Role for the EU?*, Contemporary Security Policy 26(1) 103-25.

Krasner, S (1982), *Regimes and the Limits of Realism: Regimes as Autonomous Variables*, International Organization 36(2) 497-510.

Krasner, S (1991), *Global Communications and National Power: Life on the Pareto Frontier*, World Politics 43(3) 336-366.

Krasner, S (1993), *Power, Polarity, and the Challenge of Disintegration* in Haftendorn, H and Tuschoff, C (eds.) *America and Europe in an Era of Change* (Boulder: Westview) 21-42.

La Guardia, A and Smith, M (7 December 2000), *France snubs America over EU army* (The Telegraph: London).

La Guardia, A and Helm, T (17 December 2002), *Blair seeks peace talks as Assad digs heels in* (The Daily Telegraph: London) 1.

La Guardia, A, Helm, T and Rennie, D (28 October 2005), *EU summit We will use force, Blair warns Iranians* (The Daily Telegraph: London) 8.

La Guardia, A and Rennie, D (31 January 2006), *Israel cuts funds as Hamas refuses to give up violence* (The Daily Telegraph: London) 2.

Labour Party (1996), *Road to the Manifesto: A Fresh Start for Britain – Labour's strategy for Britain in the modern world* (London: Labour Party).

Labour Party (1997), *Election Manifesto* (London: Labour Party).

Laitner, S (22 September 2005), *Brussels unveils counter initiative on data storage* (The Financial Times: London) 8.

Landler, M (January 20 2003), *Threats and Responses: Shroeder's Antiwar Stance Becomes a Balancing Act* (New York Times: New York) 13.

Lambert, R (March/April 2003), *Misunderstanding Each Other*, Foreign Affairs.

Larsen, H (2002), *The EU: A Global Military Actor*, Cooperation and Conflict 37(3) 283-302.

Latham, S (21 April 2002), *Saddam 'sends troops to help bin Laden men'* (The Sunday Telegraph: London) 22.

Lax, D and Sebenius, J (1992), *The Manager as Negotiator: The Negotiator's Dilemma: Creating and Claiming Value* in Goldberg, S, Sander, F and Rogers, N, *Dispute Resolution 2nd Edition* (Little, Brown and Company: Boston) 49-62.

Layne, C (4 April 2001), *Death knell for NATO? The Bush Administration Confronts the European Security and Defense Policy* (The CATO Institute: Washington DC).

Le Gloannec, A (1999), *Germany and Europe's Foreign and Security Policy: Embracing the British vision,* in Lankowski, C, *Break out, break down or break in?, Germany and the EU after Amsterdam* (CGS Research Report 8) 21-30.

Leader Section (12 December 2000) *Necessary deals in Nice* (The Financial Times: London) 26.

Leader (11 June 2005), *Not the time for a sordid squabble: An EU budget wrangle is a distraction from the real crisis* (The Financial Times: London) 12.

Leigh, D. and Evans, R. (9 March 2005), *Over a Quarter of MoD arms sales unit work for Saudis* (The Guardian: London).

Lewis, F (30 June 2000), *Like it or fear it, a united Europe is on its way* (International Herald Tribune: Neuille sur ville) 8.

Lichfield, J (5 December 1998), *Anglo-French summit: France and the UK blaze trail on defence* (The Independent: London).

Lichfield, J (28 May 2005), *'Oui' camp fails to muster late rally as French voters prepare to reject treaty* (The Independent: London).
Liddle, R and Mandelson, P (1996) *The Blair Revolution: Can New Labour Deliver?* (Faber & Faber: London).
Lindblom, C (1959), *The Science of Muddling Through,* Public Administration Review 19(1) 76-88.
Lindley-French, J (2002), *Terms of Engagement. The Paradox of American Power and the Trans-Atlantic Dilemma post-11th September - Chaillot Paper 52* (WEU: Paris).
Little, D (2003), *Endogenous Variables,* in Beck, M and Bryman, A (eds.) *Encyclopaedia of Social Science Research Methods Volume I* (Sage Publishing: New York) 490.
Livingstone, K (17 December 1998), *Charm is not enough - now Blair must take on Murdoch* (The Independent: London).
Long, D (2002), *The European Union and the Ottawa Process to ban landmines,* Journal of European Public Policy 9(3) 429-446.
MacCormick, N (1999) *Questioning sovereignty: law, state and nation in the European commonwealth* (Oxford University Press: Oxford).
MacIntyre, D (17 February 2004) *A Bush victory could trouble the Tories as well as Labour* (The Independent: London) 3.
MacIntyre, D (30 June 2006), *Israel Cripples Hamas with Capture of Ministers* (The Independent: London).
Majone, G (1993), *The European Community between Social Policy and Social Regulation,* Journal of Common Market Studies 31(2) 224-240.
Majone, G (1996), *Regulating Europe* (Routledge: London).
Majone, G (2000), *Democracy and Constitutionalism in the EU,* European Consortium for Political Research (ECPR) Paper, European Union Studies Association 13(2) 2-7.
Maloney, W, Jordan, G and McLaughlin, A (1994), *Interest Groups and Public Policy: the Insider / Outsider Model Revisited,* Journal of Public Policy 14(1) 17-38.
Mancini, F (1991), *The Making of a Constitution for Europe,* in Keohane, R and Hoffman, S, *The New European Community: Decision Making and Institutional Change* (Boulder Company: New York) 177-194.
Mandelson, Peter (30 January 1998), *Speech* (European University Institute: Florence).
Mann, M (1996), *Authoritarian and Liberal Militarism: a contribution from comparative and historical sociology* in Smith, S, Booth, K and Zalewski, M, *International Theory: Post-Positivism and Beyond* (Cambridge University Press: Cambridge).
Mann, N (26 October 2001) *Roger Liddle, Centre Stage Once More* (BBC Online News: London).
Manners, I (2002), *Normative Power Europe: a Contradiction in Terms,* Journal of Common Market Studies 40(2) 235-58.
Maor, M (1995), *Party Competition in Interlinked Political Markets: A Rational Choice Framework for Understanding Party Behaviour in the European and*

National Political Arenas in Dowding, K and King, D, *Institutional Rational Choice* (Oxford University Press: Oxford) 114-133.

Maloney, J (2000), *Path Dependence in Historical Sociology*, Theory and Society 29(4) 507-548.

Maples, J (7 December 1998), *Oral Defence Questions* (House of Commons: London) Cols.10-11.

Maples, J (22 November 1999), *Debate in the House of Commons* (Hansard: London) Column 381.

March, J (1994) *A Primer on Decision Making: How Decisions Happen* (Free Press: New York).

March, J and Olsen, J (1984) *The New Institutionalism: Organizational Factors in Political Life*, American Political Science Review 78 734-49.

Marshall, J (3 December 1998) *Answers to Oral Questions* (House of Commons: London) Col.1083.

Massie, A (23 March 2003), *US power and a willingness to employ it rankled most* (The Sunday Times: London) 21.

Massingberd, H (17 September 2002), *A very special relationship as Britain again stands shoulder to shoulder with its transatlantic ally* (The Daily Telegraph: London) 1.

Massy-Beresford, H (24 January 2006), *European UAV makers urged to work together* (Flight International: London).

Marks, G, Hooghe, L and Blank, K (1996), *European Integration since the 1980s. State-centric Versus Multi-Level Governance*, Journal of Common Market Studies 34(3) 343-78.

Mataly, J (1993), *Beyond Intergovernmentalism: The Quest for a comprehensive framework for the study of integration*, Co-operation and Conflict 28(2) 181-210.

Mathiopoulos, M and Gyramati, I (1999), *Toward European Defence*, The Washington Quarterly 22(4) 65-76.

Mbaye, H (2001), *Why national states comply with supranational law: Explaining implementation infringements in the European Union 1972-1993*, European Union Politics 2(3) 259-281.

McElvoy, A (October 5 1997), *Goodbye Party, hello people. First New Labour now New Britain. After watching the Prime Minister in action at Brighton last week Anne McElvoy believes she has discovered his real political aims* (The Sunday Telegraph: London) 27.

McInnes, C (1998), *Labour's Strategic Defence Review*, International Affairs 74(4) 823-848.

Mearsheimer, J (1990), *Back to the Future. Instability in Europe After the Cold War*, International Security 15(4) 5-56.

Mearsheimer, J (1994), *The False Promise of International Institutions*, International Security, 19(3) 5-49.

Melman, S (1970), *Pentagon Capitalism: The Political Economy of War* (McGraw Hill: New York).

Menon, A (May 2000), paper given at Department of Nottingham Invitational Speaker Series.

Menon, A (25 July 2000), *Evidence to the House of Lords Committee on the European Union (Sub-Committee C)* (The Stationery Office: London).

Menon, A (2000), *House of Lords Committee on the European Union (Sub-Committee C)* (London: The Stationery Office).

Menon A and Hurrell, A (1996), *Politics Like No Other? Comparative Politics, International Relations and the Study of the EU*, West European Politics 19(2) 386-402.

Menon, A and Weatherill, S (2002), *Legitimacy, Accountability and Delegation in the European Union*, in Arnull, A and Wincott, D (eds.) *Legitimacy in the European Union After Nice* (Oxford University Press: Oxford) 113-131.

Meyer, C (2005), *DC Confidential* (Weidenfeld and Nicolson: London).

Miliband, D (17 October 2001), *European Communities (Amendment) Bill* (House of Commons: London) Col.1255.

Milne, S (16 January 2003), *Direct Action may become a necessity* (The Guardian: Manchester) 24.

Milner, M (16 September 2002), *Single Currency: Work in Progress* (The Guardian: Manchester)

Milward, A (2001), *The European Rescue of the Nation State* (Oxford University Press: Oxford).

Minder, R (9 December 2004), *EU stalls over lifting China arms embargo* (The Financial Times: London).

Ministry of Defence (30 July 1997), *MoD Press Release 096/97, 'Strategic Defence Review seeks 'Smart Procurement'* (The Ministry of Defence: London).

Ministry of Defence (December 2000) *Performance Report, Cm 5000* (Ministry of Defence: London).

Ministry of Defence (13 February 2001), *Press Release, Inter-Allied Confederation of Reserve Officers Annual Seminar, European Defence – The Facts and the Myths* (Ministry of Defence: London).

Ministry of Defence (15 July 2002), *MoD Announcement, 'Gordon Brown announces billions extra for defence', SR2002/MOD* (HM Treasury: London).

Ministry of Defence (2003) *The Government's Expenditure Plans 2002-3 to 2003-4* (London: The Stationery Office).

Ministry of Defence (2003), *Paragraph 12 – 'Methodology, Key Findings and Shocks', Strategic Trends* (Joint Doctrines and Concepts Centre: Shrivenham).

Moens, A (1998), *NATO's dilemma and the elusive European defence identity*, Security Dialogue, 29(4) 463-75.

Moravcsik, A (1990), *Negotiating the Single European Act*, in Keohane, R and Hoffman, S, *The New European Community* (Boulder Community Press: New York) 41-84.

Moravcsik, A (1991), *Negotiating the Single European Act: National Interests and Conventional Statecraft in the European Community*, International Organization 45(1) 19-56.

Moravcsik, A (1992/3), *Liberalism and International Relations Theory* (Center for International Affairs Working Paper Series 92-6: Harvard University).

Moravcsik, A (1993a), *Introduction: Integrating International and Domestic Theories of International Bargaining,* in Evans, P, Jacobson, H and Putnam, R, *Double Edged Diplomacy* (University of California Press: California) 3-43.

Moravcsik, A (1993) *Preferences and Power in the European Community: A Liberal Intergovernmentalist Approach,* Journal of Common Market Studies 31(4) 473-524.

Moravcsik, A (1994), *Why the European Community Strengthens the State: Domestic Politics and International Cooperation* (Harvard University: Cambridge).

Moravcsik, A (1995), *Liberal Intergovernmentalism and Integration: A Rejoinder,* Journal of Common Market Studies 33(4) 597-626.

Moravcsik, A (1997), *Taking Preferences Seriously: Liberalism and International Relations Theory,* International Organization 54(4) 513-553.

Moravcsik, A (1997), *Does the European Union Represent an n of 1?,* ECSA Review X(3) 1-5.

Moravcsik, A (1998), *The Choice for Europe: Social Purpose and State Power from Messina to Maastricht* (Routledge / University College London Press: London).

Moravcsik, A (1999), *The Choice for Europe - Current Commentary and Future Research (Reply to James Caporaso, Fritz Scharpf, and Helen Wallace)* Journal of European Public Policy 6(1) 157-179.

Moravcsik, A (1999), *The Choice for Europe: A Reply to Helen Field,* Australasian Journal of European Integration 1(1) 86-88.

Moravcsik, A (29 November 2000) *Correspondence 'PhD research concerning Liberal Intergovernmentalism'.*

Moravcsik, A (12 July 2003), *Correspondence from Andrew Moravcsik, 'Question LI'.*

Moravcsik, A (27 January 2006), *Future of Europe* (The Financial Times: London) 2.

Moravcsik, A and Nicolaidis, K (1998), *Keynote Article: Federal Ideals and Constitutional Realities in the Treaty of Amsterdam,* The European Union 1997: Annual Review of Activities, Special Issue of Journal of Common Market Studies 13-38.

Moravcsik, A and Nicolaidis, K (1999), *Explaining the Treaty of Amsterdam: Interests, Influences, Institutions,* Journal of Common Market Studies 37(1) 59-85.

Morth, U (2000), *Competing Frames in the European Commission,* Journal of European Public Policy 7(2) 173-189.

'Multi-Annual Strategic Programme', European Council (published 8 December 2003), <http://www.eu2006.at/includes/Download_Dokumente/MAPEN.pdf>, accessed 16 November 2006.

NATO (2000), Factsheet, Strengthening European Security and Defence Capabilities (NATO: Brussels).

'The National Security Strategy of the USA', The Whitehouse (published online September 2002) <www.whitehouse.gov.nsc.nss.pdf>, accessed June 2006.

Neuman, W (2000), *Social research methods. Qualitative and quantitative approaches (Fourth edition).* (Allyn and Bacon: Boston).

Nevins, J (2002), *The Making of 'Ground Zero' in East Timor in 1999*, Asian Survey 42(4) 643.

Nice European Council (10 March 2001), *Nice European Council: Presidency Conclusions, IV Common European Security and Defence Policy, Paragraphs 13 and 14 & Annex VI* (European Council: Nice).

Noonan, M (19 April 2004), *Correspondence 'ESDP'*.

Norgaard, A (1994), *Institutions and Post Modernity*, Cooperation and Conflict 29(3) 245-287.

Norman, P (1 December 2000), *Prodi warns of chance that Nice meeting might fail* (The Financial Times: London) 11.

North Atlantic Council (24 April 1999), Summit (Washington DC).

Norton-Taylor, R (27 May 2005), *Landrovers 'used in Uzbek killings'* (The Guardian: Manchester).

Norton-Taylor, R et al (1996), *The Scott Report and Its Aftermath* (Victor Gollancz: London).

Norton-Taylor, R and MacAskill, E (2002), *£1bn arms push to India* (The Guardian: Manchester).

Number 10 Downing Street (5 June 2000), *New Head of Cabinet Office European Secretariat Number 10 Downing Street Press Briefing* (Downing Street: London).

Number 10 Downing Street (22 June 2001), *Improving Public Services / Changes at the Centre Number 10 Downing Street Lobby Briefing* (Downing Street: London).

Nye, J (1990), *Bound to Lead* (Basic Books: New York).

Oakes, M (2 May 2001), *European Security and Defence Policy: Nice and Beyond, House of Commons Research Paper 01/50* (The Stationery Office: London).

Observer (24 June 2005), *Mr Blair Goes to Europe* (The Financial Times: London), 14.

Olsen, J (2000), *Garbage can, new institutionalism and the study of politics*, American Political Science Review 95(1) 191-198.

Ordeshook, P (1986), *Game Theory and Political Theory* (Cambridge University Press: New York).

O'Sullivan, A (21 July 2004), *Israeli UAVs recognized as world leaders* (Jerusalem Post: Jerusalem).

Oxford Research Group (September 2004), *Escaping the Subsidy Trap: Why Arms Exports are bad for Britain* (Oxford Research Group: Oxford).

Page, L (2006), *Lions, Donkeys and Dinosaurs* (William Heinnemann: London).

Palmer, N (30 November 2002), *Interview*.

Papandreo, G (6 May 2003), *The Future of Europe after Iraq, Lecture delivered at St Antony's College* (University of Oxford: Oxford).

Parker, G and Thornhill, J (29 December 2005), *European navigation satellite a challenge to US* (The Financial Times: London).

Parker, G (19 May 2003), *Blair to set out bottom line on new EU Treaty* (The Financial Times: London) 3.

Parker, G (26 October 2005), *Brussels moves to slay image of 'bureaucratic monster'* (The Financial Times: London) 8.

Parris, M (5 July 2003), *Iraq is a world problem. It needs a world solution* (The Times: London) 24.

Parry, G, Moyser, G and Day, N (1992), *Political Participation and Democracy in Britain* (Cambridge University Press: Cambridge).

Parsons, C (2000), *Domestic interests, ideas and integration: lessons from the French case*, Journal of Common Market Studies 38(1) 45-70.

Patten, C (29 January 2003), *Iraq: Speech to the European Parliament, Speech/03/34* (European Parliament: Brussels).

Patten, C (20 March 2003), *Speech by the Rt Hon Chris Patten CH, European Parliament Iraq Debate, Brussels, Speech/03/148* (European Parliament: Brussels).

Patten, C (29 January 2003), *Iraq speech to the European Parliament* (European Parliament: Brussels).

Patten, C (12 March 2003), *Speech by the Rt Hon Chris Patten, 'Iraq: European Parliament Debate in Plenary, Introduction: the ambition of the common foreign and security policy* (European Parliament: Brussels).

Peel, Q (14 December 2000), *Britain and Spain 'biggest Nice winners'* (The Financial Times: London) 10.

Peel, Q (6 May 2003), *The failure of Blair's European Policy* (The Financial Times: London) 21.

Peterson, J and Bomberg, E (1999), *Decision Making in the European Union* (St Martins: New York).

Phillips, D (1983), *After the wake: post-positivistic educational thought*, Educational Researcher, 12(5) 4-12.

Phythian, M (2001), *The Politics of British Arms Sales since 1964* (Manchester University Press: Manchester).

Phythian, M (2004), *The Perfect Intelligence Failure? US pre-war intelligence on Iraqi weapons of mass destruction*, Politics and Policy 34(2) 400-424.

Pierson, P (1994), *A Historical Institutionalist Account - Working Paper 5.2* (Harvard Center for European Studies: Cambridge).

Pierson, P (1996), *The Path to European Integration: A Historical Institutional Analysis*, Comparative Political Studies 29(2) 123-163.

Pierson, P (2000), *Increasing returns, path dependence and the study of politics*, American Political Science Review 94(2) 251-67.

Pierson, P and Skocpol, T (2004), *Historical Institutionalism in Contemporary Political Science* (Harvard University: Cambridge).

Pilisuk, M and Hayden, T (1965), *Is there a military industrial complex which prevents peace?: Consensus and Countervailing Power in Pluralistic Systems*, Journal of Social Issues XXI(3) 67-117.

Pollack, M (1995), *Creeping competencies: the expanding agenda of the European Community*, Journal of Public Policy 14(2) 98-145.

Pollack, M (1997), *Delegation, Agency, and Agenda Setting in the European Community*, International Organization 51(1) 99-134.

Pollack, M (2002), *The Engines of Integration: Delegation, Agency and Agency Setting in the European Union* (Oxford University Press: Oxford).

Pond, E (1999), *Kosovo: Catalyst for Europe*, The Washington Quarterly 22(4) 77-92.
Popper, K (1959), *The Logic of Scientific Discovery* (Hutchinson: London).
Popper, K (1963), *Conjectures and Refutations* (Routledge: London).
Popper, K (1968), *The Logic of Scientific Discovery* (Penguin Books: London).
Popper, K (1974), *Conjectures and Refutations: The Growth of Scientific Knowledge* (Routledge: London).
Portillo, M (1996), *'A British View'*, in The Framework of United Kingdom Defence Policy (The Stationery Office: London).
Potsdam Summit (1 December 1998), *Final Declaration, Franco-German Summit*, Potsdam, 1st December 1998.
Potts, D (2002), *Tactical Combat with the New C4ISTAR A British Perspective* (Wehr and Wissen: London).
Prodi, R (26 March 2003) *Statement on Iraq* (Brussels).
Pryce, R (1989) *The Dynamics of European Union* (Routledge: London).
Ptiffner, J (2004), *Did President Bush Mislead the Country in his Arguments for War with Iraq?*, Presidential Studies Quarterly 34(1) 25-46.
Puchala, D (1999), *Institutionalism, Intergovernmentalism and European Integration*, Journal of Common Market Studies 37(2) 317-331.
Putnam, R (1988), *Diplomacy and Domestic Politics: The Logic of Two Level Games*, International Organization 42(3) 427-460.
Putnam, R (1993), *Appendix – Diplomacy and Domestic Politics: The Logic of Two Level Games*, in Evans, P, Jacobson, H and Putnam, R (eds.) *International Bargaining and Domestic Politics – Double Edged Diplomacy* (University of California Press: London) 431-69.
Quadripartite Committee Descriptions, The, House of Commons website, <http://www.parliament.uk/parliamentary_committees/quad.cfm 2005>, accessed 16 November 2006.
Redwood, J (10 December 2002) *Correspondence*.
Regelsberger, E, de Schouthette de Terverant, P and Wessels, W (eds.) (1997), *Foreign Policy of the European Union: From EPC to CFSP and beyond* (Reinner: Colorado).
Rennie, D (28 October 2002), *Time for talking on Iraq to stop America tells UN* (The Daily Telegraph: London) 14.
Rennie, D (26 June 2003), *Bush gives Europe his US policy wish list* (The Daily Telegraph: London) 16.
Rennie, D and Helms, T (30 November 2005), *Blair ready to surrender EU rebate with no payback France refuses to agree any cuts to CAP subsidies* (The Daily Telegraph: London) 1.
Rhodes, R and Dunleavy, P (1995), *Prime Minister, Cabinet and Core Executive* (St Martin's Press: New York).
Richardson, J (1996), *European Union: Power and Policy Making* (Routledge: London).
Richardson, L (1993), *British State Strategies after the Cold War*, in Keohane, R, Hoffmann, S, and Nye, J (eds.) *After the Cold War* (Harvard University Press: Cambridge) 148-169.

Rifkind, M (13 January 2004), *Interview*.
Risse-Kappen, T (1996), *Exploring the Nature of the Beast: International Relations Theory and Comparative Policy Analysis Meet the European Union*, Journal of Common Market Studies, 34(1) 53-80.
Robertson, G (7 December 1998) *Oral Defence Questions* (House of Commons: London) Col. 8.
Robertson, G (11 December 2003), *This ain't your Daddy's NATO - final speech as Secretary General of NATO* (NATO: Brussels).
Robertson, G (1999), *NATO in the new Millennium*, NATO Review 47(4) 6.
Robertson, G (17 March 2003), *Statement: By NATO Secretary General Lord Robertson, Press Release (2003)025* (NATO: Brussels).
Robertson, G (11 March 2004), *Interview*.
Roeber, J (August 2005), *Hard-wired for Corruption* (Prospect Magazine: London).
Rogers, P (1998), *New Grand, Old Assumptions: Analytical Limitations in the SDR*, Disarmament Diplomacy, Issue Number 28.
Rosamond, B (March 1999), *Globalization and multi-level governance in Europe'*, paper for conference on Globalization and its implications for Europe and the United States (Atlanta).
Roth, N (9/10 February 2000), *The New European Security and Defence Policy (Panel Summary)', for 'The Future of Europe Conference of the European Union Centers'* (The German House: New York).
Roy, A (2 April 2003), *War in the Gulf* (The Guardian: Manchester) 2.
Ruane, K (2000), *The Rise and Fall of the European Defence Community. Anglo-American Relations and the Crises of European Defence, 1950-55* (Palgrave: Basingstoke).
Rueschemeyer, D and Stephens, J (1997), *Comparing Historical Sequences: A Powerful tool for Causal Analysis*, Comparative Social Research 17(1) 55-72.
Rummel, R and Wessels, W (1983) *Federal Republic of Germany: New Responsibilities, Old Constraints*, in Christopher Hill (ed.) *National Foreign Policies and European Political Cooperation* (Allen & Unwin: London) 34-55.
Rumsfeld, D (22 January 2003), *Briefing at Foreign Press Centre* (Foreign Policy Centre: Washington).
Rush, M (ed) (1990), *Parliament and Pressure Politics* (Clarendon Press: London).
Rutten, M (2001) *From Saint Malo to Nice. European Defence: Core Documents* (Institute for Security Studies: Paris).
'Saferworld Briefing for Select Committee Members – Sep 2005', Saferworld website, <http://www.saferworld.co.uk/QSC-briefing5.htm> accessed 21 October 2005.
Sandholtz, W (1992), *High Tech Europe: The Politics of International Co-operation* (University of California Press: California).
Sandholtz, W (1993), *Choosing Union: Monetary Politics and Maastricht*, International Organization, 47(1) 1-40.
Sandler, T and Hartley, K (1995), *The Economics of Defence* (Cambridge University Press: Cambridge).

Sandler, T and Hartley, K (1995), *The Political Economy of NATO: Past, Present and into the 21st Century* (Cambridge University Press: Cambridge).

Sands, P (13 September 2005), *Tackling Terrorism: is Britain setting the world a good example?* (The Times: London).

Santa de Feira Council (19/20 June 2000), (European Council: Santa de Feria).

Sbragia, A (ed.) (1992) *Europolitics: Institutions and Policy Making in the New European Community* (Brookings Institute: Washington DC) 257-293.

Schake, K (2001), *EU Should Duplicate NATO Assets* (Centre for European Reform: London).

Schake, K, Block-Laine, A and Grant, C (1999) *Building a European Defence Capability*, Survival 41(1) 20-40.

Scharpf, F (1998), *The Choice for Europe: Selecting cases and testing hypotheses*, Journal of European Public Policy 6(1) 164-168.

Scheurich, J (1997), *Research Methods in the Post Modern* (Falmer: London).

Schmitter, P (1996), *Imagining the Future of the Euro-Polity with the Help of New Concepts* in Marks, G, Scharpf, F, Schmitter, P and Streeck, W (eds.), *Governance in the European Union* (Sage: London) 1-14.

Schwandt, T (1997), *Qualitative Inquiry: A Dictionary of Terms* (Sage Publications: California).

Sciolino, E (31 May 2005), *The French Decision: The Aftermath, French No Vote on the Constitution Rattles Europe* (New York Times: New York).

Scott, R (1996), *Report of the Inquiry into the Export of Defence and Dual-Use Goods to Iraq and Related Prosecutions* (House of Commons Papers 115: London).

Secretary of State for Foreign and Commonwealth Affairs (February 2000), *IGC: Reform for Enlargement. The British Approach to the European Union Intergovernmental Conference 2000, CM4595* (The Stationery Office: London).

Seldon, A (ed.) (2001), *The Blair Effect – The Blair Government 1997-2001* (Little, Brown and Company: London).

Shaw, T (6 September 1995), *Euro laws in danger, says judge* (The Daily Telegraph: London) 11.

Shepherd, A (2000), *Top-down or Bottom up: is security and defence policy in the EU a question of political will or military capability?*, European Security 9(2) 13-30.

Shepherd, A (2006), *Irrelevant or Indispensable? ESDP, the 'War on Terror' and the Fallout from Iraq*, International Politics 43 71-92.

Sherwell, P (22 January 2006), *Iran extends nuclear plant in secret Satellite images show facilities now bear alarming similarities to weapons factories* (The Daily Telegraph: London) 24.

Short, C and Rifkind, M (15 November 2003), *Too close for comfort? Is our special relationship with the US a happy fact or a dangerous fantasy?* (The Guardian: Manchester) 24.

Shrivesley, R (27 February 2002), *How Labour's wizards spun themselves to a standstill: Government efforts to evade the truth have deepened crisis* (The Financial Times: London) 20.

Sintra Meeting (28 February 2000), *'The Toolbox Paper' Meeting of European Union Defence Ministers* (Sintra).

Simitis, C (26 March 2003), *Presentation of the conclusions of the Spring European Council to the European Parliament by the President of the European Council, Prime Minister Costas Simitis* (European Parliament: Brussels).

Simpson, A (8 May 2003), *Correspondence*.

Silvestri, S (1999), *Atlantic and European Defence after Kosovo*, The International Spectator, XXXIV(3) 11-20.

Sloan, S (1997), *Congress and NATO enlargement*, US Information Agency Electronic Journal, 2(4).

The Small Arms Survey website, <www.smallarmssurvey.org>, accessed 18 September 2006.

Smith, M (1998), *Rules, Transgovernmentalism, and the Expansion of European Political Cooperation*, in Sandholtz, W and Stone Sweet, A (eds.) *European Integration and Supranational Governance* (Oxford University Press: Oxford) 304-333.

Smith, M (2003), *Institutional Moments, Policy Performance and the future of the EU Security / Defense Policy*, European Studies Association Review 16(1) 3-5.

Smith, S, Booth, K and Zalewski, M (eds.), *International Theory: Post-Positivism and Beyond* (Cambridge University Press: Cambridge).

Solana, J (26 March 2003), *The Unity of Iraq must be preserved* (Die Welt: Berlin).

Sowemimo, M (2001), *Evaluating the success of the Labour Government's European Policy*, Journal of European Integration 2(3) 343-68.

Spear, J (27 March 2001), *Interview*.

Squire, R (3 December 1998), Oral Questions (House of Commons: London) Col. 1105.

Stavrianakis, A (2007), *Too close for comfort? NGO Strategies for Change in the UK Arms Trade*, PhD Thesis (University of Bristol: Bristol).

Steele, R (2004), *Information Peacekeeping and the Future of Intelligence*, International Journal of Intelligence and Counter-Intelligence 17(2) 265-285.

Stephens, P (1997), *Politics and the Pound* (Macmillan: London).

Stephens, P (24 June 2005), *Actions must follow words at Europe's moment of decision* (The Financial Times: London) 19.

Stevenson, R and Preston, J (February 1 2003), *Threats and Responses: Bush meets Blair amid signs of split on UN war role* (New York Times: New York).

Stewart, W (28 February 2003), *Putin holds out olive branch to Whitehouse* (The Daily Express: London) 5.

Stone, D (1996), *Capturing the Political Imagination: Think Tanks and the Policy Process* (Frank Cass: London).

Stone Sweet, A and Caporaso, J (1996), *From Free Trade to Supranational Polity: The European Court and Integration* (Political Relations and Institutions Research Group).

Stone Sweet, A and Sandholtz, W (1997), *European integration and Supranational Governance*, Journal of European Public Policy 4(3) 297-317.

The Strategic Defence Review (1998), *Essays 10-1, The Strategic Defence Review* (The Stationery Office: London).

The Strategic Defence Review (1998), *Essays 1-3, The Strategic Defence Review* (The Stationery Office: London).

Straw, J (September 2001), *Mission Statement - Foreign and Commonwealth Office* (HMSO: London).

Straw, J (9 January 2003), *The United Kingdom and the Muslim World* (FCO: London).

Straw, J (11 February 2003), *Iraq: A Challenge we must confront – Speech to the International Institute of Strategic Studies* (FCO: London).

Sullivan, A (14 April 2002), *Victory for Bush in Iraq will bring peace in Israel* (The Sunday Times: London).

Sullivan, A (2 February 2003), *Come on In: The Anglosphere is Freedom's New Home* (The Sunday Times: London).

Talbott, S (1999), *America's Stake in a Strong Europe*, Reprinted in Rutten, M (2001) 54-59.

Tapsell, P (1998), *Oral Questions Concerning European Council, Vienna* (House of Commons: London) Col.613.

Taverner, M (24 November 2003), *Europe's Peace Shield*, Aviation Week and Space Technology.

Taylor, T (1991), *Great Britain*, in Jopp, M, Rummel, R, Schmidt, P (eds.), *Integration and Security in Western Europe. Inside the European Pillar* (Boulder: Westview) 136-145.

Taylor, T (1998), *Smart Procurement and Partnerships with Industry*, The Journal of the Royal United Services Institute 143(2) 41.

Theodoulos, M (31 January 2002), *Europeans wary over US hostility to Tehran* (The Times: London).

Tigner, B (16 July 2001), *EU Group to Discuss Unifying Defense Market* (Defense News: New York).

Tisdall, S (16 November 2000), *Embryonic European Defence Force Inches Forward* (The Guardian: Manchester).

Tonra, B (1997), *The Impact of Political Cooperation,* in Jorgensen, K (ed.) *Reflective Approaches to European Governance* (Macmillan: Basingstoke) 181-198.

de Torrente, N (2004), *Humanitarian Action Attack: Reflections on the Iraq War*, Harvard Human Rights Journal 17.

Toulouse Council (29 May 1999), Franco-German Defence and Security Council (Toulouse).

Treaty of Nice (10 March 2001), *Treaty of Nice- Amending the Treaty on European Union, The Treaties Establishing the European Communities and Certain Related Acts (2001/C 80/01)* Official (Journal of the European Communities: Brussels).

The Amsterdam Treaty 1998.

Tweedie, N (18 May 2002), *Beware of the Euro-Army, says Major* (The Daily Telegraph: London) 2.

United Nations (8 November 2002), *Security Council Resolution 1441(2002)* (New York).

Usborne, D (22 January 2003), *France breaks ranks on Iraq* (The Independent: London) 1.

Uttley, M (2001), *Defence Procurement and Industrial Policies*, in Croft, S, Dorman, A, Rees, W and Uttley, M, *Britain and Defence 1945-2000, A Policy Re-evaluation* (Pearson /Longman: London) 115-134.

Verbeek, B (1998), *Whither the Study of Governmental Politics in Foreign Policy Making*, Marshon International Studies Review 41 205-255.

de Villepin, D (2 March 2003), *Villepin on Resolution 1441 and Iraqi Crisis* (Ministry of Foreign Affairs: Paris).

de Villepin, D (11 December 2002), *Speech to the National Assembly on Iraq and Enlargement* (Ministry of Foreign Affairs: Paris).

Wagner, W (2001), *Foreign policy capacities and state preferences in CFSP: Assessing the rationalist explanation of German French and British CFSP policies*, in Willa, P and Levrat, N (ed.), *Actors and Models: Assessing the European Union's External Capability and Influence* (University of Geneva: Geneva) 20-45.

Wagstyl, S (9 December 2005), *Croatian War Crimes Suspect Arrested* (The Financial Times: London) 8.

Walker, K (31 January 2003), *7 Euro leaders back Iraq war* (The Daily Express: London) 10.

Walker, M (3 June 1999), *Europe takes first steps to common defence policy* (The Guardian: Manchester).

Walker, M (3 June 1999), *Summit and Nothing: Today's Cologne summit looks set to continue the European Council of Minister's tendency to make plans rather than take action* (The Guardian: Manchester) 21.

Walker, M (9 April 2004), *Join Europe – and shrink* (United Press International: Washington).

Wallace, H, Caporaso, J, Scharpf, F and Moravcsik, A (1999), *Symposium on The Choice for Europe*, Journal of European Public Policy 6(1) 155-179.

Wallace, W (23 May 2003), *Interview*.

Walter, F (28 June 2003), *Durchwelsten until 2006?* (Die Welt: Berlin).

Waltz, K (1979), *Theories of International Politics* (Random House: New York).

Waltz, K (1986), *Reflections on Theory of International Politics. A Response to My Critics*, in Keohane, R (ed.) *Neorealism and Its Critics* (Columbia University Press: New York) 322-345.

Waltz, K (1993), *The Emerging Structure of International Politics*, International Security 18 44-79.

Washington Declaration (4 April 1949) (Washington).

Ward, S and Marshall, A (28 September 1995), *Two other international courts in Luxembourg and the Hague have the right to challenge Britain's sovereignty* (The Independent: London) 19.

Watson, R (16 August 2002), *Bush Speaks Softly, but still carries a big stick* (The Times: London).

Watt, N (27 January 2006), *EU Inquiry May Call Cheney* (The Guardian: London) 27.

Weaver, K and Rockman, B (eds.) (1993), *Do Institutions Matter? Government Capabilities in the United States and Abroad* (The Brookings Institute: Washington).

Weber, K (1997), *Institutional choice in international politics: a glimpse at EU member's industrial policies* (International Studies Association: Toronto).

Webster, P (21 March 2003), *Eight leaders rally 'new' Europe to America's side* (The Times: London) 1.

Webster, P (28 October 2005), *Blair hints at military action after Iran's 'disgraceful' taunt* (The Times: London) 4.

Wendt, A (1992), *Anarchy is what states make of it: The social construction of power politics*, International Organization 46(2) 391-425.

Wendt, A (1994), *Collective Identity Formation and the International State*, American Political Science Review 88(2) 384-396.

Werner, W and de Wilde, J (2001), *The Endurance of Sovereignty*, European Journal of International Relations 7(3) 283-313.

WEU Council of Ministers (19 June 1992), *Western European Union Council of Ministers Petersberg Declaration* (Brussels).

White, M (22 December 1998), *Bombing of Iraq a triumph of an old foreign policy* (The Guardian: Manchester).

White, M (18 September 2001), *Blair will tour site of atrocity after talks with Bush* (The Guardian: Manchester).

White, M (8 December 1999), *Thatcher decries European Army* (The Guardian: London).

White, M (18 December 2003), *Interview*.

White, M (19 December 2005), *Blair Says Budget Rebate Will Increase* (The Guardian: Manchester) 11.

Wilkinson, D (1999), *Unipolarity without Hegemony*, International Studies Review 1(1) 141-172.

Williams, J (19 April 2004) *Correspondence*.

Wilson, G (2 June 1999), *Cook under fire on EU army deal* (The Daily Mail: London) 4.

Wincott, D (1995), *Institutional Interaction and European Integration: Towards an Everyday Critique of Liberal Intergovernmentalism*, Journal of Common Market Studies 33(4) 597-609.

Winkler, B (1999), *Is Maastricht a good contract?*, Journal of Common Market Studies 37(1) 39-58.

de Witte, P (20 April 2004), *Interview*.

Wolf, K (1999), *The New Raison d'etat as a Problem for Democracy in World Society*, European Journal of International Relations 5(3) 333-363.

Woods, N (ed.) (1996), *Explaining International Relations since 1945* (Oxford University Press: Oxford).

Yoo, J (2003), *International Law and the War in Iraq*, American Journal of International Law, 77(3) 563-576.

Yost, D (2000), *The NATO capabilities gap and the European Union*, Survival 42(4) 97-128.

Young, H (27 July 1999), *Blair is a European. He must speak now* (The Guardian: London and Manchester).

Young, O (1999), *Comment on Andrew Moravcsik 'A New Statecraft? Supranational Entrepreneurs and International Cooperation*, International Organization 53(4) 805-810.

Index

Aerospace and Defence Industries Association of Europe (ASD) 127
Afghanistan campaign 24, 105, 115
Al-Qaeda 96-7
Amsterdam Treaty 2, 58, 64, 70-1, 125-7
Anglo-sphere 87
Arms trade 1-7, 13-14, 117-141, 143-8
    EU Code of Conduct 118-9, 133
    manufacturers 117-135, 143-8
    'off the shelf' equipment 7, 26
Association of European Space Industry 127

BAE Systems Plc 118-137
Berlin-Plus Arrangements 36, 106
Blair, Tony (Prime Minister) 2, 21-37, 47-48, 99-104, 107, 110, 115
    'Heart of Europe' speech (1997) 2, 23, 28, 60, 77
    Memo to Permanent Under Secretaries (PUS) 29
Blix, Hans 98
British budget rebate 108-113
Brok, Elmar 44-5, 126
Bush, President George W. 35, 96, 115
    'Axis of Evil' speech 96, 110
    Bush Doctrine 96
    National Security Strategy 96, 102

Cabinet Office 2, 15-6, 21-39, 47, 57, 72, 108, 134
    Cabinet Committees 16, 29
    (E)DOP 29
    European Secretariat 15, 23, 35, 47, 57, 62, 72, 147, 151
Campbell, Alistair 34
Chinese government 109, 118, 139
Clinton, President William 27, 35
Cologne Council (June 1999) 59-65
Comité des Représentants Permanents (COREPER) 41, 55, 62, 72, 150, 151
Common Agricultural Policy (CAP) 112-5

Common Foreign and Security Policy (CFSP) 49, 53, 56, 70, 76, 82, 102
Cook, Robin 54, 99
core executive 9

Defence Attachés, UK 120-4, 136
Defence Exports Services Organisation (DESO) 120-5, 133-6
Defence Intelligence Staff (DIS) 133
defence savings 26
Defence Working Group 122
Department for International Development (DFID) 133-8
Department for Trade and Industry (DTI) 1-32-8
    arms export licence 132-3, 138
    Export Control Organization 135
    F680 Process & 'Ratings' 133-8
    'smart front end committee' 133
Deputy Supreme Allied Commander Europe (DSACEUR) 50, 66, 69
Directorate of Export Services Policy (DESP) 133-4
domestic interest groups 4, 9, 23, 30-1, 37, 40-2, 49, 60, 147
Downing Street, Number 10 15, 31, 48, 86-9, 147-52
    Downing Street Policy Unit 15

Ecouen informal ministerial meeting (September 2000) 67
epistemic communities 147-8
Errera, Phillipe 54
EU-3 110, 118
European Association of Aerospace Industries and Eurospace 127
European Commission 18, 39, 45-6, 74, 95, 101-5, 117-132, 139
European Court of Justice (ECJ) 51
European Defence Agency (EDA) 117-25, 130-1, 139

European Defence Industries Group 122, 127
EU defence industrial base 5, 126
European Parliament (EP) 44, 46, 74, 78, 107-8, 112, 115, 127, 140, 144, 152
European Security and Defence Policy (ESDP) 6-7, 31-6, 45-55, 63-4, 67, 71-3, 90-3, 143-6
 EU Political and Security Committee (PSC) 64-71
 Military Committee 64-6, 69, 71, 123
European Security Strategy 106
eurosceptics 26, 33, 153

Fischer, Joschka 64-5, 100-1
Foreign and Commonwealth Office (FCO) 25-7, 31-9, 54, 57, 59, 67, 86-9, 134-5, 147
 Secretary of State for Foreign and Commonwealth Office 68, 101
formal Europeanization 1, 6, 39, 75-94,
French government 35-7, 54-68, 80-88, 90, 98, 101-4, 112-3, 123

Galileo satellite system 119, 120, 128
George, Bruce 59
German government 50, 55, 62-4, 85-7, 97-105, 110
 Presidency of the EU (1999) 62
Global War on Terror (GWOT) 132
 'extraordinary renditions' 109
 Hague Programme (June 2005) 109
Good Friday Agreement 34
Grant, Charles 30, 47, 78
Group of Personalities 125-6
Guthrie, Charles 25, 31, 49

Hatfield, Richard 23, 28-39, 53-9, 66, 69, 73
Helsinki Council (December 1999) 44, 59, 65, 71, 91
 'Headline Goals' 65-7, 91
High technology industries 5, 25, 122, 140
Homeland security 7, 24, 108-9, 117, 126-132, 141-149
Hoon, Geoffrey 32
House of Commons 33, 61, 73, 81
 Parliamentary Rebels 61
 Quadripartite Committee 138
 Select Committee on Defence 32
 Standing Committees on the Intergovernmental Conference 81
House of Lords 33
 Select Committee on the European Union 32
Hussein, Saddam 96-104

Informal Europeanization 1, 41-3, 89, 95, 107, 112-3, 130
Institutional Choice theory 84
Intergovernmental Negotiations 43, 52, 72-3, 81, 111, 122, 129, 149-51
 log-rolling 62, 65, 149
 'red-lines' 54-5, 61, 67, 72, 88
 side-payments 42, 62
 states as the principal units in the international system 6, 17, 39, 43, 46, 51, 149
 the gate-keeper role of states 39, 43, 60, 62, 81
 threats of exclusion 62
 'two-level' game 42, 149
 'voice opportunities' 80
 'win-sets' 2, 42, 53, 62, 67, 68, 73
Iraq 95-116
 US-UK invasion (March 2003) 8-9, 103-4, 153
 UN Security Council Resolution 678 99
 UN Security Council Resolution 1441 97-100
 weapons of mass destruction 96-104
Israel-Palestine problems 100, 110-1, 115, 119

Jones-Parry, Emyr 23, 31, 35, 45, 53-4, 56-7, 66, 73, 147

Key, Robert 22, 34, 59
Kosovo 23, 27, 47-8, 50, 63-4, 86

Labour Party 2, 21, 24, 25, 28
 Parliamentary Labour Party (PLP) 34, 46
 1997 manifesto 2, 25, 28, 46-7, 59
Liberal Intergovernmentalism (LI) 3-6, 12, 18, 22, 37, 40, 51, 64-5, 74-6, 152
 aggregation of interests 7, 36-7, 49, 137, 147
 creating value in negotiations 40

Index

claiming value in negotiations 40, 57
convergence of interests 3, 6, 10, 39-43, 55-6, 59-60, 72, 74, 80, 152
domestic interest groups 4, 9, 23, 30-1, 37, 40-2, 49, 60, 147
domestic producer groups 2-4, 30, 128, 152
'major governments' 5, 52, 80
'policies' and 'preferences' 1-6, 9, 22, 24, 33, 36, 39-42, 60, 72
'positive' and 'negative' externalities 3, 5, 37, 152
Liddle, Roger 5, 15, 29, 35, 47, 48, 66
Lindblom, Charles 23, 36-7
successive limited comparisons 23, 35-9
Lisbon Agenda 7, 10, 112, 118
London bombings (7 July 2005) 100, 129-30, 152

Maastricht Treaty 44, 53, 55, 58, 61, 81
Madrid Train Bombings (2004) 100, 129-30, 152
Mandelson, Peter 29, 35, 147
MBDA 130, 134
Members of the European Parliament (MEP) 44, 73, 125
Military Industrial Complex 25, 148
'pork-barrel politics' 7
'Milwardian' rescue of the nation state 1, 21, 81
Ministry of Defence (MoD) 16, 21, 28-31, 37, 47, 56, 66, 125, 134
Expenditure Plans 28
Secretary of State for Defence 29, 32-5, 48, 136-7
Moravcsik, Andrew 3-6, 12, 41-4, 60, 62, 76, 83, 93

'Napoleonic' style of government 2, 33
National Archives 16
30 and 50 year rules 12, 16
NATO 3, 5, 21, 34-5, 47, 50-2, 59, 63, 66, 69-70, 152
Anglo-Saxon dominance 56, 58, 79
decoupling, duplication and discrimination 59
'out of area' tasks 48, 50, 63
'peace enforcement' tasks 49-50, 65, 100

Turkish concerns 70
Neofunctionalism 17-18
Nice Intergovernmental Conference 53-74
Enhanced cooperation 72
Presidency Report on ESDP 68-71
non-governmental organizations (NGOs) 13, 120, 128, 138
Saferworld 138
Nordic region 91

Operation Artemis 106, 150
Operation Concordia 106

Papandreo, George 102-3
Patten, Lord Christopher 99, 102-5, 114, 123, 128
Petersberg Tasks 49, 56, 62-7, 128, 131
Pörtschach (1998) 21-38, 53, 56, 85
positivism 11-2
'as-if' positivism 11
challenges of interviewing 11-17
post-positivism 11-2
snowballing strategy 17
triangulation 11, 14, 16
Potsdam meeting (December 1998) 55-6
Presidency of the EU 106-116
presidential government in the UK 28, 36
Private Finance Initiatives (PFI) 34
Prodi, Romano 102-3, 132

QINETIQ 123
Qualified Majority Voting (QMV) 84, 92

Raytheon 130
realism 79-80
balances of power 22, 75, 77, 79, 85, 88
regime coordination 79-80
'shocks' in the international system 85-6, 91
Robertson, Lord George 29, 32-5, 45, 47, 58, 70, 147
Rumsfeld, Donald 8, 98
'new' Europe 8, 98
'old' Europe 8, 98, 100
Russian government 98-9

Saint-Malo meeting (December 1998) 53-74
Saudi Arabia 117, 121, 137
Al-Yamamah deal 137

Scott Report (1996) 13, 137-8
September 11, 2001 (9/11) 96, 105, 109, 132, 139
Serious Fraud Office 137
Short, Claire 99
Schroeder, Chancellor Gerhard 98, 105
Single European Act (SEA) 1986 18
Single European Currency (EURO) 18, 21-6, 29, 46-8, 84, 143
Sintra Council (February 2000) 53-4, 65, 73
   'Toolbox Paper' 53, 65-7, 73
Smith, Iain Duncan 46, 61
Solana, Javier 64, 102-3, 124
sovereignty 75-94
   pooling sovereignty 19, 75, 83-5, 90-1, 145
   Westphalian sovereignty 144-5
state-private network 117, 121, 123, 126, 130, 140, 144, 147-8
Strategic Defence Review (SDR) 5, 7, 26, 33, 49
Straw, Jack 101

Thales 128, 130
Thessaloniki Council (June 2003) 123
Think-tanks 4, 143-4
   Centre for European Reform 30, 47-8, 149
   Chatham House 14
   Demos 148-9
   European Institute for Security Studies 30

Foreign Policy Centre 30
   Royal United Services Institute 30, 148
Treaty of Rome 41, 125
Tsatos, Dmitris 44

UK government as an 'awkward partner' in Europe 24, 112-5
UK-US 'special relationship' 24, 79, 87, 113
UK's Permanent Representative to the EU (UKREP) 35, 151
United Nations (UN) 50, 96, 77
   United Nations Security Council 97-9, 103, 107
   UN Security Council Resolution 678 99
   UN Security Council Resolution 1441 97-100
   War Crimes Tribunal 110
   Weapons Inspectors 98-9
United States 25, 36, 47-8, 55, 82-3, 96, 98, 113
   Central Intelligence Agency (CIA) 78, 109, 120
   Defense Department 23
   Pentagon 66, 78, 88-9
   State Department 23, 27, 34, 47, 66, 78, 88-9
'uploaded' preferences 1, 39, 121

Wall, Sir Stephen 15, 29, 34-5, 47, 147
Witney, Nick 121-2, 124, 139

Yugoslavia 27, 30, 82, 100